NOT ONLY THE POOR

NOT ONLY THE POOR

The Middle Classes and the Welfare State

ROBERT E. GOODIN
University of Essex

JULIAN LE GRAND
London School of Economics and Political Science

with

John Dryzek   D. M. Gibson
Russell L. Hanson   Robert H. Haveman
David Winter

London
ALLEN & UNWIN
Boston   Sydney   Wellington

Allen & Unwin, the academic imprint of
Unwin Hyman Ltd
PO Box 18, Park Lane, Hemel Hempstead, Herts HP2 4TE, UK
40 Museum Street, London WC1A 1LU, UK
37/39 Queen Elizabeth Street, London SE1 2QB, UK

Allen & Unwin Inc.,
8 Winchester Place, Winchester, Mass. 01890, USA

Allen & Unwin (Australia) Ltd,
8 Napier Street, North Sydney, NSW 2060, Australia

Allen & Unwin (New Zealand) Ltd in association with the
Port Nicholson Press Ltd,
60 Cambridge Terrace, Wellington, New Zealand

First published in 1987

British Library Cataloguing in Publication Data
Goodin, Robert E.
Not only the poor : the middle classes and the welfare state.
1. Welfare State——History   2. Middle classes——History
I. Title   II. Le Grand, Julian
361.6'5'0880622   HN16

ISBN 0–04–336094–7
ISBN 0–04–336095–5 Pbk

Library of Congress Cataloging-in-Publication Data
Goodin, Robert E.
Not only the poor.
Bibliography: p.   Includes index.
1. Middle classes.   2. Welfare State.
I. Le Grand, Julian.   II. Title.
HT684.G57 1987   361.6'5   86–32249
ISBN 0–04–336094–7 (alk. paper)
ISBN 0–04–336095–5 (pbk. : alk. paper)

Typeset in 10 on 12 point Monophoto Bembo
by Latimer Trend & Company Ltd, Plymouth
and printed in Great Britain by
Billing and Sons Ltd., London and Worcester

Contents

Part Four   The Challenge to the Welfare State

Part Five   Conclusion

List of Tables and Figures

Preface

The chapters of this book are all concerned with the involvement of the non-poor in the welfare state. Each is individually free-standing: they have been written by a variety of different hands, for a variety of different purposes and from a variety of different angles. We make no pretence to systematic coverage of all aspects of the welfare state, even in the three states (the United Kingdom, the United States and Australia) that we do discuss. The collective impact of all these independent exercises nonetheless seems to us to be enormous: the non-poor seem to play a very important role indeed in the basic life processes of the welfare state, and to benefit in important ways from that involvement.

Although each of the ten chapters that comprise this book is signed separately, one or the other of the principal authors (Goodin, Le Grand) have either authored or co-authored all but two of them. We are grateful to Bob Haveman and Russ Hanson for lending their special expertise to the American side of this study, and to all our other co-authors for letting us impose our continuing preoccupations upon them.

Despite these differences in each chapter's provenance, the book is not simply a collection of diverse papers loosely grouped around a common theme. Instead, the chapters draw on a wide variety of evidence and argument to tell parts of what we believe to be the same story: a story whose essential features we try to bring out in an introductory and, particularly, in a concluding chapter. In this connection, we should emphasize that the arguments in these particular chapters are ours alone; they do not necessarily represent the views of the others whose work is included here.

Some of these chapters have not been published before. Previously published chapters have generally been revised for inclusion in this volume. We have also attempted to make the book as accessible to as many people as possible. Some of the arguments, by their nature, are rather technical; but we have, wherever possible, relegated the more technical aspects to appendices.

Many people have provided vital assistance in the preparation of this book. Acknowledgements specific to each chapter will be found among the notes to the chapter concerned. But here we should thank Brian Barry and A. H. Halsey, in particular, for comments on the overall conception of the book as a whole.

We also have some other more general debts to be acknowledged. Our collaboration on this book grows out of the time we spent together in 1983 as Visiting Research Fellows on the Social Justice Project in the Research School of Social Science at the Australian National University. We would like to take this opportunity to thank again our colleagues on that Project – especially its director, Pat Troy – and around the ANU more generally for their generous support, both intellectual and material. Le Grand also enjoyed the support of a Nuffield Foundation Research Fellowship during part of this period, for which he is grateful. Later stages of this work have been carried out under the auspices of the Welfare State Programme of the Suntory–Toyota International Centre for Economics and Related Disciplines at the London School of Economics, of which Le Grand is co-director and from which we have both benefited. There, too, we are deeply indebted not only to our sponsors but also to Tony Atkinson, the judicious director of the Centre and co-director of the Programme.

We have been blest with a succession of talented research assistants – Janette Ryan, Gina Roach and Chris Davies. Our task has also been eased enormously by the excellent secretarial assistance of Norma Chin at the ANU and of Jane Dickson, Administrative Secretary to the Welfare State Programme.

October 1986

Robert E. Goodin and Julian Le Grand

NOT ONLY THE POOR

PART ONE

Background

Chapter 1

Introduction

ROBERT E. GOODIN and
JULIAN LE GRAND

This book concerns the involvement of the better-off in the life-processes of the welfare state – its birth, growth and sustenance. Our concern, stated colloquially, is with the relations between the 'middle classes' and the welfare state. Stated more precisely, it is with the relations between the 'non-poor' and the welfare state.[1]

Under some of the most standard interpretations of the purposes of welfare programmes, the non-poor are officially not meant to benefit directly from them. It is our thesis that the non-poor nonetheless play a crucial role in (variously) creating, expanding, sustaining, reforming and dismantling the welfare state. In some cases, the motives of the non-poor are wholly altruistic – the activities of the middle-class campaigners working with the Child Poverty Action Group in Britain are an honourable example. Far the more common pattern, however, is for the non-poor to play all these various roles in the affairs of the welfare state with an eye to their own direct benefit. That is what we shall hereafter refer to as the *'beneficial involvement'* thesis.

In the course of these chapters, we shall show that some appreciation of this beneficial involvement at crucial junctures is essential for understanding, *inter alia*, the conditions under which welfare states emerge and enjoy dramatic spurts of growth, the particular shapes that these programmes take, and the circumstances under which they will come under successful and unsuccessful attack. At the same time, appreciating the crucial role of the non-poor in these processes can also help show both defenders and opponents of the welfare state where it is vulnerable to political attacks and why. From this, they can infer whether the welfare state is worth defending – or attacking – and, if either, how best to do so.

In what follows, we hope to show that the non-poor do play a major and (for them) beneficial role in the life of the welfare state. Whether or not they must necessarily do so is, of course, another matter. We leave our ultimate conclusions on the *inevitability* of beneficial involvement of the non-poor in the welfare state to the final chapter of this book. We will, however, be reflecting indirectly on this question as we go along, since how avoidable the beneficial involvement of the non-poor is in the future depends in large part upon how they have managed to find a beneficial role for themselves in the past.

Likewise, we leave to our final chapter any reflection upon the *undesirability* of the beneficial involvement of the non-poor in the welfare state. To foreshadow, we will there argue that, if the beneficial involvement of the non-poor or middle classes is inevitable, that may (in at least one sense) be no bad thing. But the sense in which it would be 'no bad thing' is a sense rather different from the one in which many have understood the welfare state and some of its most central goals and purposes.

These goals will be discussed in more detail shortly. But, according to all the conventional understandings, the welfare state has as one of its most central aims that of *redistribution*. It has always been regarded as at least in part as a mechanism whereby the distress among the poorer elements of society is relieved at the expense of the better off members of society.[2] In so far as the non-poor are themselves involved in the welfare state in such a way as to make them, along with the genuinely poor, beneficiaries of such transfers, then to that extent the redistributive effects of the transfers are thereby diminished. Welfare state programmes characterized by beneficial involvement of the non-poor thus defeat, or at least seriously compromise, one of their own most central purposes. And that is made all the worse if – as occasionally happens – people's poverty has a 'positional' aspect (Hirsch, 1976; Sen, 1983), so the non-poor's benefiting actually makes the poor *worse* off than they otherwise would have been.

Strictly speaking, of course, programmes are not the sorts of things that can have purposes or goals or aims of their own. Only people can possess such things. Talking about the aims of a programme is just an elliptical way of talking about the aims that people have in creating and supporting such a programme. And if the middle classes have been crucial in creating and sustaining welfare programmes from which they in turn derive benefits, then maybe the programmes are fulfilling at least some of their founders' purposes, after all.

Still, even the most cynical observer would have to concede that there is something deeply wrong with such arrangements. Even if benefiting the non-poor is the hidden intention of some (or, indeed of many) of those who are responsible for creating and sustaining the welfare state programmes, it is rarely their avowed intention. And at least some people – both those who are potential beneficiaries and those who are not – presumably support the programmes for precisely the high-minded reasons that are reflected in the rationales that are officially offered. At the very best, announcing redistributive aims without having any intention of fulfilling them would, in the circumstances, constitute a clear case of fraud. So, too, would announcing redistributive aims and all the while intending to thwart them as far as you can.

We would not want to argue that the welfare state fails in its redistributive tasks altogether. Certainly the welfare state is, at some time and in some areas, a remarkable redistributive success. What we do want to argue, however, is that its redistributive efforts are always liable to be compromised – and are often in fact compromised – by the beneficial involvement of the non-poor in such programmes. And sometimes even those programmes that appear on the surface to be clear redistributive successes, effecting substantial transfers from non-poor to poor, might at a deeper level be seen to be providing substantial benefits to the non-poor as well. Any programme that can be conceptualized as an insurance scheme, along the lines proposed by Goodin and Dryzek in Chapter 3 below, would be like that: superficially, the transfer is from the fortunate to the unfortunate, but the security and peace of mind produced by such schemes constitutes a clear benefit for the fortunate themselves.

Moreover, the transfer may not be genuinely from the fortunate to the unfortunate. Insurance programmes are sometimes justified as 'redistribution over the life cycle', transferring resources from a person's richer years to that same person's poorer years. At the end of the day, the same amount of money that has been taken away from Sally in her earning years will have been paid back to Sally in her non-earning years. In many ways, the realization of that fact is precisely what motivates people who are not presently poor to support programmes that seem to be transferring their tax monies to the poor. But before we embrace this argument too warmly as a way of increasing support for programmes favouring the poor, it is important to note what is really going on here. In so far as the 'life cycle insurance' thesis truly is an accurate characterization of the programme, then it is not really a programme for aiding the poor at all. Or – less provocatively put – it is a programme for aiding those who, while presently poor, are not poor over most of the course of their lives. In one way, what really counts in determining whether people are poor is whether they are poor *now*: that must undeniably be one of the policymaker's prime concerns. In another way, however, programmes providing nothing more than 'life cycle insurance' often benefit people who are, taking their lives as a whole, anything but poor (Aaron, 1977).

The Goals of Welfare Policy

As the above discussion suggests, we cannot proceed further without a more precise notion of the goals and purposes of the welfare state, particularly those concerned with redistribution. The welfare state – or, more precisely, the set of programmes and policies that make up the welfare state – can serve many purposes. These, as phrased in popular discussion or even in government documents, are often vague and ill-defined. It seems, however, reasonable to categorize them under three headings. The first is concerned with interpersonal *redistribution*, the second with *allocative efficiency* (corresponding, respectively, to Musgrave's (1959, p. 5) distinction between the distributive and allocative functions of government). The third is concerned with social cohesion or *community*. We shall look at each in turn.

Our concern here will be with the announced goals of social welfare programmes, their official intentions and public justifications. It may of course be true that welfare programmes serve other functions as well, either intentionally or unintentionally. It is often said, for example, that an unacknowledged purpose of the welfare state is 'regulating the poor' (Piven and Cloward, 1971), maintaining support for and undermining opposition to the established political order in times of economic distress. That may or may not be the effect of welfare state expenditures; it may or may not be an effect intended by state managers. But it is not their announced intention, and so lies outside our purview here. We will confine our attention narrowly to the justifications that can be given publicly for welfare state activities.

REDISTRIBUTION

Redistribution as an aim may derive from more fundamental concerns, such as the promotion of equity or social justice, or the exercise of charitable compassion.[3] Among the compassionate, at least, redistribution may also be justified on the grounds of efficiency (Hochman and Rogers, 1969). Perhaps for that reason, there are many possible ways in which the objective can be interpreted. The better to distinguish them, it is useful to classify the various interpretations.

There are at least four ways in which redistribution aims might be classified. First, they may be concerned with *equality* or they may be concerned with *minimum standards*. That is, the objective of redistribution might be a fully egalitarian one, or one only concerned with ensuring that no one in the community falls below a specified minimum of some kind. Second, they may be concerned with policy *inputs* – the instruments of policy, such as medical care or teaching resources – or they may be concerned with policy *outcomes* – the variables that policies are trying to affect, such as health itself or educational skills. Third, they may be aimed at the *whole population*, or they may be aimed at *specific categories* (the elderly, the disabled, the ill). Fourth, they could be concerned with the *access* to a service or they could be concerned with the *amount* of the service used.

Some illustrations may help. The aim of 'equal treatment for equal need', often ascribed to health care policy, clearly refers to equality rather than minimum standards; to a policy 'input', treatment, rather than a policy 'output', health; and it concerns specified groups, those in need of various kinds of treatment. On the other hand, the expression 'a decent home for every family', versions of which often appear in government statements concerning housing policy, refers to minimum standards (of decency); it concerns a policy output (quality of housing); and it refers to everyone in the population.

The fourth method of categorization requires a little more elaboration. It concerns the distinction between amounts and 'access'. Often policy objectives are formulated in terms of access or opportunity. Thus 'equality of opportunity' is frequently mentioned as a desirable goal for educational policy, 'equality of access' as an objective for

health policy (one British Government document on health policy –
UK DHSS, 1976 – even referred to 'equality of opportunity of
access'). Unfortunately, it is rarely, if ever, specified precisely what
these terms mean. It has been suggested (Le Grand, 1982b, p. 15) that
they are most easily interpreted in terms of the personal or private
costs faced by the individuals affected by the relevant policies. Thus
'equality of access' to medical services means that every individual
should face the same personal cost of, say, a visit to a family
practitioner or a day spent as a hospital in-patient; 'equality of
opportunity' in education means that everyone faces the same
personal cost of, say, spending an extra year in school or college or of
sending a child to kindergarten. 'Cost' in this context refers to all the
costs associated with the relevant service; thus, as well as any charges
that may be levied for use of the service, it should include any travel
costs and any income foregone as a result of spending time travelling
to, waiting for, and actually using the services. Further, it may be
interpreted in terms of money, or, more ambitiously, in terms of the
utility or satisfaction foregone.

Objectives framed in terms of cost (access, opportunity) should not
be confused with those framed in terms of amounts used. Thus equal
education for equal ability is not the same as equality of the personal
cost of education; equal treatment for equal need is not the same as
equality of personal cost of medical care. If full equality of personal
cost exists, then there may still be variations in the amount of the
service consumed or used, depending on the *demand* for the service of
the individuals concerned. The point can be made with examples.
Thus, of two individuals with the same income, same ability and
facing the same personal cost of, say, going to university, one may
choose to take up the offer of a university place, while the other
chooses not to. Or, of two individuals with the same diagnosed
illness, one may choose to undertake further professional treatment,
the other to rely on his or her body's recuperative powers.

We have emphasized this distinction because it can represent a
fundamental philosophical divide between types of distributional
policy. A policy concerned with equality of cost – equality of access
or opportunity – is generally based on a more individualistic
philosophy than one concerned with equality of amount used. The
former is designed to ensure that everyone *begins* at the same place,
the latter at ensuring that everyone *ends* at the same place.[4] One
incorporates a belief in individual responsibility and rationality,

where individuals are left free to make their own choices; the other represents a more paternalistic (or less optimistic) view where individuals have to be directed by some means or another to make the choices that society deems desirable. Any attempt to discuss the distributional impact of a particular policy has to be clear as to which of these two philosophies the policy concerned represents.

There is a further distinction that has appeared in the debate concerning inequality measurement (see, particularly, Kolm, 1976) and will be mentioned on occasion subsequently in the book. This is between what might be termed 'absolute' and 'proportional' egalitarians. Put simply, an absolute egalitarian is concerned with the absolute differences between rich and poor in whatever index is the focus of social concern (income, well-being, use, access, etc.) and the proportional egalitarian with proportional differences.

An example may help. Suppose the focus of concern is income, and we are contemplating the difference in income between two individuals, one earning £30,000 per year and the other £10,000. Suppose a government programme were introduced that gave the first individual an increase in income of £1,500 and the second an increase of £1,000. Proportional egalitarians would note that the first person's income had increased by only 5 per cent, while the second person's income had increased by 10 per cent. As a result, the ratio of their incomes had fallen. Hence they would conclude that inequality had fallen. Absolute egalitarians, on the other hand, would see only that the richer individual had received an increase of £500 more than the poorer person, and so that the absolute gap between their incomes had increased by that amount. Hence they would conclude that inequality had risen.

In practice, debates over distributional issues, such as those concerned with wage bargaining or the progressivity or regressivity of tax changes, generally concern proportional changes, from which we might conclude that most people are proportional rather than absolute egalitarians. This is a little curious, for the rationale for being a proportional egalitarian is not immediately apparent. In the example above, for instance, it does seem odd to maintain that inequality in income has fallen, when the absolute difference has increased.

A possible justification for proportional egalitarianism lies in the difference between income and well-being. Those people who are proportional egalitarians in terms of income are perhaps absolute egalitarians in terms of well-being or utility; the reason why they emphasize proportional differences in income is that, because of the phenomenon of diminishing marginal utility of income, they believe these correspond more closely to absolute differences in utility than do absolute differences in income. Thus, in the example, they might believe that the 5 per cent increase in income for the richer person results in a smaller absolute increase in utility than that resulting from the 10 per cent increase in income for the poorer person. Hence inequality – in terms of well-being – has indeed fallen.

Whether proportional or absolute egalitarianism is the more defensible we here leave as an open question. Our point here is merely that either represents a coherent position.

EFFICIENCY

It is a standard proposition in economics that certain commodity and factor markets may fail to achieve allocative efficiency, and that some form of state intervention may be thereby justified. We cannot discuss here in detail the enormous literature concerning this issue (for references, and for a more substantial introduction to the arguments as they apply in various welfare areas, see Le Grand and Robinson, 1984b). But, briefly, we can say the following.

For markets to be efficient, it is necessary for certain conditions to be fulfilled. Both consumers and producers must be perfectly informed; there must be no natural or other forms of monopoly; there must be no externalities. Now, these conditions are not always met in key areas of welfare provision. In medical services and, to a lesser extent, education, there is a clear imbalance between the information that consumers possess and that possessed by suppliers, an imbalance that confers a measure of monopoly power on the latter. In areas such as insurance against loss of earnings due to old age, unemployment or sickness, the imbalance is the other way round. Individuals are often in a better position than insurance companies to know the likely risk of their encountering the relevant hazard, thus creating the problem technically known as 'adverse selection'; insurance companies cannot monitor individual behaviour sufficiently closely so as to deter individuals from increasing the relevant risks once insured, thus creating the problem of 'moral hazard'. Hence there is a need on *efficiency* (not redistributive) grounds for social insurance – for government intervention to promote redistribution over the life-time. Increasing returns to scale, and hence problems of 'natural' monopolies, arise in hospital provision, the provision of rural schools, and in the joint provision of various forms of social insurance. Externalities arise when the use of a service by an individual confers benefits on other individuals not directly concerned. This phenomenon characterizes several welfare areas: for instance, immunization from medical diseases, house improvements, the acculturation role of education.

The existence of these market imperfections does not, of course, imply that state intervention in the relevant markets will necessarily improve matters. Many of the factors causing these imperfections also create problems for state intervention. Thus, for example, suppliers' monopoly of information on medical services creates difficulties for the efficient organization of the British National Health Service (Le Grand and Robinson, 1984b, p. 49). Also, state intervention creates efficiency problems of its own. The lack of direct accountability to users may cause waste and other inefficiencies; the provision of services at subsidized prices may encourage the use of services whose marginal social costs exceed their marginal social benefits; the taxation necessary to fund the state's activities may create adverse incentives for work and savings.

It is not our purpose here actually to assess the efficiency consequences of market or state forms of resource allocation. Rather, it is simply to draw attention to the fact that a case can be made for state welfare in terms of promoting allocative efficiency and, therefore, that efficiency considerations must be taken into account as one of the objectives of the welfare state.

COMMUNITY

A case for the welfare state might also be couched in terms of notions of 'community'. The end here in view would be a sense of social cohesion and fellow-feeling, and the sort of behaviour (non-egoistic, altruistic mutual aid) that naturally follows from such sentiments. In marked contrast to the strict reciprocity of the market's 'exchange relationship', the social welfare sector embodies a 'gift relationship': people give what they can and receive what they need, without any expectation of return. In this way, the welfare state is said to contribute to a sense of social unity. At one level, everyone's partaking of common 'rights of citizenship' symbolizes everyone's common membership in a single-status moral community. At another level, the mode of administration of some welfare programmes sometimes enhances social interactions across class boundaries (e.g. in bus queues and doctors' waiting rooms). At yet another level, welfare-state transfers tend to break down the grossest form of cross-class inequalities and in that way remove barriers to the emergence of a 'common culture' (Tawney, 1971, p. 43).

Again, the existence of *anomie* should not necessarily be taken to imply that state action taken to remedy it, through welfare programmes, will necessarily be a success. The communitarian rationale for the welfare state is problematical at many levels. The precise meaning of 'community' is unclear; and it can be made clear only by raising the discussion to such a level of abstraction as to make the notion woefully imprecise in its practical applications (Plant, 1978). Furthermore, the precise nature of the putative connection between social welfare programmes and fellow-feeling is obscure: is the relationship meant to be a logical one (turning on the definition of 'membership' in the community, as some 'social rights' theorists imply), or is it merely an empirical one? Are welfare programmes meant to be the cause of fellow-feeling, or their consequence? And so on.

Further still, it seems doubtful that the evidence will *fully* bear out any of these versions of the communitarian argument. Well-integrated communities (e.g. ancient Athens) have existed without a welfare state; welfare states, far from engendering or reflecting a feeling of 'oneness' with the needy, often (as in the US, perhaps) serve only to keep them at arm's length from the prosperous. Thus it seems that the welfare state is neither a necessary nor sufficient condition – neither a necessary cause nor inevitable consequence – of fellow-feeling (Goodin, forthcoming, ch. 4). At most, it might be a contributing factor. That in itself may be important, however.

THE RELEVANCE OF TRADE-OFFS

Those discussions of other goals besides redistribution are necessarily sketchy. We are under no illusion either that our listing of the other goals the welfare state might serve is complete, or that our treatment of those we do discuss is in any way exhaustive. Still, those remarks serve to indicate the range of other possible goals. For present purposes, that will suffice.

The reason it will suffice is that the existence of those goals other than redistribution could be regarded, for the purposes of the present discussion, as simply irrelevant. That is *not* to say that redistribution is the only important goal of the welfare state; it is not even to say that redistribution is the most important among its many goals. Instead, it is merely to say that there is no logically necessary trade-off between redistributive and other sorts of goals. The pursuit of these other sorts of goals is, in principle, *separable* from the pursuit of redistribution. That being the case, it may not be necessary to sacrifice anything in terms of redistribution in order to achieve any of the other goals we might have in mind for the welfare state. That is the sense in which we say those other goals may be irrelevant.

It would matter whether redistribution was *the* principal aim, or merely *a* principal aim, of the welfare state only if there were some necessary trade-off between redistribution and other goals. Our concern in this book is, specifically, with the beneficial involvement of the non-poor in the welfare state. So the trade-off that must concern us is this: might the beneficial involvement of the non-poor in the welfare state, which is *prima facie* undesirable from the point of view of redistribution, be necessary and good from the point of view of efficiency or community?

Superficially, it may seem that there may be some such necessary trade-off. Many of the efficiency gains in view can be had only if everyone is subject to the same policy. Community spirit can be engendered only by everyone participating in the same programmes and activities. And so on.

But as Crosland (1956, p. 145) pointed out long ago, universal use of a service is importantly different from universal *free* use. In economists' language, it may be possible to devise means tests that extract consumer surplus from better-off users of a service without affecting their level of use. Put less technically, it is one thing not to means-test access to a service; it is quite another not to use means tests to charge those who can afford to pay for their usage of those universally available services. Universal use of the former sort is what is required for the purposes of efficiency or community as we just discussed. Universal free use of the latter sort is what might constitute a threat to redistributive aims.[5] Since the one does not necessarily entail the other, there is no *automatic* trade-off between redistribution and other goals on this point. Efficiency and community can be promoted by making services of the welfare state universally available, while redistribution is promoted by transfers or by levying increasingly larger user fees for these services upon those who can afford to pay more for them.

To say there are absolutely *no* trade-offs between redistributivist and other sorts of goals is, of course, an exaggeration. Even if the Crosland strategy works to remove the necessity of some of the trade-offs between redistribution and community, that strategy may still entail some costs in terms of efficiency: letting everyone use the same services, but charging some people more for them than we charge others (and charging still other people nothing at all for them) amounts to 'price discrimination', and that may entail inefficiencies of a familiar form. Similarly, to the extent that the transfers create disincentive effects, there may be some efficiency loss. However, none of these are *necessary* consequences of redistributive measures, and their significance in practice is ultimately an empirical question.

While we cannot therefore completely dismiss the issue of trade-offs, we still believe that downplaying it is a useful antidote to the standard occupational hazard among economists of overplaying it. As Atkinson (1987) rightly complains, economists spend all too much time probing the trade-offs – between equality and efficiency, social justice and work disincentives – entailed by social policies, and all too little ever asking whether those policies really work to accomplish what they set out to accomplish. Here we hope to restore that question to its rightful place at centre stage by asking, 'Is the welfare state really redistributive?'

This is a useful question to address, even if some trade-offs turn out to occur in practice. Suppose that, for some reasons, it turns out that the goals of community or efficiency can be pursued only (or, anyway, best) through some mechanism that entails the beneficial involvement of the non-poor in the welfare state. This book will still have performed the undeniably useful purpose of showing that there is the price to be paid, in terms of redistributive goals, for pursuing those other goals in such ways.

Plan of the Book

The strategy in the following chapters is to trace the beneficial involvement of the non-poor through various stages in the life-cycle of welfare-state programmes: their origins, their development and their possible decline. An essential – and necessarily rather technical – preliminary is an assessment of the methodological difficulties that arise in establishing the extent of that involvement – or, more generally, the distributional impact of the welfare state. Accordingly, this is the subject of Chapter 2, where Le Grand addresses issues such as the role of taxation, general versus partial equilibrium analysis, valuation of benefits, incidence, externalities and capital expenditures.

Part Two demonstrates the beneficial involvement of the non-poor in the origins of the postwar welfare state. Thus in Chapter 3 Goodin and Dryzek use a case study of Britain and a cross-national regression analysis involving twenty-two other countries to argue that the dramatic expansion and alteration of the welfare state during and after the Second World War can best be explained by the pervasive uncertainty experienced by everyone, poor and non-poor alike, in consequence of that war.

Part Three discusses aspects of the beneficial involvement of the non-poor in the development and present practices of the welfare state, and reflects upon some of the mechanisms whereby that beneficial involvement is effected. Thus in Chapter 4 Haveman attempts to quantify the extent to which the non-poor benefit from the American welfare state. In Chapter 5 Le Grand summarizes some of the evidence concerning the distributional impact of the British social services and discusses some possible ways in which that impact could be changed. In Chapter 6 Goodin and Le Grand demonstrate both the way in which the non-poor have infiltrated the Australian social security system, and the mechanism that enabled that infiltration to be so successful. In Chapter 7 Goodin, Le Grand and Gibson again draw on Australian evidence to argue that the geographic location of publicly-provided services will often tend to be biased against the poor, and hence favour the better off.

Part Four deals with the role that the non-poor have played and are playing in the current 'crisis' of the welfare state, particularly in Britain and America. In Chapter 8 Le Grand and Winter use econometric evidence to establish that the middle classes have played a prominent role in the successful defence of the British welfare state against the attack mounted by the Conservative Government of Mrs Thatcher. In Chapter 9 Hanson argues a similar case with respect to the middle classes in the defence of key elements in the American welfare state under the Reagan Administration, where federalism also acts as a crucial intervening variable.

Finally, having illustrated the beneficial involvement of the non-poor in the birth and life and possible decline of the welfare state over time, we are in a position to reflect in Part Five on both the inevitability and the undesirablity of the phenomenon. This is the task of our conclusion in Chapter 10.

Notes

We gratefully acknowledge the comments of Tony Atkinson, John Dryzek, Bob Haveman, John Hills and Philip Pettit on earlier drafts of this chapter.

1   We phrase 'middle classes' in the plural, in deference to the growing body of sociological findings pointing to the plurality of class locations. The problem of defining social class is a large and complex one – and, happily, one that we can afford to skirt for the purposes of this book. For present purposes, all that matters is that there is a large, identifiable body of persons who are beneficially involved in welfare state programmes who are 'non-poor'. What matters for the sake of our argument here is merely that they are not poor – whatever else they may be. Nothing in our argument would be affected one way or another whether they turned out to be non-poor members of the working classes or non-poor members of the middle classes or, indeed, non-poor members of the upper classes.

2   Or – what is only a slightly longer version of the same basic story – the welfare state is supposed to redistribute resources from categories of people who are generally richer to categories of people who are generally poorer (e.g. families with children; the disabled). The rationale and basic tendency of the rule is plainly redistributive, even though in any particular application of it the beneficiary might be richer than the benefactor.

3   The conceptions of justice and compassion are not the same, even though they are sometimes confused. Justice refers, in some sense, to people's due: to what they merit as of right, for example. Compassion refers to the desire to provide help to others, regardless of what they may or may not 'merit'. The distinction is apparent in the old proverb: 'be just before you are generous'. For a discussion of the possible motivations for redistribution, see Tullock (1983, ch. 1).

4   This broadly corresponds to Nozick's (1974, ch. 7) distinction between end-state and process models of distributive justice.

5   'Might', because even universal free use would not necessarily constitute a threat to redistributive aims, provided we could pay for those programmes by taxing (only) the rich, as John Dryzek has rightly pointed out to us.

Chapter 2

Measuring the Distributional Impact of the Welfare State: Methodological Issues

JULIAN LE GRAND

Many of the arguments advanced in subsequent chapters of this book depend upon evidence drawn from various studies concerning the distributional impact of the welfare state. Hence it seems important first to address some of the methodological difficulties involved in such studies, and to see what problems they present for interpreting the evidence. Such is the task of this chapter.

Although, as will become apparent, many of the issues overlap, it is convenient to group them under six headings: taxation, partial versus general equilibrium analysis, valuation, benefits to suppliers, capital expenditure and externalities. Some of the issues are technical and hence inevitably require technical discussion; however, so far as possible, these have been kept to a minimum, and, in one case, relegated to an appendix. The discussion draws heavily upon some of my previous work (Le Grand, 1982b, Appendix A; 1985; 1986); it has also, of course, been influenced by other discussions of methodology in this area, such as Peacock and Shannon (1968), Prest (1968), Aaron and McGuire (1970), Webb and Sieve (1971), Peacock (1974), Boreham and Semple (1976), Field, Meacher and Pond (1977) and O'Higgins (1980).

Taxation

A common objection to many studies of the distributional impact of
public expenditure is that they ignore taxation. The redistributive
effect of a particular public programme, it is argued, cannot properly
be assessed simply by looking at the beneficiaries from that programme; it is also necessary to take account of those who bear the
cost. It is the *net* redistributive consequences of a programme that are
of interest, not simply the effects of the expenditure on its own.

Against this, it might be argued that both conceptually and in
practice public expenditure and taxation are quite separate distributional instruments. The distributional impact of a given tax is usually
assessed independently of the incidence of the public expenditure it
'finances', for the good reason that, in the absence of ear-marked
taxes, it is impossible to say which tax 'finances' which item of public
expenditure. Indeed, in a world of general revenues and deficit
financing, the 'financing' of a particular programme could be
attributed partly or wholly to government borrowing, as much as to
taxation. The point is reinforced by the fact that, as any student of
public finance is aware, taxes (or government borrowing) do not
actually 'finance' public expenditure; rather, they 'permit' public
expenditure by reducing aggregate demand so as to permit a
government undertaking a given amount of spending to meet its
macro-economic targets.

However, if it were agreed that some analysis of the taxation 'costs'
of public expenditure programmes were appropriate, how might this
be undertaken? There is no simple answer to this question.

A commonly used approach is 'to determine the proportion of a
government's total expenditure that go for a particular programme
and then to apply that proportion to the total taxes paid by the
[household]' (Hansen and Weisbrod, 1971, p. 515). Algebraically, if
E_j is the amount of public expenditure on the j'th programme, E,
total public expenditure, and T_i the taxes paid by the i'th household,
then the part of the cost of the programme incident upon the i'th
household, C_i, is:

$$C_i = \frac{E_j}{E} \cdot T_i$$

The second procedure is to allocate costs according to the proportion of total taxes that a household pays. This proportion, once

determined, is applied to the amount of expenditure on the programme to determine the apportionment of costs. Thus, if it were discovered that a particular household (or, more plausibly, group of households) was paying 5 per cent of total taxes, then the part of the cost incident on that group is assumed to be 5 per cent of the expenditure on the programme. Algebraically, the cost is allocated according to the formula:

$$C_i = \frac{T_i}{T} \cdot E_j$$

where T is total tax payments.

The two approaches are very similar. Indeed, if the government balances its budget, then $T = E$ and the two formulas are identical. Both seem plausible; however, both are in fact quite arbitrary, as we shall now see.

Hansen and Weisbrod (1971) have stated the basic argument. The only correct way, they maintain, to determine the allocation of the costs of a particular programme is to ascertain who would have benefited if the government had not allocated funds to the programme. Thus, if it could somehow be known that the government would have cut taxes had it not funded the programme, the costs are incident upon those who would have benefited from the tax reduction. This solution to the problem Hansen and Weisbrod term the 'marginal tax allocation' approach.

Now in fact it is possible to accept the logic underlying the marginal approach and yet to arrive at the same allocation of costs as would be obtained from the use of the customary approaches. What is required is an assumption about how the government would alter tax rates if it were not to fund the programme. Thus, if the government decides to change the overall tax rate applying to the i'th group, t_i, by an amount Δt_i, then the cost incident upon the group under the marginal approach is $\Delta t_i \cdot Y_i$, where Y_i is the tax base to which the overall rate is applied. If this is to yield an equiproportional allocation as in, for instance, the first approach, then:

$$\Delta t_i \cdot Y_i = \frac{E_j}{E} \cdot T_i = \frac{E_j}{E} \cdot t_i \cdot Y_i$$

Therefore:

$$\frac{\Delta t_i}{t_i} = \frac{E_j}{E} \tag{2.1}$$

which is constant for all i.

Similarly, the second approach implies a proportional tax rate change given by:

$$\frac{\Delta t_i}{t_i} = \frac{E_j}{T} \tag{2.2}$$

Thus the assumption required for the two methods of allocation to be 'correct' is that the government would change the overall tax applying to each group in such a way that the *proportional* change in the rate was (a) the same for all groups, and (b) equal to the proportion of the government's total expenditure (or total tax revenue) that go to fund the programme.

So the customary approaches carry with them a specific counter-factual hypothesis concerning what the government would do if it were not to fund the programme. However, as Hansen and Weisbrod ask, why should it be assumed that the government would act in this way? There seems little empirical basis to suppose that the government, in the absence of the programme, would reduce taxes in such a way as to conform to either of conditions (2.1) or (2.2); and yet this is precisely what these approaches imply. Nor is the assumption even a particularly plausible one. For in practice there are a large number of taxes that are paid by any one group, and the assumption requires that the government adjusts some or all of the *separate* tax rates for each tax, so that the overall rate change corresponds to (2.1) or (2.2) – hardly a likely course of action.

Is there any kind of non-arbitrary counterfactual hypothesis that can be made about government behaviour if it were not to fund a particular programme? There are three general options, any of which the government might choose in such a situation. First, it could direct the funds to another expenditure programme within the public sector. In this case, the costs of funding the original programme are incident upon those who would have benefited from these other projects, had they been undertaken. Second, it could allocate the funds to the private sector, by a reduction in some or all tax rates. This is the course of action discussed above and, as was mentioned, the costs are then incident upon those on whom the tax reduction would have been incident. Third, it could 'absorb' the funds in the budget surplus or deficit. The government need not allocate the money to any sector, public or private, but could simply increase its budgetary surplus or decrease its deficit. In that case the costs are incident upon those who would have gained from the macroeconomic consequences of such a change.

Now, in an attempt to predict which of these options the government might pursue, it might be possible to eliminate the third. For, if the government were pursuing a 'finely-tuned' stabilization policy, it would presumably be reluctant to upset its policy by indulging in uncompensated reductions in expenditure. However, in the absence of sustained research into government behaviour, it would seem impossible to predict accurately which of the other two options might be chosen in the hypothetical situation of expenditure being reduced. Moreover, to add to the difficulty, even if the particular option could be predicted, its exact form would also have to be forecast. Thus, if it were decided that the money would be directed into a current expenditure programme, the question as to which programme would have to be faced. Similarly, if a reduction in taxes were chosen as the most likely course of action, predictions would have to be made concerning which taxes would be reduced and by how much.

Faced with this problem, Hansen and Weisbrod suggest either avoiding it altogether by ignoring the distribution of costs, or by comparing the distribution of benefits 'with some magnitude, such as *total* taxes paid, which does not require a determination of whose tax dollars finance a particular expenditure' (1971, p. 517). This procedure is actually the one followed in the British government's annual estimates of the distribution of taxes and benefits in the UK (for a recent example, see UK CSO, 1985). But it is inherently unsatisfactory. It is simply meaningless to compare the absolute value of taxes paid to finance all public programmes with the benefits received from just one of them. The only way such a procedure might make sense is if total tax payments were compared with the aggregate value of the benefits from *all* public programmes (including defence, police, highways, etc. as well as social services); even here, the counterfactual hypothesis is being made that if all public expenditure were eliminated, so would all taxation, leaving, for instance, government borrowing unchanged.

What can be done? There are two ways round the difficulty. One is to concentrate on questions concerning the distributional impact of public policies that do not require the positing of a counterfactual hypothesis. Basically these concern the attainment of a specific objective, such as equal treatment for equal need, or a minimum standard of housing. We can, at least in principle, observe whether under existing policies these objectives have been achieved or not, without having to postulate some alternative. Thus, we can see whether there exists, under current policies, equal medical treatment for equal need, equality of access to education, minimum standards of housing or whatever. This is essentially the procedure followed in Le Grand (1982b).

However, this procedure does rather limit the range of possible questions. It rules out, for example, important questions of interest such as: has programme X achieved greater equality in private disposable income? Is programme X redistributive? In such cases the only solution is to make the counterfactual nature of the discussion explicit. That is, statements of the kind 'programme X is redistributive' have to be replaced by statements that incorporate one or more counterfactual hypotheses. For instance, suppose it was discovered that higher income groups received five times as much subsidy from a particular programme as lower income groups. Then we can conclude that the programme redistributes income from poor to rich (that is, perversely) as compared with a situation where it is eliminated, if and only if were it eliminated: (1) there would be no other prices or incomes changes; and (2) the savings would be used (say, through a combination of tax cuts and social security payments) to raise everyone's income equally. Indeed, one could go further and say that the programme is (perversely) redistributive as compared with any situation where the savings were used to increase individuals' disposable incomes, except where the absolute increase in income for the rich is more than five times as great as that for the poor. Although such statements are much more cumbersome than the neat 'X is redistributive', they can be sensibly interpreted, whereas the other cannot.

Partial versus General Equilibrium

Most studies of the distributional impact of public expenditure (and indeed of taxation) are partial in nature. For instance, it is conventionally assumed that the only changes that occur are related directly to expenditures on the programme (or tax) under investigation; the programme is assumed to have no impact on the economic or other behaviour of the individuals involved, and hence no impact on earnings, savings or other prices. Thus, in many studies the distributional impact of a particular item of public expenditure is estimated by adding the amount of that expenditure directly incident upon a particular individual (or household or group) to the private income of that individual (household, group); it is thereby assumed that there is no change in the use of the service concerned as a result of the public expenditure, no change in the individual's pre-benefit income, no change in his or her consumption of other commodities, and no change in work effort or savings patterns.

We can illustrate the stringency of the conditions required for these assumptions to be correct by use of a simple algebraic example. Suppose a household pays taxes, T, on an income Y, and spends all its after-tax income on two commodities, 1 and 2, which are competitively supplied at prices P_1 and P_2 and of which it buys amounts X_1 and X_2. Then:

$$Y - T = P_1 X_1 + P_2 X_2$$

Now suppose the government decides to subsidize commodity 1, thus reducing the price faced by the household to zero. Letting superscripts 0 and 1 denote the values of the variables before and after the policy change respectively, the real value of the household's private disposable income (the income available for expenditure on commodity 2) after the change then is:

$$\frac{Y^1 - T^1}{P_2^1}$$

The increase in real income due to the policy change is therefore:

$$\frac{Y^1 - T^1}{P_2^1} - \frac{Y^0 - T^0 - P_1^0 X_1^0}{P_2^0} \tag{2.3}$$

Now the real value of the expenditure by the government on providing commodity 1 free to the consumer is:

$$\frac{A_1^1 X_1^1}{P_2^1} \tag{2.4}$$

where A_1^1 is the average cost of producing commodity 1. The question therefore is under what conditions (2.4) will equal (2.3). There are three sets of such conditions: first, that $X_1^1 = X_1^0$, $P_2^1 = P_2^0$, $A_1^1 = P_1^0$, $Y^0 = Y^1$ and $T^0 = T^1$; second, that some or none of the above equalities hold, but T is manipulated by the government such that (2.4) is brought equal to (2.3); third, that by chance the variables take on exactly the right values after the change such that (2.4) equals (2.3). The last two conditions seem unlikely to be fulfilled, to say the least. One assumes the government to possess a remarkable degree of fiscal skill; the other requires an extraordinary combination of circumstances. Unfortunately, the first set of conditions are almost equally stringent. They require that the household's demand for the commodity is totally inelastic ($X_1^0 = X_1^1$), that it is produced under constant returns to scale ($P_1^0 = A_1^1$),[1] that no other prices are affected ($P_2^0 = P_2^1$), that the household's money income is unchanged ($Y^0 = Y^1$), thereby requiring that the change in real income available for private use does not affect members of the households' ability or incentive to work, and that the government does not alter its taxes on the household ($T^0 = T^1$), even though it has increased its expenditure.

More down-to-earth illustrations of the difficulties involved can be provided by looking at some specific cases. For instance, consider *higher education*. Most higher education students in most countries are subsidized in one way or another, either through paying subsidized fees, through receiving subsidized loans or through receiving direct grants. Who actually benefits from this subsidy? The conventional answer is the students themselves, or perhaps their parents. But this need not necessarily be the case. If the subsidy were withdrawn, then, so long as the demand for higher education was not totally inelastic, there would be a fall in demand for that education and hence in the supply of graduates. So long as the employers' demand for graduates was not totally elastic, this in turn would imply a rise in the wages that graduates could command and hence in employers' costs. Employers (or, depending on the extent to which they could pass on cost increases in price increases, their customers) would therefore face greater costs if the higher education subsidy were withdrawn. Hence to that extent they are partial beneficiaries of the subsidy. Only if the demand for education were totally inelastic would *all* the benefit from the subsidy accrue to the students (or their parents).

That this is a significant problem in practice can be illustrated by reference to the demand for university places in the United Kingdom. Pissarides (1982) has estimated the elasticity of demand with respect to changes in the relative present values of earnings of manual workers and university graduates as approximately unity. Since he included the grant currently paid to British students in higher education as part of the income of university graduates during the period 18–21, any reduction in the grant due to a reduction in public subsidy will reduce the present value of graduates' earnings streams; so any such reduction would also be associated with a unitary price elasticity. This suggests therefore that a substantial withdrawal of public subsidy would lead to a substantial fall in the supply of graduates. Unpublished work at the Centre for Labour Economics at the London School of Economics suggests that the demand elasticity for graduates may be very low. If this is true, then, together with the relatively high elasticity of demand for university places, it suggests that there may be significant shifting of the public subsidy to education – and the assumption in most of the studies in this area (including my own, Le Grand, 1982a) that the whole of the subsidy is incident upon the nominal recipients is wrong.

Another example concerns *housing*. In most developed countries, owner-occupied housing is subsidized through the tax system. Owner-occupiers either receive tax relief on mortgage interest payments; or they are not taxed on their imputed income (for a discussion of the relationship between these two kinds of tax-expenditure, see Le Grand, 1982b, p. 91). Assessing the incidence of this subsidy raises important issues, ones that underline the difficult theoretical problems involved.

Suppose the supply of owner-occupied housing is totally inelastic. Then the introduction of a housing-related subsidy, such as the exemption of mortgage interest payments from tax, would simply raise the price of housing by exactly the amount of the subsidy: a once-and-for-all gain to those lucky enough to own housing at the time (and their descendants), but with no subsequent gains to anyone else. In particular, owner-occupiers who have bought their house since the introduction of the subsidy will apparently have no benefit from it. Now suppose the supply of housing was totally elastic. Then the introduction of a housing-related subsidy would have no effect on house prices; all the benefits will accrue to all owner-occupiers, including those who have bought their houses since the introduction of the subsidy. Thus, the incidence of the subsidy thus depends crucially upon the elasticity of housing supply.

Actually, the situation is still more complicated than this. For it depends on the counterfactual hypothesis chosen. If one compares the position of current owner-occupiers with that *which would have existed had the subsidy never been introduced*, then, if the supply of housing is partly or wholly inelastic, the benefit to those who bought houses subsequent to the introduction of the subsidy would be partly or wholly offset by the rise in house prices. If, on the other hand, the comparison is between the position of current owner-occupiers and that *which would exist if the subsidy were eliminated tomorrow*, then the same argument would suggest that, since house prices would fall, they would be the principal losers. So whether or not current owner-occupiers can be viewed as benefiting from housing-related tax-expenditures in the presence of an inelastic supply of housing will depend on the choice between two counterfactual hypotheses. Since theory offers us no guidance as to which we should select, either may be appropriate; again, however, it is important to specify which is being used in particular cases.

Overall, it is clear that in an ideal world, general equilibrium analysis would be the only correct procedure. However, even in the tax field the gaps in the data required for such analysis are enormous, and they are yet greater in the analysis of public expenditure. Partial equilibrium studies may therefore be the only feasible method of approach; but their weaknesses need to be acknowledged.

Valuation

A common criticism of empirical work on the impact of public expenditure is that the studies concerned measure the distribution of subsidy rather than of benefits. That is, the studies measure the distributional impact of a public service on a particular group by the costs to the public purse of the use of the service by that group, rather than by the *value* of the service to the individual concerned. Since the distribution of the latter may be quite different, concentrating only upon the former may give a misleading impression of the actual impact.

Now, in an ideal world it might be preferable to measure, say, the distribution of consumer surplus rather than the distribution of costs. As Timothy Smeeding has argued 'most economists agree that [consumer surplus] is the proper measure for ranking in-kind transfers to evaluate their impact on economic well-being and the income size distribution because it translates the market value of goods into cash values conceptually equivalent to the money incomes to which they are added' (Smeeding, 1984, p. 145; see also Smeeding and Moon, 1980; Smeeding, 1982).

However, the practical and theoretical problems are immense. First, the measurable proxy for consumer surplus (the area under the Marshallian demand curve) is only an accurate indication of the value individuals place on a service if the income elasticity of demand for the service is zero. Second, any comparison of consumer surpluses across individuals requires that the marginal utility of income to each individual be the same: an implausible requirement when the comparison is being made across different income groups. Third, the data requirements are considerable; in particular, to construct the relevant demand curves, it is necessary to obtain individual money valuations of their use of the service concerned.

The third problem could be resolved if market valuations were available. However, since for virtually all the services concerned private markets are non-existent, very small or heavily distorted, it is not clear whence such valuations would come. Alternatively, questionnaires could be used; but these are unreliable, since respondents face no particular incentive to tell the truth (and indeed if they suspect the information they reveal may be used in some way detrimental to their interests – such as in assessing their tax burden – may have a positive incentive to lie). Preference-revelation mechanisms have recently been devised involving payments to or from individuals whereby individuals can maximize the payments they receive (or minimize the ones they make) if they reveal their preferences for a commodity correctly (see Varian, 1984, for a useful summary). But these have the rather implausible requirement that individuals' true preferences for the commodities concerned are independent of the size of the transfers involved; also, they have yet to be tried out on any significant scale.

Aaron and McGuire (1970) have shown that, for a public good, if households' utility functions are identical and additively separable between the public good and all other commodities, then a household's money valuation of the public good will be inversely proportional to the marginal utility of its income.[1] But apart from the inherent implausibility of the assumptions, this procedure does not solve the problem of the unavailability of data, for it is now necessary to obtain information concerning differences in households' marginal utilities of income.

It is possible in come cases to use consumer theory to draw some *qualitative* conclusions about the distribution of benefits from information concerning the distribution of use. For those who are interested, an illustration is provided in an appendix to this chapter. However, to obtain *quantitative* information concerning the distribution of benefits presents almost insurmountable difficulties. Perhaps the best that can be done is simply to acknowledge that in general it would be better to measure benefits than costs, but practical considerations dictate concentrating only on the latter.

Benefits to Suppliers

It has now become commonplace to assert that the many public services are run in the interests of their suppliers as well as their users. That this is indeed quite plausible can be illustrated by a simple example, where the government purchases a service from suppliers and sells it to consumers at a subsidized price. This situation is illustrated in Figure 2.1 where D and S are the supply and demand curves for the commodity, P_1 is the market price and P_2 is the subsidized price. To meet the extra demand created by the subsidy, the government has to increase the price paid to suppliers to P_3. This results in an increase in consumers' surplus of the darker dotted area and an increase in suppliers' surplus of the lighter dotted area (the total subsidy is given by the two areas plus the striped triangle). The relative sizes of the surpluses will of course depend on the elasticities

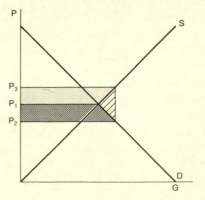

Figure 2.1 *Supplier and consumer benefits from price subsidy*

of the supply and demand curves; but even if they were the same, since there are likely to be far fewer suppliers than consumers, *per head*, the value of the surplus involved is likely to be much greater for the former. Only if the supply curve were totally elastic, or if the demand curve were totally inelastic would there be no increase in suppliers' surplus and only in those cases would the conventional assumption that all the benefits are incident on consumers be correct.

Capital Expenditure

Another common practice in public expenditure incidence studies is to confine the analysis to the current expenditure, thus omitting capital expenditure. This is usually justified on the grounds that the benefits from that expenditure accruing to individuals using the services in the future should not be attributed to those using them in the present (see, for example, Peretz, 1975, p. 9). However, this argument has been criticized on two grounds. First, some parts of what is generally considered to be current expenditure in certain areas (such as education and health care) also yield benefits that accrue in the future; therefore consistency would require that these too should be omitted (Boreham and Semple, 1976, p. 292). Second, the argument implies that elements of past capital expenditure should be allocated as well as current expenditure, a procedure that is rarely followed (Boreham and Semple, 1976, p. 274; Peretz, 1975, p. 9).

The first criticism is slightly misplaced. If the intention is to calculate the distribution of the public expenditure undertaken in a particular year, it is incorrect to omit some of that expenditure (whether nominally 'current' or 'capital') on the grounds that it yields benefits in the future. Rather, the procedure should be to allocate such expenditure (subject to appropriate discounting) to those who are going to receive the future benefits. These may be the current users of the service (as in the case of education), or they may be future users (as in the case of a motorway in the process of construction). The second criticism, however, is more legitimate. Strictly speaking, public expenditure on a particular service in a given year should include the opportunity cost of the capital used (its value in an alternative use); and therefore any estimate of the distribution of that expenditure should also include the distribution of that opportunity cost.

Are these omissions serious? They would only be a problem if, under existing policies, the distribution of such expenditure was significantly different from that of current expenditure. Since this would require the distribution of future users of the relevant services to be different from the distribution of present users, this seems unlikely.

Externalities

Any study concerned with the distributional impact of public expenditure has to identify accurately who are the actual beneficiaries of that expenditure, that is, those on whom the expenditure is incident. Two problems arise here. First, there is the question of public goods: commodities, of which the classic example is military defence, which are non-excludable and non-rival in consumption and hence whose use (or the benefits therefrom) cannot be allocated to any specific individual or group of individuals. Related to this problem, and of more relevance to the welfare state is the question of externalities. An individual's use of a particular service may benefit (or cost) not only the individual himself or herself, but others as well, that is, it may generate an 'external' benefit (or cost). A classic example is the case of vaccination, where if I decide to be vaccinated against a particular disease then this not only reduce the chances of my getting the disease, but also reduces the chance of your catching it off me. Other examples include the reduction in congestion on roads due to public transport subsidies and the increase in the value of properties adjacent to a house recently refurbished. If such externalities exist, then to assume that public expenditure in a particular service is incident only upon the direct users of that service, as is done in almost all the relevant studies, is incorrect.

In practice, most studies of public expenditure fail to consider externalities. It is difficult to know what impact this failure has on their results concerning the impact of public expenditure on inequality. However, it is worth noting that, to have a serious effect on the conclusions of the book, it would be necessary for any externalities that exist to be distributed in an opposite direction to that of the distribution of internal benefits. Since this does not appear to be particularly plausible at least so far as the services relevant to the welfare state are concerned, it is likely that even if these problems were properly taken into account, the basic conclusions would remain intact.

A Concluding Word

In this chapter, I have discussed some of what seem to be the principal dangers that confront those who venture into the difficult territory of researching the distributional impact of public policy. A legitimate criticism of the discussion is that it is rather better at pointing out problems than at presenting solutions. However, many of the problems concerned have been with us for a long time; their very longevity indicates that they have no easy answers. Perhaps the most that can be expected from researchers in the area is that they show an awareness of the problems concerned, and of the extent to which those problems might limit their analyses.

Appendix: The Distribution of Benefits

Consider the following simple model. Suppose there are only two commodities: X, privately supplied and G, publicly supplied. (G may or may not be a public good in the Samuelsonian sense.) All individuals have identical utility functions $U(G, X)$ with the usual properties. Then:

$$MV = U_g/\lambda \qquad (2.5)$$

where MV is the marginal valuation placed on a unit of G by each individual, U_g is the marginal utility of that unit and λ is the marginal utility of income. Holding G constant, differentiate (2.5) with respect to Y. This gives:

$$\frac{d(MV)}{dY} = \frac{U_{gx}dX/dY}{\lambda} - \frac{U_g d\lambda/dY}{\lambda^2} \qquad (2.6)$$

where $d(MV)/dY$ is the change in the marginal valuation of any unit of G with respect to changes in income.

Now, given that the utility function has normal properties (such that $U_g > 0$ and $d\lambda/dY < 0$), the second term on the right hand side of (2.6) is negative. Then if $U_{gx} \geqslant 0$ and if the privately provided commodity is a normal good ($dX/dY > 0$) then $d(MV)/dY > 0$. That is, the marginal valuation of each unit of G will increase with income, if the utility function is additively separable ($U_{gx} = 0$), or if the

marginal utility of the publicly provided commodity increases with
the consumption of the private commodity ($U_{gx} > 0$).

What does this imply about benefits? First, note it means that, for
publicly provided commodities that meet the necessary conditions
($U_{gx} \geqslant 0$), the demand (MV) curve for the better off will always lie
above that for the poor. This in turn must imply that the better off
will derive greater consumer surplus from any publicly-provided
good that is supplied at a uniform price (which may or may not be
zero). Moreover, this will be true even if non-price rationing is
employed, providing again that the form of rationing is uniform.
This is illustrated in Figure 2.2, which shows the distribution of good
G (assumed for the purpose of the diagram to be not a Samuelsonian
public good) for both (a) price, and (b) non-price rationing. D_p and
D_r in both diagrams are the demand curves for the poor and rich
respectively; in (a), the commodity is supplied at a price P, and in (b)
it is supplied free, but an amount $\bar{G}$ is allocated alike to both rich and
poor. The consumer surplus for the poor in each case is the dotted
area, obviously smaller than the consumer surplus for the rich (the
dotted area plus the striped area).

Since most of the public services with which we are concerned
probably do meet the necessary conditions (that is, their marginal
utility increases, or at least remains constant, as private consumption
increases), it is likely that, if they were supplied at a uniform price or
by uniform non-price criteria, benefits would increase with income.

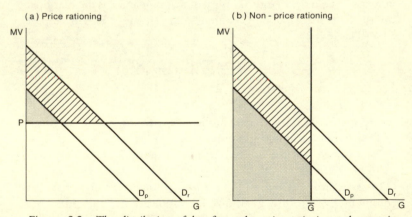

Figure 2.2   *The distribution of benefits under price rationing and non-price rationing*

Hence, for such services at least, observation of a pro-rich distribution of use or subsidy would be consistent with a pro-rich distribution of benefits. More interestingly, the analysis suggests that an equal (or even, under some circumstances, a pro-poor) distribution of use might be associated with a pro-rich distribution of benefits.

Notes

1. This result, incidentally, is true under these assumptions not just for public goods, but also for any commodity that is consumed equally by households – a point not made by Aaron and McGuire (1970).

PART TWO

The Origins of the Welfare State

Chapter 3

Risk-Sharing and Social Justice: The Motivational Foundations of the Post-War Welfare State

ROBERT E. GOODIN and JOHN DRYZEK

Much political behaviour can be interpreted as the pursuit of more or less naked self-interest. Occasionally, though, individuals do apparently exhibit some concern for their fellow human beings. The result is a less cold and dismal world – and one in which moral philosophers can find a role. Our focus here, however, is more on practical problems than philosophical ones. We shall be less concerned with questions of what moralists should demand of people than with questions of how such demands could be enforced upon people.

Specifically, we will be asking how it has been possible to evoke, from people who are not themselves poor, support for policies aiding those less fortunate than themselves. We propose to address this question by exploring the sources of support for the most broadly-based institution presently available for promoting social justice, the welfare state.[1]

There are three caveats to be entered straightaway. First, our focus is on *post-1945 expansions* of programmes that had their origins much earlier – in some cases, as early as the turn of the century.[2] Such a focus is arguably misplaced. Some would say that it is more significant to introduce a programme for the first time than to extend it many years later; and those looking for continuities can surely find them in the formal shells of these programmes. But emphasizing the continuities would overlook what seems to us far more significant, namely, the sharp discontinuity that occurred between prewar and postwar social security expenditures, and the way in which this happened in some countries but not in others. That is what most needs to be explained, if the question is one of people's motivations for pursuing social justice.

Second, we do indeed intend to focus tightly upon these *motivational* questions. Of course, there are also various cultural, social-structural and institutional factors at work in the growth of welfare states (Wildavsky, 1985; Wilensky, 1975; Flora and Heidenheimer, 1981). In the end, all these factors will have to be blended together into one large super-model. Here, however, we shall focus narrowly upon certain individualistic and intentional factors that will, in our view, have to be incorporated in any plausible larger model.

Third, we shall focus on the growth of *social security* programmes, not on the growth of public expenditures in general or even on the growth of social spending broadly conceived. The latter might include programmes of public provision for health, housing, education, regulation and so on. There are good reasons, however, for believing that some of these policies are special cases (Wilensky, 1975, ch. 1); with regard to others, long runs of data are often missing. We shall therefore follow the lead of various earlier commentators (Rimlinger, 1971; Wilensky, 1975; Jackman, 1975) and confine our attention to social security programmes, understood as, basically, income-support programmes.

Setting Altruism Aside

In so far as it is seen to be anything other than a mere social-structural epiphenomenon, welfare-state benevolence is ordinarily explained in terms of 'altruism' and 'sympathy'. This theory has its joint origins in the works of David Hume (1739, bk. 3; 1777) and Adam Smith (1790, pt. 1, sec. 1, ch. 5, para. 5). To this day, it continues to find adherents among both social theorists and economists (Baker, 1979; Margolis, 1982; Wilson and Wilson, 1982). Recently, for example, economists have appealed to just such 'interdependencies in people's utility functions' to make out a case for the Pareto optimality of (some) redistribution, to explain post-disaster charitable relief and so on (Hochman and Rogers, 1969; Dacy and Kunreuther, 1969; De Alessi, 1967; 1968; 1975).

Such explanations do not, however, take us very far. What enters into these models as assumptions (altruistic preferences) emerges virtually unchanged as conclusions (altruistic behaviour). It is, as Brian Barry (1977, p. 279) says, 'a pretty thin performance', rather 'like a conjurer putting a rabbit in a hat, taking it out again, and expecting a round of applause'.

Still, even though it is not a very powerful explanation, it may none the less be a true one so far as it goes. At some level, this simply has to be true. Family life is pretty well incomprehensible unless you assume mutual benevolence and sympathy of roughly this form (Becker, 1982). But, alas, this theory is unlikely to be true at the level it needs to be in order to explain such generalized benevolence as is practised through the welfare state. It is one thing to care for those particular individuals, known and beloved to us, that constitute our own families. Extending such sentiments from those who share our genes to all those who merely happen to share the same coloured passport is another thing altogether.

Were this otherwise – if people's benevolence and sympathies really did extend to all their fellow countrymen – then the welfare state would be the least dramatic of the consequences. Systematic revisions would be required right across the range of our social and political theory and practice.

The notion of 'self-sacrifice', for example, would become incoherent. If people were altruistic, in the sense of internalizing others' interests as their own, then when 'sacrificing' themselves to aid others they would really just be pursuing their own extended interests. At the very least, that is untrue to the phenomenology of self-sacrifice: that is just not how it *feels* to perform an act of self-sacrifice. Both philosophical arguments (Overvold, 1980) and social-psychological findings (Batson and Coke, 1981) converge on the conclusion that such skepticism is well-founded. Bishop Butler (1726, sermon 9), it seems, was right to say that the altruist's object is the other's happiness itself, and not just the satisfaction of the altruist's own desire for the other's happiness.

Or, to take another example, notice the objection lodged by William Thompson, an early feminist, against James Mill's assumption that women need not be given the vote because their interests would be internalized by their fathers or husbands. Thompson (1825, p. 19) protests:

The pretext set up to exclude women from political rights, namely, the inclination of men to use power over them beneficently, would, if admitted, sweep away the grand argument itself for the political rights of men; inasmuch as it would prove men to be inclined to use power, though without limits or checks, beneficently, over at least half their race. Whence the argument founded on the contrary assumption, that of the universal love of power for selfish purposes, must fail.

Now, Thompson's own claim is tenuous at best. A man's wife or daughter stands in a very different sort of relationship to him than do anonymous fellow-countrymen; and it is entirely plausible (although by no means certain) that he might internalize her interests without simultaneously internalizing those of everyone else in his community. But those who explain the welfare state in terms of 'altruism' and 'sympathy' must, of course, assert that latter, more dramatic proposition: they must claim that one's altruism and sympathies extend to some significant degree to strangers (indeed, to *all* needy strangers in the community) as well as to those to whom one is personally connected. If that were true, then Thompson's point would really begin to bite; civil and political rights really would be superfluous. If we are uncomfortable with that conclusion, then we had better reconsider the premiss that leads so inexorably to it.

Or, to take a final and more mundane objection to the altruism move, notice that it would imply that one should give less to worthy causes, the more others are giving. Intuitively, that is implausible: that is just not what is means to *care*. Empirically, such evidence as we have on the economics of philanthropic contributions suggests that that is simply not how people really behave (Sugden, 1982).

The model of altruism – internalizing others' pains and pleasures as one's own – is thus variously flawed. It is theoretically thin. Its implications are implausible. In so far as empirical evidence can be brought to bear on the topic, its predictions would appear to be mostly false. In short, this standard explanation of welfare-state benevolence fails.

Uncertainty and Morality

Having set to one side explanations based on altruism, we propose to try a different tack. We start from twin presumptions. The first is that the welfare state is essentially (in its intentions, if not necessarily its effects) an instrument of social justice. The second is that justice is essentially a matter of impartiality. Utilitarians say so; Kantians agree; and that, at least according to the modern conventional wisdom, pretty well exhausts the viable alternatives. For present purposes, we shall simply take that as given.

There are various devices for deducing what actions impartiality might demand of us: Adam Smith's impartial spectator, Richard Hare's universalizability, John Rawls's original position and so on. Representative of these devices is John Harsanyi's 'equiprobability model of moral value judgments'. A theme introduced in Harsanyi's first published article, and one to which he has constantly returned, is that:

> a value judgment on the distribution of income would show the required impersonality to the highest degree if the person who makes this judgment had to choose a particular income distribution in complete ignorance of what his ówn relative position . . . would be within the system chosen. This would be the case if he had exactly the same chance of obtaining the first position (corresponding to the highest income) or to the second or the third, etc., up to the last position (corresponding to the lowest income) available within that scheme. (Harsanyi, 1953, pp. 434–5; see similarly 1982, pp. 44–8).

This formulation leaves to one side the practical question of motivations – of why people might actually choose to be impartial, moral or just – that is of particular concern to us here. Harsanyi himself acknowledges:

> Of course, it is not really necessary that a person who wants to make a moral assessment of the relative merits of [two alternatives] . . . should be literally ignorant of the actual social position that he does occupy or would occupy under each system. But it *is* necessary that he should at least try his best to disregard this morally irrelevant piece of information when he is making his moral assessment. Otherwise his assessment will not be a genuine moral value judgment but rather will be merely a judgment of personal preference.

He goes on to claim that:

> each individual will . . . have *moral preferences*, which may or may not have much influence on his everyday behavior but which will guide his thinking in those – possibly very rare – moments when he forces a special impersonal and impartial attitude, that is, a moral attitude, upon himself. (Harsanyi, 1982, pp. 44, 47, italics in original; see similarly 1955, p. 315)

But nowhere does Harsanyi explain what gives rise to these 'very rare moments' or what causes people to put their egoistic interests into abeyance and act instead on their moral preferences. To put the question bluntly: why should we take a moral point of view, acting as if we were equally likely to occupy any position, when we know fully well which one we will in fact occupy?

We suggest that the impetus might be, broadly speaking, of either of two possible kinds. One is that the circumstances do not really allow people to pursue their egoistic interests, anyway. Then they can safely act on their principled concerns without any real cost to their selfish ones. This can happen in any number of ways, for any number of reasons. But the most general, and politically the most interesting, lies in the nature of mass electoral politics. There, the infamous 'voter's paradox' rears its head: since there is virtually no chance that any one vote will alter the electoral outcome, there is virtually no point in anyone going to the polls. Still, people do flock to the polls. The most plausible explanation, in our view, is that they are pursuing goals that do not depend for their satisfaction upon changing electoral outcomes. The same thing that makes the pursuit of egoistic advantage through mass politics irrational also frees us to pursue (nonconsequentialistic) moral principles in the selfsame arena (Goodin and Roberts, 1975; Benn, 1979; Goodin, 1986, pp. 86–91).

What this may mean for the welfare state depends, of course, upon what sort of principles people internalize. Followers of Samuel Smiles's ideology of 'self-help' might, as a matter of principle, insist that people should be made to stand on their own two feet (Smiles, 1859; cf. Goodin, 1985c). Among those, however, who feel the moral force of the welfare ideal at all, this eclipsing of selfish concerns by principled ones in the context of mass-electoral politics might explain why public welfare provision so far outstrips private (voluntary) contributions to social welfare.

There is of course a long history of explanations of the welfare state along the lines of principled behaviour. This is especially true among sociologists and cultural historians (Robson, 1976). But it is also true among philosophers. When pressed to specify what provides the motive force to compel people to adhere to his principles of justice, Rawls (1971, sec. 86) explains in one belated section of *A Theory of Justice* that it is a 'sense of justice', upon which people will act more-or-less automatically once his elaborate apparatus has given it direction.

A social scientist might once again reply that that may be true but, if so, it is not very interesting. The objection above was 'altruism in, altruistic behavior out'. The objection here is 'principles in, principled behaviour out'. An even more important reply might come from social reformers: it may be true, but we would not like to count on it. What they seek – and what we need – is a method for evoking moral behaviour from people who are not predisposed in that direction already.

An analysis couched in terms of principled behaviour might be useful for explaining certain marginal details of welfare-state provision. It is not, however, a very powerful tool for explaining the existence or nonexistence of the welfare state as such. At that level, the explanation comes dangerously close to becoming yet another tautology: voters create welfare states because their moral principles make them want to do so. Why that should be the case remains to be explained.

The second sort of impetus for people to act on the basis of 'moral preferences', defined in terms of Harsanyi's equiprobability criterion, is that people might be genuinely uncertain about their own positions. Then people would choose impartially, not because they are acting *as if* they were uncertain, but rather because they *really are* uncertain. They show concern for the outcomes for people in all positions, not as a matter of moral principle, but rather as a matter of self-protection.

Supporting various mechanisms for taking care of those in need is, under conditions of gross uncertainty, just a way of taking care of yourself. These institutions are, on this model, just insurance schemes, wherein everyone pools his own risks with the *ex ante* indistinguishable risks of everyone else. This is a common theme among modern political economists.[3] But notice that this argument is acknowledged even by that infamous Social Darwinist, William Graham Sumner, in his thoroughly mean analysis of *What Social Classes Owe Each Other*.[4]

Of course, some redistribution inevitably occurs within these insurance schemes. The lucky never need to draw on them, even though they have been paying their premiums for a long time. The unlucky who draw on them will typically draw out far more than they paid in. That is inherent in the logic of insurance (Zeckhauser, 1974). But the redistribution is utterly incidental to the true purpose of the programme. Participation in insurance schemes, and any redistribution that occurs in consequence, can be explained in purely egoistic terms of self-protection.

This is a plausible model of welfare-state activities. Indeed, the notion of 'social insurance' itself features largely in the early history of most welfare states. Notice, for example, how the original initiatives – workmen's injury compensation schemes, old age pensions, death, invalidity and even unemployment benefits – are all typically described in those terms, and are to some extent organized along those lines. In Britain, such things are covered by what is called 'National Insurance', in the US by the 'social security insurance program' or 'unemployment insurance'.[5] Judging from their form, at least, the original initiatives of the welfare state seem to serve essentially an insurance (i.e. risk-sharing) function.

There remains the problem of explaining why the need for any such insurance should be felt so deeply and so widely as to justify state action. After all, for a group of egoists to regard compulsory, society-wide risk-pooling schemes as just – fully just, in the sense of Harsanyi's equiprobability criterion – the uncertainty must be both profound and pervasive. In the limiting case described by Harsanyi, any given individual must be totally unaware of what position he will in fact occupy; and that must be true for each individual in the society. Furthermore, actuarial calculations will become completely impossible, leading to the total collapse of private insurance markets and making state intervention absolutely necessary, only if similarly profound uncertainty surrounds the magnitude of the risks that all alike are facing.

It is rare for these conditions to be completely satisfied. Social commentators have long appreciated that:

> Security is the chief end of civilization, and as it progresses, the fortunes of individuals are upon the whole made less liable to derangement. This very security may tend to make men careless of the welfare of others and . . . may [thus] be noted as an impediment to benevolence. (Helps, 1845, p. 14)

Such propositions are echoed by countless philosophers (Harman, 1975, pp. 12–13; Benn, 1978), economists (Zeckhauser, 1974, pp. 215–17) and social reformers. As the eminent turn-of-the-century British campaigner for old-age pensions, Charles Booth (1892, p. 201), poignantly notes,

> If the chances of poverty were equal, none could say that they lost while another gained by paying for a general scheme of pensions. They are not equal. 'One of the few lessons' (says Mr Leslie Stephen)

'which I have learnt from life, and not found already in copy books, is the enormous difficulty which a man of the upper classes finds in completely ruining himself even by vice, extravagance, and folly; whereas there are plenty of honest people who in spite of economy and prudence can scarcely keep out of the workhouse'.

Under ordinary circumstances, then, people have a pretty clear idea of what, broadly speaking, the future might hold for them.[6] But then again, welfare states do not emerge or, more especially, undergo dramatic expansions under ordinary circumstances. It usually takes some pretty dramatic events – if not quite so dramatic as the limiting case that Harsanyi describes – to lay the necessary foundations. Each welfare state, of course, has a history all its own. But here we shall be exploring one characteristic path to the welfare state, namely, the way in which welfare states grow out of periods of deep and widespread uncertainty in which the barriers to redistribution-through-insurance have largely collapsed. Moreover, under conditions of such profound uncertainty, actuaries will be unable to assess risks with any confidence, and hence prudent private brokers will refuse to supply insurance. The state alone is capable of filling this gap.

When a large proportion of the population is profoundly unsure what its relative standing in the future society will be, then partiality and impartiality are fused, and institutions for promoting social justice serve self-interest as well. Not all welfare-state innovations can be traced to this source.[7] But we shall argue that this is what underlay the greatest recent round of expansions.

Here we shall focus in particular upon the impetus that the Second World War gave to the development of welfare states.[8] What the benefits and burdens of war might be, and how they might be distributed, has presumably always been somewhat uncertain at a war's outset. But with the advent of modern total war these uncertainties have come to run more deeply and to be spread more widely. Perhaps the most dramatic (but hardly the only) example would be how, during the Battle of Britain, no one could say for certain where the bombs would land. At least at the outset, no Londoners, rich or poor, could be all that confident that they or their property were immune – or even substantially less at risk than the average. Nor, as the bombings spread, and especially with the advent of the wildly erratic buzz bombs, could many other Britons. As Titmuss (1950, p. 506) points out in his distinguished volume in the

Official Civil History of the war, 'Damage to homes and injuries to persons were not less likely among the rich than the poor.' He exaggerates slightly – the rich could move to the country, or to the Irish Free State, in a way that the poor could not. Still, his claim is largely correct. Witness the fact that Titmuss's own London home was itself bombed twice during the war (Gowing, 1975, p. 406).

The pervasive uncertainty following from indiscriminate bombing and various other aspects of the war seems to have had precisely the consequences we would predict:

> The assistance provided by the Government to counter the hazards of war carried little social discrimination, and was offered [equally] to all groups in the community. The pooling of national resources and the sharing of risks were not always practicable nor always applied, but they were the guiding principles. (Titmuss, 1950, pp. 506–7)

In a latter essay on 'War and Social Policy', Titmuss (1958, p. 85) goes on to say that 'the acceptance of these social disciplines ... made necessary by war, by preparations for war, and by the long–run consequences of war, must influence the aims and content of social policies not only during the war itself but in peacetime as well' (see similarly Douty, 1972, pp. 586–7; cf. De Alessi, 1975).

Our thesis, then, is that the pervasive uncertainty of wartime led to new popular demand for risk-spreading and broke down old barriers to it, and that that provides a powerful (if only a partial) explanation for the dramatic postwar upsurge in welfare states.[9] The remainder of this chapter is devoted to putting that thesis to the test. We shall argue, in the next section, that it was the uncertainty associated with the war that provided the major impetus to the growth of the postwar British welfare state. In the next, we shall go on to show that this was the case not only in Britain but also throughout the developed world.

The British Case

The British case has, deservedly, received a good deal of attention from those concerned with both empirical and normative aspects of modern welfare states. Indeed, it gave the phenomenon its name (Briggs, 1961, p. 221). While it was hardly the progenitor of every type of social service, and is by no means the world's most developed welfare state today, the United Kingdom pioneered or expanded to an unprecedented degree many social programmes that have since become familiar throughout the Western world. Both defenders (Furniss and Tilton, 1977) and critics (Friedman and Friedman, 1980, pp. 82–118) of the modern welfare state look to the British experience for evidence to substantiate their claims.

Many accounts of the development of the British welfare state treat it as a prime example of social change effected by an avowedly socialist government backed by a strong electoral mandate (Williams, 1967). Evidence to support this view is easily found. The 1945–50 period was characterized by a number of pieces of landmark social welfare legislation: the Family Allowances Act of 1945; the National Assistance, National Insurance, National Health Service and Housing Acts of 1946; the Children Act of 1948; and the Housing Act of 1949.

Such accounts, however, tend to ignore developments during the war, before the 1945 election of the Labour government. The wartime coalition government, though containing a large Conservative majority, often pursued domestic policies of a fairly radical nature (Addison, 1975, p. 14; see similarly, for Australia, Butlin and Schedvin, 1977, ch. 21). Many of the apparent innovations in social policy of the 1945–50 period turn out to be affirmations of functions already being carried out by the public sector. From the vantage point of 1982, Michael Foot, then leader of the Labour party, looked back to the wartime period, not to 1945–50, as Britain's high point of democratic socialism in operation.[10]

A cursory examination of the early years of the war does indeed reveal a great deal of activity on the social-services front. Perhaps the best remembered of these is the Beveridge inquiry into Social Insurance and Allied Services, set up in 1941 and reporting in 1942 (Beveridge, 1942). More concretely, however, 1940 and 1941 witnessed a flurry of activity in which a number of social services were established, expanded or reformed as Britain faced military disaster and the threat of attack on its national territory. Among these were cheap meals and free milk for schoolchildren, immunization and other health programmes, expansion of hospital services, increased pensions (under the Old Age and Widows Pension Act of 1940), the abolition of means testing for social service payments, assistance to evacuees, and aid to those suffering damage to life, limb or property as a result of the war (under the War Damages Act of 1941).

Furthermore, in 1940 the Unemployment Assistance Board became simply the Assistance Board and expanded its clientele to include pensioners and those suffering from war damage (Titmuss, 1950).[11]

The period of the war and its aftermath, taken as a whole, clearly witnessed a marked growth in the proportion of national income devoted to public spending. Peacock and Wiseman (1961, p. 27) ascribe this growth to what they call a 'displacement effect'. Admittedly, they do formally acknowledge the sort of influence that here most concerns us, saying that rising perceptions of what constitutes a 'tolerable burden' of taxation might be 'a consequence of changed ideas induced or encouraged by [the war] itself'.[12] But their main emphasis, both in their original book (Peacock and Wiseman, 1961) and elsewhere (Peacock, 1960, p. 14; Peacock and Wiseman, 1979, pp. 14–17), is on the supply side rather than the demand side of the government-revenue equation. During wartime, the populace becomes accustomed to the dramatically higher levels of taxation necessary to finance the war effort. While the war lasts, most of the funds thus raised have to go to the military. But the war's end presents a golden opportunity for politicians and bureaucrats to divert public funds to their pet domestic projects, as military expenditures wind down while tax revenues remain high.[13]

The basic Peacock–Wiseman displacement theory, then, refers to a 'wartime weakening of the checks that inhibit the growth of public spending' (Peacock and Wiseman, 1961, p. 62). As they explain the phenomenon.

> People will accept, in a period of crisis, tax levels and methods of raising revenue that in quieter times they would have thought intolerable, and this acceptance remains when the disturbance itself has disappeared. As a result, the revenue and expenditure statistics of the government show a displacement after periods of social disturbance. Expenditures may fall when the disturbance is over, but they are less likely to return to the old level. The state may begin doing some of the things it might formerly have wanted to do, but for which it had hitherto felt politically unable to raise the necessary revenues. (Peacock and Wiseman, 1961, p. 27)

It is our contention that as an account of the growth of the postwar British welfare state this is at best incomplete, at worst mistaken, and that our risk-sharing explanation provides a superior account. In what follows, we shall attempt to compare empirically the relative merits of these two hypotheses.

The crucial test is one of timing. Peacock and Wiseman's displacement hypothesis would predict a major leap in total government expenditure towards the beginning of the war, owing to high defence-related expenditures. On their hypothesis, however, the bulk of the increase in social security expenditures would not be expected until the end of the war, when the military's claim on the public purse declines. Any sharp discontinuity in social security spending at the end of the war would be broadly consistent with the displacement hypothesis. Our risk-sharing explanation, in contrast, would predict much more of an increase in social security spending when uncertainty first increases – i.e. towards the beginning of the war – with only incremental growth thereafter. Other things being equal, a jump in social security expenditure at the beginning of the war would be consistent with the risk-sharing thesis; a jump at the end of the war would best support displacement; and a sharp increase after the war would suggest that the programme of the Labour government was the major explanatory factor. When, then, did the major increase occur?[14]

A time series of government social security expenditures in constant prices for the years 1931–53 is presented in Table 3.1 and graphically in Figure 3.1. (War pensions were excluded in the computation of this series, in order to control for the subsequent direct demands upon social security entailed by wartime expansion of the armed forces.) At first glance this series would seem to lend support to the displacement hypothesis, inasmuch as the major increase in social security spending occurred between 1944 and 1946.

This pattern, though, tells only part of the story. During the war years, a number of programmes justified as part of the war budget were *de facto* social security measures. Included here would be war gratuities, assistance to evacuees and compensation for personal injuries resulting from air attack. Financially, perhaps the most significant were the War Risks and War Damage Insurance programmes organized by central government and applicable to property damage. Government took on this insurance task as the private sector had announced its refusal to insure against war risks in 1936, with full responsibility being assumed by the government with the passage of the War Damage Act of 1941 (Titmuss, 1950, p. 15).

Table 3.1 displays War Risks and War Damage Insurance premiums and payments (in constant prices) alongside the time series for social security expenditures, narrowly defined. The time distribution

Table 3.1   *UK Social and Military Expenditure Statistics, 1931–53*[a]

Year	(1) Social security spending[b]	(2) Total social services spending[c]	(3) War risks–War damage		(4) Military spending
			Premiums	Payments	
1931	134	270			204
1932	139	275			203
1933	136	272			156
1934	134	271			156
1935	136	280			155
1936	129	283			151
1937	125	287			133
1938	132	306	0	0	139
1939	118	n.d.	7	0	322
1940	110	n.d.	60	18	1544
1941	104	n.d.	136	107	1769
1942	105	n.d.	108	85	1966
1943	108	n.d.	80	71	1908
1944	106	n.d.	38	40	1824
1945	121	n.d.	18	58	1539
1946	206	n.d.	3	46	581
1947	194	n.d.	0	87	279
1948	191	n.d.		50	233
1949	192	n.d.		54	216
1950	187	561		29	217
1951	179	550		21	284
1952	194	556		16	333
1953	212	580		16	317

Notes:
[a] All figures in £ million, 1913 prices. The deflator used is a price index for public authorities goods and services.

[b] Social security spending comprises 'National Insurance Benefits' (expenditures on unemployment, sickness, and contributory pension national insurance benefits) and 'Other Grants to the Personal Sector' (non-contributory pensions; national assistance grants; unemployment allowances, billeting allowances; milk and vitamin allowances; and grants to universities and colleges). The grants to universities and colleges, although clearly not pertaining to social security, cannot be disaggregated for the entire series; but for the last year for which it can be, 1938, it constitutes only a very small part of the total (about 3 per cent). Also included in social security spending are local government 'Grants to Persons' (expenditures on outdoor relief, school meals and milk, and scholarships and grants to university students). War pensions are deducted from this total.

[c] Total social services spending included central and local government expenditures on education and child care, health services, national insurance (unemployment, sickness and pension benefits), national assistance (poor relief and family allowances), housing (subsidies and capital expenditures) and food subsidies. War pensions are deducted.

Sources: see Dryzek and Goodin (1986, pp. 16–17).

of the payouts made under this scheme is irrelevant for our purposes: it does not even bear any strong relationship to the timing of the actual damage.[15] In any case the damage that actually occurs does not matter so much for our purposes as the *perceived threat* of damage occurring. It is the perceived threat that drives our uncertainty dynamic. The waxing and waning of those perceived threats is better reflected in the time distribution of War Risk and War Damage premiums. The premium total represents the amount of money the country as a whole was willing to commit to risk-sharing.[16] The time distribution of premiums is unimodal, peaking in 1941. This profile is presented, together with that of social security expenditures, in Figure 3.1.

A composite measure of 'total risk–pooling effort' may be computed by adding social security expenditures and War Risks–War Damage insurance premiums. Quite clearly, this effort peaks in the early years of the war. At war's end, the war-related premiums fall to

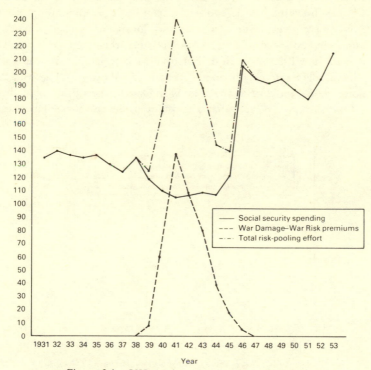

Figure 3.1 *UK social security spending, 1931–53*

zero. Concurrent with this decline is a rise in social security expenditure *per se*. This rise may be interpreted as a continuation of the special wartime programmes: as a very different kind of 'displacement', here of funds away from these special programmes into permanent programmes of insurance protection.[17] The net effect is that social security spending in the postwar period is at a consistently higher level than in the prewar period. But this upward shift was arguably made possible by the war-related social insurance schemes. This result is consistent with the risk-sharing account of the growth of the postwar British welfare state and is inconsistent with the competing explanations emphasizing the displacement of military revenues or the election of a postwar Labour government.

Figure 3.1 pertains to social security expenditures, construed narrowly as social insurance programme expenditures. To do full justice to the rival displacement thesis, perhaps we should examine all programmes that stand to gain from the displacement of funds from military uses to social ones at the war's end. For this purpose, Table 3.1 also lists 'total social service expenditure', representing total government expenditure (central and local) on housing, health, education and social security. Unfortunately, these data are unavailable for the 1939–49 period; but at least comparable prewar and postwar data can be obtained.[18] These are shown in Figure 3.2, alongside the series of War Risks–War Damage premiums.

Once more, it is clear that a substantial increase in welfare state

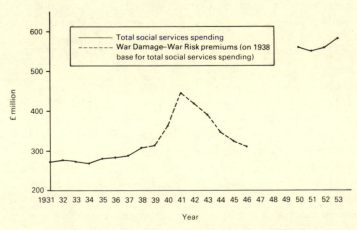

Figure 3.2   *UK total social services spending, 1931–53*

spending occurred somewhere between 1938 and 1950. This incomplete series cannot tell us exactly where the jump came. Figure 3.2 does demonstrate, however, that a substantial part of that jump *could* have been accounted for if War Risks–War Damage insurance premiums were regarded as part of the category of total social security expenditures. A line drawn parallel to that representing 1931 to 1938 social service spending, but elevated by the amount represented by the 1941 peak in War Damage–War Risk premiums, would make a remarkably good fit to the observed 1950–53 social service spending series. Once again, it seems not to be necessary to hypothesize the widespread displacement of expenditures to explain the growth of the postwar welfare state, however broadly it is conceived.

The crucial question for the displacement hypothesis to answer is this: if postwar displacement of wartime military spending accounts for the postwar growth of social spending, then why is *so little* of the wartime military spending thus displaced? Military expenditures, in constant prices, are listed alongside social security and total social service expenditures in Table 3.1. A cursory examination of that table reveals that the postwar jump in social spending (of either sort) constitutes only a tiny fraction of wartime military expenditures.

This is even more apparent from Figure 3.3. Our risk-sharing hypothesis predicts that total risk-pooling efforts should be continuous between war and postwar periods. Evidence of such continuity has been found in Figures 3.1 and 3.2. The displacement hypothesis would lead us to expect a similar continuity between wartime military expenditures and postwar social spending. Figure 3.2 thus displays total military and social expenditures (the latter being conceived firstly as social security expenditures alone, and then as total social service expenditures). Unlike Figures 3.1 and 3.2, Figure 3.3 shows a sharp discontinuity at the end of the war. Social expenditures rise, as Peacock and Wiseman predict, but not by nearly as much as military expenditures fall. Where did the rest of that non-displaced military spending go, and why? And why did not the rest of it go in that way, too? Those must be deeply embarrassing questions for Peacock and Wiseman's theory. The sharp discontinuity at war's end revealed in Figure 3.3 thus constitutes yet another piece of empirical evidence supporting our risk-sharing explanation over their displacement one.

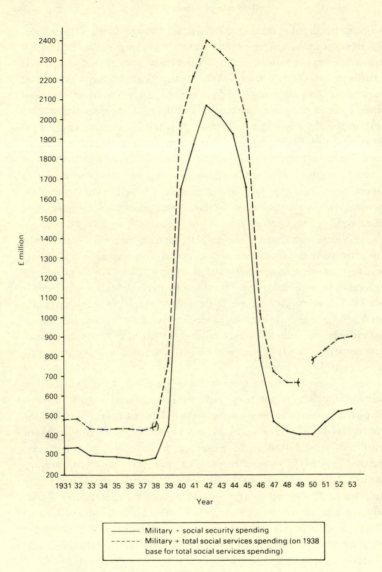

Figure 3.3 *Combined UK military and social spending, 1931–53*

The picture of the British case we have been painting may further be elaborated by digging a little further beneath the aggregate expenditure statistics. A number of striking patterns can be observed in the types of social policies and programmes introduced in the early years of the war. Here there is a pronounced 'concentration effect' in public expenditure; responsibility for many functions shifted from local to central government (Peacock and Wiseman, 1961). For example, commencing in 1938 (in anticipation of the war) responsibility for hospital services shifted from local to national authorities (Titmuss, 1950, p. 55). Arguably, this shift provided much of the impetus for the subsequent establishment of the National Health Service. According to Peacock and Wiseman, reasons of technical efficiency (i.e. a recognition that the larger governmental unit may be the more cost-effective provider of a service) underlay the concentration process; however, they also concede that pressure for equality of treatment across local government units was also an important factor (Peacock and Wiseman, 1961, pp. iv–xxv).

In fact, the concentration process can be interpreted as risk-spreading in action. Localities pool their risks by transferring responsibility to a higher level of government. The upshot is that if Coventry, for example, gets bombed, it is not Coventry alone that will carry the burden of repairing property, healing the injured or providing shelter for the homeless or income for the disabled and their families. The fact of substantial *deconcentration* of expenditures in the postwar period, when such uncertainties diminished, is further support for our interpretation of this phenomenon (Foster, Jackman and Perlman, 1980, pp. 80 ff.).

Another important development in social policy during the early years of the war was an increase in the scope of coverage of social programmes. Prior to the war, most programmes were aimed at the indigent. The profound uncertainty concomitant with the outbreak of war meant a large increase in the proportion of the population perceiving itself to be at risk. 'Bombs, unlike unemployment, know no social distinctions' (Fraser, 1973, p. 193). The consequence was a shift from income-specific to universalistic programmes. Universalistic innovations in 1940–41 included such things at the 1940 Old Age and Widows Pension Act and the broadening in scope of the functions of the National Assistance Board (Fraser, 1973, p. 195). Further, it became clear that the quality of the services appropriate to 'poor relief' now needed to be upgraded considerably, given their increased coverage (Titmuss, 1950, p. 506). This development made for greater expense.

The universalistic approach to the provision of social services reached its apogee in the Beveridge (1942) report. Beveridge specified that the entire population should be covered by social insurance, that there should be no means testing for eligibility and that both contributions and benefits should be flat rate. The report's proposal received an enthusiastic reception from all social groups. In a survey taken shortly after its publication, 86 per cent of those responding believed that the proposals should be adopted; the figure for 'employers' was 73 per cent, for 'upper income' respondents 76 per cent, and for members of the professions 91 per cent (Addison, 1975, pp. 271–8).

After 1945, the universalistic principles, though generally accepted as the guiding principles for social policy, became progressively diluted. Means testing (in fact, if not in name) made a gradual comeback. This is precisely as the risk-sharing hypothesis would predict. In a period in which all the population faced significant risks, one would expect social programmes to be universalistic in nature. Once things return to normal, programmes become more category-specific. The wartime consensus, as reflected in Beveridge, was a product of the very special circumstances of the war. One would not expect it to persist with full force long into the postwar period (Harris, 1981).

A Cross-National Comparison

Much evidence can, then, be adduced in support of our contention that the postwar expansion of the British welfare state had its origins in wartime risk-sharing. The findings from the British case might not, however, be generalizable across countries. Single-case analyses are always flawed, since for any one country some key variables (such as 'total wartime uncertainty' and 'total pressure for displacement of expenditures') can only appear as constants. Hence we now turn to a comparative analysis of the growth of the welfare state. The comparative method can turn constants into variables.

The United Kingdom, though often treated as the exemplary case, was hardly unique in experiencing considerable growth in the size of its welfare state in the wartime period. Countries throughout the developed world experienced similar expansions during that period, as Table 3.2 reveals. The risk-sharing explanation would predict that

Table 3.2   *Social Security Spending as a Proportion of National Income*[a]

Country	1933	1949	Proportionate change[b]
Australia	2.4	4.1	0.708
Austria	13.6	9.9	−0.272
Belgium	4.0	11.4	1.850
Canada	5.0	5.4	0.080
Czechoslovakia	8.9	10.4	0.169
Denmark	5.0	8.2	0.640
Finland	2.9	6.0	1.069
France	6.9	11.6	0.681
Germany	11.7	13.0	0.111
Greece	1.3	3.0	1.308
Ireland	6.7	7.5	0.119
Italy	3.1	9.2	1.968
Japan	0.2	4.0	19.000
Netherlands	5.2	8.9	0.712
New Zealand	10.1	9.5	−0.059
Norway	6.2	6.4	0.032
Poland	1.3	7.1	4.462
South Africa	0.7	3.5	4.000
Sweden	6.2	9.4	0.516
Switzerland	4.7	6.1	0.298
United Kingdom	7.6	10.4	0.368
United States	3.3	3.1	−0.061
Yugoslavia	1.2	10.6	7.833

Notes:
[a] Excluding benefits to war victims.
[b] (1949 minus 1933)/1933.
Sources: See Dryzek and Goodin (1986, appendix).

increases in the size of a country's welfare state during and after the war should vary directly with the degree of uncertainty experienced.

Here we intend to undertake an empirical test of this hypothesis, once again comparing its performance with that of the competing 'displacement' explanation. In fact, we shall be undertaking several closely-related empirical tests. Each of the variables involved in these tests admit of alternative operationalizations and some of the cases might be thought to be especially problematic. We have, therefore, adopted the strategy of reporting, in Table 3.3, the results for a baseline 'Standard Regression' using the full set of cases and the operationalizations we regard as the most appropriate. Then, in Table 3.4, we report how these results would change if any of the alternative specifications were employed.

Our dependent variable for this cross-national empirical test is based on the difference between pre-war and post-war levels of social security expenditure as defined by the International Labour Organisation.[19] The ILO definition includes social insurance (sickness, maternity, invalidity, old age, death and employment injuries), family benefits (such as family allowances) and public assistance. To fall under this definition these schemes must also be either set up by legislation or have a public or semi-public body assuming obligations and administering the scheme (ILO 1952). We exclude benefits such as pensions to war victims or their widows, since the postwar level of such benefits is naturally a direct function of a country's involvement in the war; to include these in our dependent variable would produce an illegitimate upward bias in the perceived effect of uncertainty on the difference between prewar and postwar welfare state expenditures.[20]

The only prewar year for which expenditure figures are widely available is 1933. The first postwar year for which this is true is 1949. Hence we will specify change in social security spending as the difference between 1933 and 1949 levels.[21] Our dependent variable is operationalized as the proportion change in social security expenditures, i.e. the difference between 1949 and 1933 expenditures, divided by 1933 expenditures.

There are, however, at least two ways in which the 'expenditures' component of this dependent variable could be operationalized. One is as social security spending in real (i.e. inflation-adjusted) currency units. The other is as the percentage of national income devoted to social security spending. Arguably, the first method best captures the growth of welfare state spending. But there are problems in obtaining reliable deflators for this time period. The second method thus seems to yield more reliable figures, and allows us to incorporate a slightly higher number of cases. The latter operationalization will therefore be utilized in our Standard Regression, though we will also report results for the former as Modification A in Table 3.4.

Our key independent variable, the degree of uncertainty a country experienced during wartime, is less easily captured. One would expect uncertainty to be greatest in countries that experienced – or expected – a high degree of destruction of life and property during the war. Alas, there are no reliable, comprehensive data on the extent of overall wartime destruction in each country.[22] We are therefore required to rely instead on two partial indicators. The first is the proportion of the prewar population killed in the war, including both military and civilian deaths. This variable is a fairly direct representation of the probability of something bad happening to an individual within a country. The second is the length of time (in months) between 1933 and 1949 during which a country either (1) was a belligerent in the war or (2) had fighting taking place on its national territory. Obviously, the more prolonged the conflict, the more pervasive the uncertainty to which individuals are exposed and the greater the likelihood that uncertainty will provoke a response through private or public action.[23]

For our Standard Regression, an Uncertainty Index was computed by standardizing and adding these two partial indicators. Recognizing that the second component (time fighting or fought over) is perhaps controversial, we will also report as Modification B in Table 3.4 results with uncertainty operationalized solely as the proportion of a country's population killed in the war.[24]

The main rival to our hypothesis, Peacock and Wiseman's (1961), takes as its key independent variable the notion of displacement. Again, there is no perfect operationalization of this concept. (Peacock and Wiseman offer none at all.) But one would expect the degree of entrenchment and experience of a country's social security bureaucracy to be strongly associated with the intensity of the displacement effect. Remember that Peacock and Wiseman (1961, p. 54) ascribe displacement in part to a weakening of the checks on upward pressures on public spending, and these pressures emanate from the pre-existing expenditure plans of government bureaucracies. One would expect such plans to be more extensive in countries the more well-established their social security bureaucracy. Our indicator of displacement in our Standard Regression is, therefore, Cutright's (1965; Jackman, 1975) measure of 'social insurance programme experience' (SIPE). SIPE is computed by adding the number of years, to 1939, that each of five categories of social insurance (work injury; sickness an/or maternity; old age, invalidity or death; family allowance; and unemployment) had been in operation.

A second, and more controversial, correlate of the potential for displacement is a country's national income per head. Several studies have offered cross-national evidence showing that the higher a country's material surplus above the level required to meet its members' basic needs, the greater its potential for redistributive programmes such as social security (Lenski, 1966; Cutright, 1967). Unfortunately, cross-nationally comparable figures for national income are unobtainable for this period; but we can use the annual energy consumption per capita as a surrogate.[25] To check for any influence of prosperity in displacement, we recompute as Modification C in Table 3.4 a Displacement Index by standardizing and adding SIPE and energy consumption per capita.

Table 3.3 reports the results of our Standard Regression. This consists of a multiple regression of the proportional change in the percentage of national income allocated to social security spending on our uncertainty and displacement variables. Operationalizations of all variables are as we have described as our 'standard' cases, and all 23 cases listed in Table 3.2 are included.

It is clear from Table 3.3 that the Uncertainty Index has a substantial positive effect (significant at the 0.05 level) on the proportionate change in social security spending. This lends support to our central hypothesis. Perversely, the displacement variable appears actually to have a *negative* effect on change in social security expenditures.

Certainly this discredits the Peacock–Wiseman explanation, in the cross-national context at least. But how can we account for this startling finding so contrary to their expectations? Perhaps the answer is that countries with an extensive social security bureaucracy in place possess what is, in effect, a 'cushion' to help them cope with times of

Table 3.3   *Regression of Change in Social Security Spending on Uncertainty and Displacement: Standard Regression*

Dependent variable: Proportionate change in social security spending, 1933–49, as percentage of national income

Independent variable	Coefficient estimate	Standard error	Standardized estimate
Uncertainty index	1.02	0.42	0.44
Displacement	-0.032	0.016	-0.36
Constant	4.93		

$R^2 = 0.366$
$N = 23$

Data and sources: See Dryzek and Goodin (1986, appendix).

pervasive uncertainty. Hence the *effective* uncertainty is reduced in countries scoring highly on our displacement indicator, in a way that is not captured in our Uncertainty Index itself. Thus, the negative correlation between the displacement variable and change in social security spending might be further evidence in support of our risk-sharing explanation of the war-related growth of the welfare state.

The results of our cross-national analysis are clearly consistent with the hypothesis that expansions of welfare states came in response to pervasive uncertainty, and clearly inconsistent with the competing displacement hypothesis. To check the validity and robustness of these results, we recomputed the Standard Regression in Table 3.3 using each of the plausible alternative operationalizations of our key variables, as described above. The re-computed results are summarized in Table 3.4.

Modification A reports the results for proportionate change in social security spending, operationalized in real terms rather than as a percentage of national income as in our Standard Regression. Here, it was necessary to control for real growth in national income over the 1933–49 period. (This growth is automatically controlled in our Standard Regression by operationalizing social security spending as a proportion of national income.) Modification B drops 'time fighting or fought over' from the Uncertainty Index, leaving proportion of the population killed in the war as the sole indicator of uncertainty. Modification C adds the energy-consumption surrogate for national income to the Displacement Index. Finally, Modification D drops Germany and Japan from the population of cases, on the grounds that thorough defeat in war and concomitant discontinuity in political institutions may have had an effect on the development of their welfare states that is qualitatively different from the experience of the other countries under examination (Olson, 1982). These modifications are not cumulative. In each case, the operationalization is as in the Standard Regression, with the sole exception of the one change explicitly identified.

The most striking feature of Table 3.4 is the robustness of our findings across these various modifications. In each case, the uncertainty variable exerts broadly the same large, positive effect on change in social security spending. The displacement variable, in each case, substantially reduces social security spending rather than increasing it. Thus, our risk-sharing hypothesis is further corroborated, and the displacement hypothesis further discredited.

Table 3.4 *Regressions of Change in Social Security Spending on Uncertainty and Displacement: Alternative Specifications*

Dependent variable: Proportionate change in social security spending, 1933–49

Standardized regression coefficients	Standard regression (Table 4.3)	Modifications[b]			
		A	B	C	D
BETA for uncertainty	0.44[a]	0.27	0.39[a]	0.37[a]	0.51[a]
BETA for displacement	-0.36[a]	-0.30	-0.44[a]	-0.50[a]	-0.22
BETA for growth control variable	n.a.	0.28	n.a.	n.a.	n.a.
R^2	0.366	0.271	0.333	0.472	0.370
N	23	21	23	23	21

Notes:
[a] Significant at the 0.05 level.
[b] *Modification A*: As Standard Regression, except dependent variable operationalized as proportionate change in social security spending, 1933–49, computed in real terms in 1933 prices rather than as percentage of national income; controlling for real growth in national income, 1933–49. *Modification B*: As Standard Regression, except uncertainty operationalized as proportion of population killed in war only. *Modification C*: As Standard Regression, except displacement operationalized by standardizing and adding energy consumption per capita (surrogate for national income per capita) and social insurance programme experience. *Modification D*: As Standard Regression, except Germany and Japan omitted from sample.
   Data and sources: See Dryzek and Goodin (1986, appendix).

Alternative Explanations

Our cross-national analysis itself puts pay to several alternative explanations of events in any one country. One might, for example, be tempted to trace the expansion of the British welfare state during and after the war to the twin facts that (1) the wartime coalition government put socialists with a well worked-out political programme into positions of real power for virtually the first time and (2) war loosened the ordinary constraints on political control of the economy. As an explanation of the British experience, that might look plausible enough. But it does not explain the pattern which emerges from our comparative analysis across countries with such very different wartime political histories.

Still, these cross-national findings are not explicable through our risk-sharing hypothesis alone. We can think of at least three alternative hypotheses which might lead us to expect broadly similar results. In order of least to most worrying, these alternatives are: (1) war damage leads automatically to postwar reconstruction spending; (2) war increases the power of organized labour, and the underclass more generally, leading to increased social spending; and (3) war increases social solidarity, which leads to increased social welfare expenditures.

The first alternative hypothesis suggests that what our uncertainty variable is really tapping is war damage. The more war damage, the more that is needed by way of postwar reconstruction. No doubt it is true that the more bombed buildings you have, the more you will need to rebuild. But very little of *that* sort of rebuilding will get coded as social security expenditure. Our aim is not to explain increases in total postwar government spending, but merely increases in social security spending. And we have been careful, in measuring that variable, to exclude the forms of social security spending that are linked most directly to the war (pensions to war victims and their dependents). Our control may miss a few indirect connections between war damage to civilian populations (e.g. long-term illnesses) and postwar social security expenditures. Still, we are inclined to regard this as a relatively marginal phenomenon.

The second alternative hypothesis maintains that war increases the bargaining power of organized labour, and the underclass more generally, which in turn increases social welfare expenditures both during the war and after. Piven and Cloward (1971) argue that it is the function of public welfare programmes to 'buy off' the poor in times of crisis. Various cross-national studies have suggested more systematically that labour movement strength correlated with social welfare spending (Stephens, 1979; cf. Jackman, 1975, ch. 6). The war certainly did improve the bargaining position of civilian employees in a wide range of war-related enterprises. They may not have engaged in any industrial action or street demonstrations. They may not even have threatened to do so. But they may not have needed to – the government, perhaps, could see the danger without having had it pointed out. It is as difficult to prove the workings of the 'law of anticipated reactions' in this context as any other, however, so this must remain no more than interesting speculation.

The third alternative explanation for our findings – the one which is closest and most threatening to our own – holds that war breeds attitudes such as 'national unity' and 'social solidarity' which are conducive to the growth of the welfare state. This, in fact, is the explanation offered by Beveridge himself. On the closing page of his report, he writes:

> The prevention of want and the diminution and relief of disease – the special aim of the social services – are in fact a common interest to all citizens. It may be possible to secure a keener realization of that fact in war than it is in peace, because war breeds national unity and readiness to sacrifice personal interests to the common cause, to bring about changes which, when they are made, will be accepted on all hands as advances, but which it might be difficult to make at other times. (Beveridge, 1942, para. 460)[26]

On this third hypothesis, we can offer a modest piece of empirical evidence. The hypothesis is, in short, that 'shared sacrifices' lead to 'social solidarity' which lead to the growth of social security expenditures during and after the war. 'Shared sacrifice' might best be operationalized through indicators of the extent and severity of wartime civilian rationing. Notice, however, that our own uncertainty hypothesis would predict a similar link between shared risks (which are what lead to shared sacrifices, after all) and the growth of welfare expenditures. So what is crucial, in differentiating this rival explanation from our own, is the importance it attaches to the intervening variable of social solidarity.

By distinguishing between different aspects of wartime rationing, we can get empirical indicators of both 'shared sacrifices/risks' and 'social solidarity'. Wartime rationing of scarce *necessities* is itself a necessity if people are not to starve. But wartime rationing of *luxuries* is not strictly necessary. Supplies being scarce, their prices would be bid up beyond the reach of the poor if it were left to the market to distribute these luxuries; but being luxuries, it is perfectly possible for the poor to do without them. If rationing is instituted for scarce luxuries, then that is a manifestation of social solidarity rather than a response to strict necessity. It is a manifestation of the view that, while the poor could do without these luxuries, they should not have to do so – the sacrifices should be spread more widely throughout society.

For an operational measure of 'social solidarity', thus conceptualized, we might focus upon the severity of the ration applied by various countries to one particular luxury good, sugar. Specifically, we will look at the 1943 sugar ration for the 'normal consumer' as a proportion of interwar sugar consumption for each country. It is obviously essential that the severity of wartime rationing be judged in light of prewar consumption patterns: a sugar ration of 250 grammes per week imposed far greater hardship on the Dutch, accustomed to consuming 401 grammes per week before the war, than did a ration of 125 grammes per week on the Italians, accustomed to only 98 grammes per week. Unfortunately, however, the paucity of data on interwar consumption patterns, combined with the paucity of information on wartime rationing itself, reduces us to a meagre 14 cases.[27]

No great faith can be placed in any empirical analysis based on so few observations. Certainly it is pointless to mount any elaborate multiple regression exercise in these circumstances. But for what it is worth, the simple correlation between growth in social security spending and severity of the sugar ration is a paltry $r = 0.04$. If the latter really is a good indicator of 'social solidarity', as we believe it likely to be, then this third alternative emphasizing that variable must be cast into doubt.

There is one final step we can take to test our risk-sharing hypothesis against all three alternative explanations at once. Notice that none of these three alternative accounts would suggest anything other than a proportionate relationship between the things we have been operationalizing in our uncertainty variable and the growth of social security spending. Our risk-sharing explanation, in contrast, would anticipate growth in social security spending to be *more* than proportional to the degree of uncertainty experienced. It is a standard axiom of utility theory, which is generally borne out by empirical decision analysis, that the typical individual is risk averse (Raiffa, 1968). If so, then the greater the objective risk, the greater will be his marginal propensity to seek insurance.

To explore this possibility, we added a variable representing the square of our uncertainty variable to our Standard Regression. The result is depicted in Table 3.5. As our explanation anticipates, there is a substantial positive association between uncertainty-squared and proportionate change in social security spending. (Indeed, this relationship is stronger than for the unmodified uncertainty variable itself.) Equally important, the percentage of variance explained is

Table 3.5   *Regression of Change in Social Security Spending on Uncertainty and Displacement, to Illustrate Risk Aversion*

Dependent variable: Proportionate change in social security spending, 1933–45, as percentage of national income			
Independent variable	*Coefficient estimate*	*Standard error*	*Standardized estimate*
Uncertainty index	0.59	0.45	0.25
(Uncertainty index)^2	0.55	0.28	0.38
Displacement	-0.040	0.015	-0.45
Constant	4.52		
$R^2 = 0.471$			
$N = 23$			

Data and sources: See Dryzek and Goodin (1986, appendix).

boosted from 36.6 per cent to 47.1 per cent by the addition of the uncertainty-squared variable to the Standard Regression.

None of this is absolutely conclusive, of course. Given all the other possible explanations, we can hardly claim to have provided *the* explanation of the growth of postwar welfare states. The most we can claim to have provided, through our notion of risk-sharing, is one explanation that is as eligible as any and more plausible than most. Still, that may be the most that any empirical researchers can honestly claim.

Conclusion

The aim of this paper has been to explore the motivational bases of moral behaviour. Our thesis is that rare moments of deep and widespread uncertainty – war being only the most dramatic example – provide one such basis.[28] Under such conditions, anyone's future might be your own. That forces each of us to reflect impartially upon the interests of all. Welfare states and suchlike constitute the appropriate institutional response.[29]

These responses get frozen and persist well beyond the moment of uncertainty that gave rise to them. Why that should happen is an interesting question in its own right. A variety of familiar factors might be at work. Inertia, bureaucratic politics, the developing constituencies of programmes, etc., all make it hard to cut programmes once they have been initiated. But these forces do not always succeed in preserving innovative institutions. Contrast the very different experiences of Britain after each of the two world wars. During the First World War there emerged a vast array of public controls upon the productive process that, in effect, amounted to the socialization of most major sectors of the economy. At the war's end, most of these controls were quickly – indeed, precipitously – abolished. The welfare reforms introduced in Britain during the Second World War met no such fate. Why?

The crucial difference was that the pervasive uncertainty associated with the Second World War changed people – their beliefs, attitudes, expectations and values – in a way that the First World War (absent mass bombing, etc.) did not.[30] The effect of that uncertainty was to expand people's moral horizons. People were forced to imagine themselves in each other's place and to evaluate social policies accordingly, at least during most of the war; and the practice carried over into peacetime as well.

The broadening of moral horizons was not, of course, irrevocable. Present events in Britain and throughout the developed world suggest that the effect may at long last be fading. Far be it from us to suggest a replay of the war just to recharge it. But we would suggest that one happy consequence of an otherwise desperately unhappy experience was to make behaviour more moral, at least for a while. Wartime uncertainty and risk-sharing seems to us to provide a particularly powerful explanation, not only of the origins, but also of the persistence and now the waning of the postwar welfare state.

Of course, people are notoriously bad at estimating the true extent of the uncertainties they are facing, and characteristically think their position more secure than it really is (Kahneman, Slovic and Tversky, 1982). The masterly University of Michigan Panel Study of Income Dynamics in the US – not a notoriously generous welfare state – found that even there 'one out of every four Americans lived in a household that received income from one of the major welfare programs at least once over a ten-year period' from 1969 to 1978. Fully half of them received welfare benefits for only one or two years, while they were ' "digging out" following a [personal] disaster of one sort or another'. Duncan (1984, p. 90) goes on to observe:

No broad demographic group in our society appears immune from shocks to their usual standard of living, shocks resulting from rapidly changing economic or personal conditions. For men, the shock often comes in the form of an involuntary job loss; for married women, divorce or the death of the spouse is often the precipitating event. Such events may not always be totally unavoidable, but few people are immune to occasional economic misfortune, and when it strikes, welfare serves as a kind of insurance for them, providing temporary assistance until they are able to regain their more customary levels of living.

The insurance rationale for the welfare state is thus still a strong one. Politically, the task before defenders of the welfare state might just be to make that fact motivationally compelling once more.

Notes

This study was originally published in the *British Journal of Political Science*, (vol. 16, 1986, pp. 1–34). We are grateful for permission from Cambridge University Press to reprint it here. The study was provoked by comments from Stanley Benn and shaped by comments from Geoffrey Best, John Champlin, Sir Norman Chester, Frank Cowell, Ivor Crewe, Diane Gibson, Dick Gunther, Sir Keith Hancock, Russell Hardin, Rod Kiewiet, Julian Le Grand, Michael Lipsky, Stuart Macintyre, Chris Pickvance, Richard Rose, Peter Self, Patricia Tulloch, Aaron Wildavsky, an audience at the Western Political Science Association annual conference in 1984 and several anonymous reviewers. Responsibility for the final product remains ours alone.

1   That is merely to say that the purpose and official public justification of the welfare state is as an instrument of social justice; whether or not it truly is a redistributive success is, as Le Grand (1982b) and other chapters in this book show, another matter. Neither do we mean to imply that, morally, concern with the less-well-off should necessarily stop at national borders; but in order to see what it might take to get a world-wide welfare state, we first need to see how we have managed to secure even a nationwide one.

2   For arguments that earlier developments might be explained along lines similar to those we here propose, see Beales (1946, pp. 6, 14), Goldthorpe (1964, pp. 48 ff.) and Freeden (1978, pp. 229–44).

3   Samuelson (1958, p. 480) muses that 'an essay could be written on the welfare state as a complicated device for self- or re-insurance.' Baumol (1982, p. 640) similarly suggests that 'a rule of fairness is a sort of insurance arrangement which selfish people accept to make sure they will not be mistreated, and pay for it by providing assurance to others

that they, too, will not be mistreated.' See similarly Buchanan and Tullock (1962, p. 193) and Goodin (1976, pp. 78–80, 115). Notice that our analysis links up to the classic welfare-economic rationale for redistribution, in so far as people are willing to buy insurance if and only if income has diminishing marginal utility for them (Olson, 1983).

4 'Environed as we are by risks and perils, which befall us as misfortunes, no man of us is in a position to say, "I . . . am sure . . . I shall never need aid and sympathy". At the very best, one of us fails in one way and another in another, if we do not fail altogether. Therefore the man under the [falling] tree is the one of us who for the moment is smitten. It may be you to-morrow, and I the next day. It is the common frailty in the midst of a common peril which gives us a kind of solidarity of interest to rescue the one for whom the chances of life have turned out badly just now' (Sumner, 1883, p. 158).

5 These differ from privately organized insurance schemes in certain respects. Premiums, for example, are not calculated on an 'individual-ized actuarial model', as private underwriters might have attempted; and, of course, participation in these public schemes tends to be compulsory. All this is explicable in terms of government insuring against people's being privately uninsurable, however (Goodin, 1976, p. 112; cf. Freeden, 1978, p. 237). In other respects, these initial pro-grammes were much more like insurance schemes than many that followed (e.g., family allowances, Aid to Families with Dependent Children). The latter programmes tended to be available to anyone in need, and were paid for out of general-fund revenue generated by ordinary taxes. The insurance-like schemes were organized around separate trust funds, fed by premium-like taxes that were collected separately and earmarked for deposit to those trust funds only. The criterion of membership in the scheme, and hence of eligibility for benefits, was payment (by oneself or on one's behalf) of those special taxes-cum-premiums. See Titmuss (1958, pp. 173–87; 1974, ch. 7) and Burns (1944; 1965).

6 Insurance companies have a good idea too, and choose whether or not to insure individuals and what premium to charge them on the basis of actuarial risks. When individuals have better information, they can outwit the actuaries. Then there will be a process of 'adverse selection', with good risks opting out, leaving only high-risk individuals in the insurance pool. Adverse selection acts as an impediment to the develop-ment of markets in insurance, which further inhibits effective redistribu-tion through insurance.

7 Some can be explained as attempts to increase economic productivity: turn-of-the-century social reforms, both in Britain and the Antipodes, and the socialization of production in Britain during the First World War are examples of that, perhaps (Beveridge, 1907; Tawney, 1943, pp. 2–7; Briggs, 1961, pp. 243–5; Rimlinger, 1966; Freeden 1978, pp. 241–4). Other welfare state innovations can best be understood in the context of war preparations, as attempts to guarantee the quality and

quantity of cannon fodder, either in the present generation or the next (Titmuss, 1958, p. 81).

8   Another factor, which fits equally well with our model (and which may in practice be hard to separate from the influence of the Second World War), is the pervasive uncertainty induced by the Great Depression (Heclo, 1981, p. 392).

9   This approximates that behaviour which Abba Lerner (1944) believes welfare economics should always commend to governments. Of course, wartime governments also had various other less high-minded reasons for introducing insurance schemes during the war. One was to guarantee the stability of economic and financial institutions predicated on the assumption that real estate would (at least on average) retain its value. Another was that insurance premiums were a convenient way of soaking up money out of the private sector and thus dampening wartime inflation. Both points were made explicit in the Chancellor's speech introducing the British War Damage Insurance scheme and in the debate that followed; see *Hansard's Parliamentary Debates* (Commons), 5th series, vol. 367 (1940–41), cols 1125–90 and 1243–99. The Australian Treasurer also explicitly evoked the latter consideration in proposing the introduction of unemployment insurance during the war, when of course most people would be employed and hence income into the fund could be counted upon vastly to exceed outflow (Watts, 1980, p. 190).

10 *Manchester Guardian Weekly*, 12 December 1982. Enoch Powell (1961/86, pp. 176–7) similarly claims that 'there is not a single social service today [1961] which was not framed more than fifteen years ago. The conception of all of them, in more or less their present form, dates from the social revolution of 1942 to 1944. Yes, you heard me correctly: I said 1942 to 1944. The General Election of 1945 was in some ways only a consequential recognition of the revolution which took place under, and inside, the Coalition Government at the height of World War II, and was announced to the outside world by a cloud of White Papers – on planning, social insurance, employment, a national health service – much as the election of a new Pope is first evinced by the smoke from the burning ballot papers'.

11 Some of these innovations – such as the War Damages Act – could be interpreted as simply part of the war effort. Others – such as pensions and school meals – had no more than a tangential connection with the actual prosecution of the war.

12 This in turn arises from the 'inspection effect', which derives (in the first instance, anyway) from a desire to assure the quality of cannon fodder, as the preface to the revised 1969 edition of Peacock and Wiseman (1961) makes clear: 'In wartime the tally of human resources for special purposes may incidentally reveal information about social, etc. conditions which was not previously available, and this new knowledge may produce a consensus of opinion in favour of new and larger public expenditures of particular kinds after the "return to normalcy"'. Hence, their explanation of the 'inspection effect' would seem to have more in

common with the familiar forces discussed in note 7 than with the wartime uncertainty which is our focus here.

13   Politicians and civil servants might, right from the beginning of the war, divert some of the revenues raised for fighting the war into their long-planned domestic projects. But this would be no more than a marginal phenomenon. For a vast majority of politicians and civil servants, winning the war would almost certainly have taken precedence over all other goals; and they would not care to endanger that outcome by more than marginally diverting revenues away from the war effort.

14   Interpretation of the timing of changes in observed expenditure can be hazardous: delayed implementation can make effects lag far behind their causes; and the anticipation of future needs might even make effects predate their causes, as Titmuss (1950, p. 54) finds with the hospital services. Peacock and Wiseman's (1961) study sheds little light on the timing of wartime increases. Their statistical series has large gaps for the period of the war and its aftermath: it shows that social welfare expenditure is much higher in 1950 than in 1938, but the intervening years are a blank. These gaps might have been what led Peacock and Wiseman to construct an explanatory account of war-related spending increases which treats the war and its aftermath as a single unit.

15   Indeed, payments peak twice, first in 1942 and then not again until 1947, well after the war's conclusion. This is partly due to the ordinary time lags in reaching settlements and disbursing funds to claimants, and partly due to the fact that government intentionally held up payments to prevent labour and material needed in the war effort from being diverted to premature civilian rebuilding projects. Indeed, at the outset of the war government proposed waiting until the war was over before making *any* payments, although it relented somewhat starting in 1940; see Titmuss (1950, pp. 282–3) and 'War damage balance sheet', *The Economist*, vol. 140 (15 December 1945), p. 883.

16   These premiums reflected, at least in the first instance, government rather than public perceptions of the level of risks: premiums were fixed by the government, and participation in the schemes was for the most part compulsory (a voluntary scheme being run only for private chattels and movable property, such as household furniture). But there is no particular reason to suppose that there was any very great divergence between the government's perception of the risk and the public's. On the contrary, it seems entirely likely that the public based its perceptions on cues (such as War Risk and War Damage premiums) given by the government itself.

17   Notice, also, that a wartime threat to capital gave rise to postwar protection against threats to labour. Specifically, those wartime schemes offering primarily protection against risks to property (the War Risks--War Damage Insurance schemes) were displaced, after the war, into social welfare programmes primarily protecting against risks to persons.

18   A continuous series is available for local government expenditures on education, housing and poor relief (Peacock and Wiseman, 1961, table A 22). This is only a small fraction of the total central plus local

government social service expenditure, however: 8.1 per cent in 1938, 3.8 per cent in 1950. Hence this series is of little use for our purposes here.

19   Suitably comparable cross-national data for other aspects of total social service spending, such as housing, health and education, were unavailable. We were also unable to obtain suitable data on the extent of programme coverage (i.e., the number of persons or percentage of the workforce covered). Even if the latter data could be found, however, they would constitute an ambiguous indicator, double-counting individuals who are covered by more than one programme; total expenditure level suffers no such ambiguity.

20   Notice that, when Peacock and Wiseman (1961, p. 33) say that 'wars generate commitments that continue into peace', it is just this sort of commitment (along with analogous 'debt commitments') that they take as their paradigm case. Even Titmuss (1958, p. 80), who usually emphasizes far deeper connections, remarks similarly at one place.

21   This is not, in fact, a bad choice of years. The former (1933) represents one of the last years of international quiescence before the gathering storm of war affected countries such as Japan, Spain, and Italy. The latter (1949) effectively represents the settled postwar situation. By then the uncertainty which had carried over into the immediate postwar period had, with the onset of reconstruction, largely disappeared.

22   One indirect indicator of destruction which we considered and rejected is the amount of US non-military aid per capita in the immediate postwar period. This financial aid (notably the Marshall Plan) was intended to promote reconstruction. Hence one would expect it to vary in proportion to the degree of destruction a country experienced. Unfortunately for our purposes, political considerations entered too strongly into decisions about both the giving and receiving of American aid for this to serve as a true indicator of wartime destruction.

23   Thus, uncertainty as indicated by this second variable is zero for non-belligerents, very low for countries (like Denmark) occupied within a few days of the beginning of the war and held by Germany for the duration, and very high for persistent belligerents like the United Kingdom and Japan. This indicator is not free from ambiguity. For example, how should resistance fighting on the national territory and civil conflict be treated? It was decided to exclude resistance fighting in all cases except Yugoslavia, where Partisans and Chetniks controlled large portions of the country during the entire period of notional Axis occupation. Civil conflict was treated as a state of belligerence.

24   'Time fighting or fought over' may be controversial as an indicator of uncertainty, because it implies that there is no uncertainty associated with full occupation by another power. Were we to include 'time occupied', however, that would drastically reduce variation in this component of the Index: virtually all countries caught up in the war at all were either fighting, being fought over, or occupied for the duration.

25   The use of energy consumption as a surrogate for national income in indicating the resource base of a country is a well-established practice in

cross-national social and political research (Taylor and Hudson, 1972, p. 291). Figures on per capita energy consumption were unavailable for the war years themselves, so we use the average of 1937 and 1949 figures for each country. Gross national product for 1950 was available for a limited number of countries in our sample; this showed a correlation of 0.84 with wartime energy consumption.

26   This theme also emerged, for example, in the course of debates on the War Damage Insurance Act. The Chancellor, introducing the measure, called it 'an instrument of justice and an act of solidarity'. Perhaps more revealing, however, was an interjection during the speech of an MP opposed to the Bill: George Benson asked, as what he thought to be a rhetorical question, 'Why is it that the Lake District owner, who is practically safe, is compelled to share the burden of the Coventry owner [who is very much at risk from German bombers]?' The *Hansard* reported records as an interjection from an Honourable Member on the opposite benches the reply, 'We are all in the war.' See *Hansard's Parliamentary Debates* (Commons), 5th series, Vol. 367 (1940–1), cols 1137 and 1166.

27   For data and sources, see Dryzek and Goodin (1986, appendix).

28   Uncertainty of a different sort might also explain the widespread tendency to adopt social security systems that shift costs and/or benefits far into the future: uncertainty about who will benefit and who will suffer naturally tends to increase with temporal distance.

29   An explanation in terms of shifting motivations really is required. It is not enough to say, as some economists might, that this is just a case of war precipitating a 'market failure' in insurance markets which the government stepped in to remedy. That leaves unexplained some of the most important particulars of the intervention, specifically, why governments failed to apply actuarial principles in setting War Damage–War Risk premiums; see Sir Kingsley Wood's speech in *Hansard's Parliamentary Debates* (Commons), 5th series, vol. 367 (1940–41), col. 126 and Hirschleifer (1953).

30   Tawney (1943, p.7) writes, 'The most extensive and intricate scheme of state intervention in economic life which the country had seen was brought into existence, without the merits or demerits of state intervention being ever discussed . . . Each addition to the structure was related to some immediate necessity of incontestable urgency . . . Once the war was over, what had been a source of strength became a weakness. War collectivism had not been accompanied by any intellectual conversion on the subject of the proper relations between the state and economic life, while it did not last long enough to change social habits. With the passing, therefore, of the crisis that occasioned it, it was exposed to the attack of the same interests and ideas as, but for the war, would have prevented its establishment'.

PART THREE

The Operation of the Welfare State

Chapter 4

US Anti-Poverty Policy and the Non-Poor: Some Estimates and their Implications

ROBERT H. HAVEMAN

The early 1960s witnessed a large and sudden increase in the concern of Americans about problems of economic poverty and disparities among blacks and whites, old and young, rural and urban, sick and well, South and North. Stimulated by the writings of Michael Harrington and John Kenneth Galbraith, President Kennedy proposed and President Johnson pursued legislation designed to fight poverty and create a 'Great Society'. As a result of these initiatives, new programmes targeted at the poor were begun; existing social welfare programmes were expanded and tilted more heavily toward the poor. As Robert Lampman stated so aptly, national policy after 1965 was heavily influenced by the question: 'What does it do for the poor?'[1]

These efforts were undertaken with optimism that poverty could be reduced, racial inequalities diminished, and efficient investments in human productivity made. Now, twenty years later, that optimism has faded. Disappointment with past efforts, a desire to cut back existing programmes, and a reluctance to embrace new social initiatives characterize the current mood. To be sure, the current view is not without basis. Poverty-related education and training efforts cannot be graded 'outstanding' – 'satisfactory with flashes of good' is about the most that can be said. Advances in health care and

access to education for the poor have occurred, and few would doubt
a decrease in employment and housing discrimination. Central cities
seem better places in which to live, and the ghettos of the poor seem
less harsh than in the 1960s, but in neither case would a judicious
observer claim a revolution. And because some of these improvements must be attributed to general economic growth and other
economic and demographic factors, many people wonder just how
much of these gains are attributable to the programmes designed to
create a Great Society.

Research about the effect of these policies on the poor is volumi-
nous. The flow of income transfers and in-kind benefits to poor
people has been documented, and the substantial contribution of anti-
poverty programmes to the well-being of low income families is
now accepted.[2] The magnitude of the impacts of income transfer
policies on the decisions and choices made by the poor – on labour
supply, saving, migration, family size and structure, and fertility – has
also been extensively assessed.[3]

Relatively little attention has focused on the overall impact of these
pro-poor policies on the much larger segment of the nation's
population that was not targeted for their benefits, i.e. the non-poor.[4]
Without such an assessment, the on-going debate over social policy is
imbalanced and not well informed. It rests far too heavily on
prejudice and predilection in place of evidence. To make such an
overall assessment is difficult, however. The impacts of some anti-
poverty policy measures on recipients can be traced in a fairly direct
way; welfare benefits or food stamps are examples. Other effects of
these measures are largely in the form of additional taxes, and
assignment of any increase in tax revenues to specific individuals is
difficult. Still other of the impacts are in the form of non-market or
spillover effects; improved health and longevity due to welfare
transfers, education programmes, or Medicaid are examples.

In this chapter, I attempt to identify the manifold effects of anti-
poverty policy on those one would expect to be adversely affected by
it – the non-poor. In some cases, numerical estimates are provided.
While speculative, these estimates indicate the effect of pro-poor
interventions on the non-poor population. While the importance of
this distributional issue is suggested in recent contributions in the
public choice literature, no framework for consistently analysing a
broad range of these effects has been set down, and no empirical
estimates exist.[5]

The Channels of Impact

Many channels exist through which anti-poverty policies – and social welfare measures more generally – affect the non-poor population.[6] A catalogue of them is as follows:

(1)   *Increase in the tax burden of the non-poor.* Because the policy changes motivated by Great Society concerns led to public spending which did not substitute on a dollar-for-dollar basis for expenditures for other purposes, aggregate public expenditures and, hence, taxes are to some extent higher than they would otherwise be. The bulk of the required increase in taxes is borne by the non-poor. This increased tax burden entails slower growth in the economic well-being of the non-poor than would have otherwise occurred.

(2)   *Spillover of social benefits to the non-poor.* Some portion of the growth in public expenditures on cash and in-kind benefits which are attributable to anti-poverty policy provide benefits directly to the non-poor. Increased spending on education, for example, has also benefited the children of the non-poor.

(3)   *Reduction in non-poor earnings.* The higher tax and benefit reduction rates (and higher taxes and benefits) faced by the non-poor resulting from increased anti-poverty expenditures cause some reduction in the labour supply of the non-poor and, hence, some reduction in their earnings.

(4)   *Increase in non-poor leisure time and home production.* The reduction in desired work effort induced by the higher tax and benefit reduction rates (and higher taxes and benefits) – described in item 3 – increases the time which the non-poor have available for leisure and home production. The value of this time partially offsets the reduced earnings.

(5)   *Increase in non-poor income from more rapid economic growth.* The improved education, training, and security attributable to anti-poverty policies leads to a more productive work force. These increased productivities lead to increases in GNP. This economic growth will result in a larger economic pie which will in some proportion be shared by both the poor and the non-poor.

(6)   *Reduction in non-poor income from increased job competition.* Anti-poverty education and training policies increase the producti-

vity of low income workers and, hence, increase competition for jobs, and reduce wage rates and earnings of those displaced by the competition. The burden of these labour-market shifts will be borne largely by the non-poor.[7]

(7)   *Increase in non-poor well-being from improved lot of the poor.* Anti-poverty policies improve the nutrition, health, education, and housing of the poor, and decrease the insecurity which poor persons bear due to income loss or irregular and extraordinary expenditure. To the extent that non-poor individuals value these improvements in the lot of the poor, their own economic well-being increases. This effect has been referred to as the benefits from 'Pareto-optimal redistribution'.[8]

(8)   *Decrease in non-poor 'status rewards'.* As Charles Murray (1984) has emphasized, the use of public benefits by the non-working poor to achieve levels of living comparable to those achieved by working, non-poor people has made them feel like 'chumps'. The satisfaction which they obtain from securing independence and escaping poverty through work is eroded.

(9)   *Increase in security of the non-poor.* The increase in effective income guarantees from expanded social welfare expenditures induced by anti-poverty policy provides a 'safety net' protecting both the poor and the non-poor. The non-poor would be willing to pay some amount for this increase in their own security. These expenditures also convey benefits to the non-poor in the form of reductions in crime and, perhaps most importantly, the defusing of civil unrest.

The Counterfactuals

To estimate the size of each of these impacts on the non-poor population over the 1965–80 period, it is first necessary to decide how much of the increase in Social Welfare Expenditures (SWE) should be legitimately attributed to the anti-poverty policies that began in the 1960s. This amount will clearly be less than the actual increase in SWE. In fact, from 1965 to 1980, SWE grew by an average of 12.9 per cent per year (see Table 4.1).

One possibility – call it Scenario *A* – is to assume that, in the absence of the War on Poverty–Great Society initiative, SWE

Table 4.1   *US Total Social Welfare Expenditures under Public Programmes (millions of current dollars)*

	1965	1980	Average annual rates of change (%)
Social Insurance	28,123	229,552	14.8
OASDI (excluding Medicare)	16,998	117,118	13.5
Medicare	—	34,992	16.8 (1970–80)
Unemployment Insurance	3,003	18,326	12.6
Workers' Compensation	1,859	13,253	13.7
Other	6,263	45,863	13.9
Public Aid	6,283	73,385	17.5
Public Assistance	4,508	17,298	9.2
Medicaid	1,367	27,394	21.7
Supplemental Security Income	—	8,226	5.9 (1975–80)
Food Stamps	36	9,083	43.7
Other	373	9,601	23.7
Health Programmes	6,246	28,119	10.4
Veterans' Programmes	6,031	21,466	8.7
Education	28,108	120,588	10.0
Elementary and Secondary	22,358	86,773	9.3
Higher	4,826	26,091	11.7
Vocational/adult	854	7,375	15.2
Housing	318	7,209	22.7
Other Social Welfare	2,066	14,036	13.4
Total	77,175	493,354	12.9

Source: Tabulated from *Social Security Bulletin*, various issues.

would have grown at the same rate as the economy as a whole over the post-1965 period. This rate of growth was 8.9 per cent, which implies that over the period the ratio of SWE to GNP would have remained constant. The difference between 12.9 per cent and 8.9 per cent implies a substantial impact of the War on Poverty–Great Society initiative on the growth of SWE. To see the impact of this assumption, we can compare the actual level of SWE in 1980 with the level that it would have attained if this scenario had held. Table 4.1 indicates that from 1965 to 1980, actual SWE grew from $77 billion to $493 billion; Scenario *A* would suggest a growth in SWE from

$77 billion in 1965 to $287 billion in 1980. In 1980, then, $206 billion of the actual level of $493 billion represents an increase in SWE which is attributable to the War on Poverty–Great Society initiative.

A far more conservative possibility would assume that the demographic trends and equity-based concerns that were already in evidence in the period before 1965 continued apace in the post-1965 period. In Scenario *B*, then, we assume that, in the absence of the War on Poverty–Great Society initiative, the growth in the *ratio* of SWE to GNP observed in the period 1950 to 1965 would have continued until 1980. This implies a growth rate of SWE of 10.7 per cent as compared to the actual growth rate of 12.9 per cent. If Scenario *B* had held, then, annual SWE by 1980 would have totalled $372 billion as compared to its actual level of $493 billion. In 1980, then, $121 billion of the actual level of $493 billion of SWE would be attributed to growth in spending which was caused by the War on Poverty–Great Society initiative.

These comparisons of Scenarios *A* and *B* indicate the implications of alternative paths of SWE growth in the absence of the anti-poverty initiatives for the level of SWE spending *in 1980*, the year for which we estimate the gains and losses of anti-poverty policy on the non-poor.[9]

Components of Gains and Losses to the Non-Poor — Some Rough Estimates

Table 4.2 presents some numerical estimates of the gains and losses to the non-poor population of the growth in public social welfare spending attributable to anti-poverty concerns. These estimates are for a single year, 1980, the final year covered by our analysis. Consider, first, item 1, the increased taxes borne by the non-poor because of the War on Poverty–Great Society effort. It is impossible to know with any accuracy how this added revenue requirement was financed.[10] Because of the growth of social insurance expenditures, a sizable share of the increase clearly came from payroll taxes. Given the relative decline in importance of corporate taxes as a source of general revenue, another sizable proportion probably came from personal income taxes.

During the 1970s, the poor were largely exempt from federal

Table 4.2   *1980 Gains and Losses to the Non-Poor from US Anti-Poverty Policy (1980 $ billions)*

Item	Gains to non-poor Scenario A	Gains to non-poor Scenario B	Losses to non-poor Scenario A	Losses to non-poor Scenario B
1. Increased taxes of non-poor required to finance increase in SWE due to anti-poverty concerns.			195	115
2. Gains to the non-poor from the spillover to them of transfers income and education, training and medical care services from increases in SWE due to anti-poverty concerns.	107	63		
3. Reduction in non-poor labour earnings from reduced labour supply due to higher tax and benefit reduction rates.			37	27
4. Increase in leisure and home production outputs due to reduction in labour supply of non-poor (see 3).	28	20		
5. Increase in non-poor incomes due to more rapid economic growth from more productive low income workers.	10	10		
6. Reduction in non-poor income from increased job competition due to more trained and educated disadvantaged workers.			X	X
7. Gains to the non-poor from reduced poverty, inequality and insecurity of poor.	X	X		
8. Decrease in well-being of non-poor from reduced 'status rewards'.			X	X
9. Increase in security of the non-poor from unexpected job or income loss or extraordinary expenses.	X	X		
Total	145	93	232	142
	(plus items 7 and 9)		(plus items 6 and 8)	

income taxes, though they probably accounted for a greater share of payroll, sales, property, and excise taxes than their income levels would indicate. Hence, it seems reasonable to allocate 95 per cent of the $121 (Scenario *A*) or $206 (Scenario *B*) billion of the required increase in 1980 revenue to the non-poor.[11] These estimates – $115 billion and $195 billion – appear as item 1 in Table 4.2.

While much of the impetus to the growth in SWE was motivated by the question 'What does it do for the poor?', not all of the increased spending went for income support to the pre-transfer poor. Plotnick and Skidmore (1975) and Plotnick (1979) have calculated anti-poverty budgets for the 1965–74 period and found that about 41 to 45 per cent of total social welfare expenditures went to poor families.[12] An update of their calculation indicates that in 1980, 45 per cent of total spending went to the pre-transfer poor; conversely, 55 per cent of these benefits spilled over to the non-poor. Assuming that the benefits to recipients of these programmes are equal to their budgetary costs, we enter gains to the non-poor from these spillovers of $63 billion (0.55 × $121 billion) for Scenario *B* and $107 billion (0.55 × $206 billion) for Scenario *A* as item 2.

Both the increased taxes (item 1) and the increased social welfare benefits (item 2) contain incentives which are likely to decrease labour supply. A recent study examined the combined effects of a reduction in social welfare programme spending and a proportional reduction in personal income tax rates on aggregate labour supply in 1980.[13] Extrapolating the results of this study to the question addressed here results in an overall 'guesstimate' of about a 2.5 (Scenario *B*) to 3.5 per cent (Scenario *A*) decrease in labour supply in 1980 attributable to the post-1965 anti-poverty policy measures and the taxes required to finance them. This leads to earnings losses of $37 and $27 billion, recorded as item 3.[14]

This loss of work time and earnings is compensated at least in part by an increase in non-marketed uses of time such as home production, schooling, or leisure. However, because individuals make the choice of fewer work hours because of the work disincentives associated with the higher taxes, the value of these increases in leisure and home production time is not equal to the foregone earnings. In the face of existing taxes and other labour market distortions, the net wage rate at the margin will be less than the gross wage rate, and it is the former at which increments of non-market time are appropriately valued. Assuming a wedge between gross and net rate of 25 per cent,[15] the value of the increase in non-market time of the non-poor is estimated to be about $28 billion (0.75 times the $37 billion of earnings losses) for Scenario *A* and $20 billion (0.75 times the $27 billion of earnings losses) for Scenario *B*. These appear as item 4.

A very rough estimate for item 5 completes the list of quantifiable items. The actual level of education and training expenditures in 1980 was $120.6 billion. If, in the absence of War on Poverty–Great Society policies, these expenditures had grown so as to maintain a constant ratio with GNP over this period, they would have been about 15 per cent lower in 1980. A similar calculation indicates that *over the entire 1965–80 period* aggregate education and training expenditures were about $126 billion higher than they would have been in the absence of the anti-poverty initiative. These direct public expenditures, however, account for only a portion of the total increase in human resource investment costs attributable to the post-1965 anti-poverty policies. Studies indicate that foregone student (trainee) income is about equal to the direct expenditures on these programmes, and that this foregone income is also to be included as a component of the total social investment in these programmes. The sum of the direct expenditures and the value of the foregone income totals about $252 billion of additional investment in human capital over the post-1965 period attributed to the War on Poverty–Great Society initiative. Assuming that this additional human capital investment existed in 1980, and that it earned a real rate of return of 5 per cent, personal income in 1980 was about $13 billion higher with these anti-poverty policy measures in place than without them.[16] With 80 per cent of this increased income retained by the non-poor,[17] $10 billion is entered as item 5.

Item 6 concerns the effects on the structure of wage rates and hours worked due to the new or expanded training and education attributable to the War on Poverty–Great Society initiatives, and to the associated affirmative action efforts to reduce labour market discrimination. Much of this increment in human capital investment and equal opportunity activities was concentrated on low skill, disadvantaged workers, who, because of their increased productivity and opportunities, became better able to compete with higher skill workers for available jobs. This increase in competition tended to reduce the wages of the higher skill individuals which had held such jobs. Because the magnitude of this effect is difficult to ascertain, we leave item 6 unquantified, but place it in the loss column for the non-poor population which contains the more skilled workers who would be adversely affected.

Items 7, 8, and 9 are also unquantifiable. The third-party gains from reduced poverty, inequality and insecurity (item 7) may be large, but no reliable estimate exists. Similarly, the loss in status rewards by the non-poor attributable to anti-poverty efforts (item 8) is claimed to be substantial by some, but again the magnitude of the effect is unknown. Finally, the increase in security from the social safety net is real for the non-poor (item 9), but again difficult to measure.[18]

Conclusion

What have we learned from these calculations, and how do they contribute to the current debate over social policy? Perhaps as no time before, the debate on federal social welfare policy is a highly polarized one. Analysts on the right argue that the post-1965 policy initiatives have simultaneously won the war on income poverty (Anderson, 1978), created increasingly serious problems of black youth unemployment, family disintegration, economic dependency, and a loss of status rewards (Murray, 1984), and led to reductions in work effort, savings, and innovation which have stifled economic growth (Gilder, 1980). Others have emphasized the serious poverty, inequality, and hardship which still exists (Danziger and Weinberg, 1986), and shown that the adverse labour supply, savings, and family structure side effects which have been created are less serious than is often asserted (Lampman, 1984).

If those holding the first view are correct, the implication is that the poor have gained income at the expense of the non-poor because of anti-poverty measures, and that these policies have at the same time harmed the non-poor by retarding economic growth, fostering a disintegration of traditional values of independence and family stability, and eroding the satisfaction from escaping poverty by one's own efforts. Perceiving these effects, it is suggested that the non-poor withdraw their support for existing social policies and, in the resulting process of dismantling, seek to induce more socially beneficial work, independence, family responsibility, and legitimate behaviour in the poor.

The framework and calculations which are presented here indicate that this view is based on a partial accounting of the full impact of social policies on the non-poor. On the basis of our examination, the War on Poverty–Great Society initiative does not appear to have imposed large net losses on the non-poor, on whose political support such efforts rely. For the year 1980 we have identified a quantifiable gross economic loss to the non-poor from the War on Poverty–Great Society measures of from $142 billion (Scenario *B*) to $232 billion (Scenario *A*). This loss was offset by a total quantifiable gain to the non-poor in 1980 of from $93 billion (Scenario *B*) to $145 billion (Scenario *A*), plus the non-quantifiable gains reflected in items 7 and 9. Assuming that the losses associated with item 6 are negligible, the $49 and $87 billion of *net* losses to the non-poor represent from 2–3 per cent of personal income in 1980. Moreover, this amount – less than one year's *growth* in personal income – will be reduced to the extent that the *net* gains experienced by the non-poor from their contribution to reducing both the hardships faced by those less well off and their own long run uncertainty (items 7 and 9), exceed whatever loss in status rewards they may have experienced (item 8).

This framework, then, contributes to setting the single-impact claims made by some into a wider perspective. If our crude estimates are anywhere close to being correct,[19] they suggest one reason why US citizens – in particular, the non-poor – have not supported wholesale dismantling of War on Poverty–Great Society measures, in spite of calls for such retrenchment from political leaders. They also suggest that with some reorientation to improve their integration, administration, incentives, and efficiency, existing social policy could be made to yield net gains to both the poor and the non-poor.

Notes

This paper was originally published in the *Political Science Quarterly*, vol. 102, no. 1 (1987), whose permission to reprint is gratefully acknowledged. Helpful comments of Sheldon Danziger, Irv Garfinkel, Edward Gramlich, W. Lee Hansen, Robert Lampman, Julian Le Grand, Donald Nichols, Robert Plotnick and Barbara Wolfe are also gratefully acknowledged, as is the questioning research assistance of Matthew Rabin.

1   Lampman (1974).
2   See Haveman (1977) and Danziger and Weinberg (1986).
3   See Danziger, Haveman, and Plotnick (1981).

4   To be sure, Piven and Cloward (1971) have stressed the political
    functions of the War on Poverty and the Great Society, viewing them as
    the price paid by the non-poor for the benefits of political and social
    stability in the low-income (largely, black) community which were
    being 'purchased'. Other participants in the debate over social policy
    have cited the higher taxes borne by the non-poor as a result of these
    initiatives, and of the deterioration in family and social structures which
    might be causally related to social welfare expenditures, and which has
    spilled over to the non-poor community. See Anderson (1978), Gilder
    (1981), and Murray (1984). None of these discussions, however, have
    attempted to systematically analyse and measure these negative and
    positive effects.

5   Le Grand (1982b) and Olson (1982).

6   A difficulty in discussing the impacts of policy measures on the non-
    poor population is the identification of who is non-poor. In any given
    year, this identification is straightforward. For example, the official
    poverty measure can be used to separate the total population into pre-
    transfer poor and non-poor groups at a given point in time. Over time,
    however, mobility into and out of poverty is substantial; families
    classified as non-poor in year 1 may well be poor in year 2. Moreover,
    because of births, deaths, and migration, the population as a whole, and
    hence the non-poor population, is composed of quite different indivi-
    duals over, say, a decade. Our discussion proceeds as if there is a constant
    group of individuals who are the official pre-transfer poor over the
    1965–80 period. A reasonable, though crude, interpretation would be to
    think of a constant group of individuals who are at the bottom of the
    distribution of some long-term (or permanent) measure of income or
    earnings capacity.

7   Fuchs (1965) described this side effect of anti-poverty policy as follows:

> Michael Harrington, author of a widely read book on poverty,
> *The Other America*, has written, 'Any gain for America's minori-
> ties will immediately be translated into an advance for all the
> unskilled workers. One cannot raise the bottom without benefit-
> ting everyone above.' This is almost precisely wrong. It is
> probably closer to the truth to say that one cannot raise the bottom
> except at the expense of those above, and those who are not far
> removed from the bottom are likely to feel the change most
> keenly. (pp. 88–9)

    In 1971, Bergmann presented a more formal demonstration of this
    effect.

8   Hochman and Rodgers (1969).

9   An alternative comparison would be to ask how much aggregate SWE
    increased *over the entire 1965–80 period* because of these policy initiatives.
    In fact, total SWE, aggregated over the period, was $3891 billion. If
    Scenario *A* had held, SWE would have totalled $3374 billion over the

1965 to 1980 period; Scenario *B* would have resulted in $3597 billion of SWE. Hence, according to Scenario *A*, the anti-poverty policy initiatives contributed $517 billion to the total of $3891 billion, or 13 per cent. If SWE had grown according to Scenario *B*, $294 billion or 8 per cent of the total would have been attributed to growth induced by War on Poverty–Great Society concerns.

10   Hansen and Weisbrod (1971) discuss the difficulties of identifying the counterfactual constellation of taxes in the absence of a public expenditure programme.

11   Pechman (1985) reports that, in 1980, the lowest fifth of all families received about 4 per cent of pre-tax but post-transfer income. Hence, allocating 5 per cent of incremental taxes from anti-poverty concerns to the poor population appears reasonable.

12   These budgets provide detailed estimates of the proportion of expenditures in the component programme areas of the Social Welfare Expenditures account which went for income support or service provision to pre-transfer poor families.

13   See Haveman (1984).

14   We take $12,904, median full-time, full-year earnings in fiscal year 1980, to be the earnings lost from a reduced person-year of full-time work in 1980. A 3.5 per cent (2.5 per cent) reduction in labour supply is about 2.9 (2.1) million worker-years, which implies a loss in earnings of $37 billion for Scenario *A* and $27 billion for Scenario *B*.

15   Pechman (1985) estimates that, in 1980, the effective rate of federal, state, and local taxes ranged was about 25 per cent over deciles 3 to 10, irrespective of the incidence assumptions used. Assuming that marginal and average tax rate are not widely divergent, the net wage rate will equal about 75 per cent of the gross wage rate.

16   For two reasons, this is a very conservative estimate. First, studies of education investments during the 1960s and 1970s concluded that these expenditures were competitive with private sector capital investments. These latter investments were producing real rates of return of up to double the 5 per cent figure (see Hansen, 1963; Mincer, 1974 and Levin, 1977). Second, these studies counted as benefits only the returns to education in the form of *earnings increases*. In fact, the benefits of education include numerous non-marketed, yet valued, impacts, including improvements in one's own health, the quality of one's children, the efficiency of one's consumption, fertility, and migration choices, and so on. Haveman and Wolfe (1984) suggest that the value of these *non-marketed effects* are likely to equal the value of the marketed returns measured in the standard, returns to education studies. These benefits, if added to those estimated in the text, would double the benefits from the initiatives credited to the non-poor in item 5.

17   About 80 per cent of total public education expenditures over the 1965–80 period went to the non-poor (see Plotnick, 1979). Hence, we assume that 20 per cent of the incremental education expenditures attributable to War on Poverty–Great Society concerns were targeted

     on the poor, and that they retained the additional returns generated by the additional human capital.

18 See Aharoni (1981).

19 The crude and tentative nature of the quantitative estimates should again be emphasized. They represent 'order-of-magnitude' impacts on the non-poor of a broad spectrum of policy changes, and in many cases deviate from estimates consistent with the principles of applied welfare economics (cost–benefit analysis). Given the magnitude of the policy shift, no formal cost–benefit analysis could be undertaken without a full general equilibrium model. Moreover, the programmes grouped together are too diverse and too complex (with contradictory incentive effects and alterations of budget constraints) to warrant a full cost–benefit evaluation. Indeed, obtaining reliable estimates of the efficiency gains and costs of any single programme is a major undertaking.

     Indeed, our accounting framework, it should be noted, neglects a variety of economic effects on the non-poor which could be attributable to War on Poverty–Great Society concerns. We will mention three. First, we have neglected the potential effect of the growth of public social spending and associated taxes then on the aggregate savings rate. This effect has been much researched and debated in the literature, especially in the context of increases in social security benefits. A reasonable and, perhaps, consensus estimate is that the dissavings effects at issue are positive but small (see Danziger, Haveman, and Plotnick, 1981) and would primarily alter the well-being of the non-poor.

     Second, we have only considered the changes in public social spending attributable to War on Poverty–Great Society concerns. These concerns also generated substantial changes in regulatory policy, primarily in the affirmative action-equal opportunity area. These regulatory changes also carry gains and losses to the non-poor. On balance, the losses are likely to exceed the gains although probably not for non-poor blacks and women. See Bergmann (1971), who formulated a model for estimating the effect on white incomes of a reduction in discrimination.

     Finally, some have asserted the many public social welfare expenditures were undertaken largely to subsidize producer interests – food programmes for agricultural interests, housing programmes for construction industry interests, research programmes for consulting firm and university interests. We have neglected the implied quasi-rents of producers in our accounting, nearly all of which would have gone to the non-poor.

Chapter 5

The Middle-Class Use of
the British Social Services

JULIAN LE GRAND

There are valid reasons for providing social services publicly and, indeed, for providing some free at the point of use. However, it is important to rid ourselves of some false assumptions. There was a time when many people in Britain believed that state provision of such services as health care, education, housing, even transport, free or at heavily subsidized prices, would in itself be a significant contribution to redistributing income to the poorest members of the community. Inequalities would diminish and a classless society would be a little nearer attainment. These dreams were not fulfilled and it is important to understand the reasons. Some lie in the tax structure which finances these services; but there is also a large amount of evidence suggesting that most of the services mentioned actually benefit the middle classes at least as much as the poor, and in many cases more than the poor. Why this is and what might be done about it is the principal theme of this chapter.

Who Benefits?

We begin with a brief summary of the facts concerning the distribution of public expenditure on the principal social services. Table 5.1 divides the services into those whose distribution is pro-poor, those that are equally distributed and those that are pro-rich. The column of figures gives an indication of the relevant numbers,

Table 5.1   *The Distribution of Public Expenditure on the British Social Services*

Service	Ratio of expenditure per person in top fifth to that per person in bottom fifth
Pro-poor	
Council housing (general subsidy and rent rebates)[a]	0.3
Rent allowances	not available[b]
Equal	
Nursery education	not available[b]
Primary education	0.9
Secondary education, pupils over 16	0.9
Pro-rich	
National Health Service	1.4[c]
Secondary education, pupils over 16	1.8
Non-university higher education[d]	3.5
Bus subsidies	3.7
Universities	5.4
Tax subsidies to owner-occupiers	6.8
Rail subsidies	9.8

Notes:
[a] The estimates pre-date the introduction of housing benefit.
[b] See note 1 to this chapter.
[c] per person ill.
[d] Polytechnics, colleges of education, technical colleges.
   Source: See note 1 to this chapter.

showing the average expenditure on people in the top fifth of the population, in income and occupational terms, expressed as a ratio of average expenditure on people in the bottom fifth. The figures refer to different groups and times. They are drawn from the author's much larger study and should be taken as indicative only.[1]

Generally they relate only to actual service spending by public authorities. With the exception of housing they exclude the benefits taxpayers receive from various tax allowances. These are even more heavily pro-rich. On the other hand, the figures exclude social security spending, much of which is pro-poor (UK Central Statistical Office, 1985, p. 107, Table 3), and spending on the personal social services, much of which is pro-poor.

It is clear from Table 5.1 that the bulk of the services listed are either distributed equally or favour the better off. Only the housing programmes aimed at council and private tenants benefit primarily the poor. The expenditure on the National Health Service is actually equally distributed in the limited sense that the average poor person receives about as much as the average rich person. But this does not take account of the fact that the poor suffer more ill health than the rich; so per person ill, they receive less. State expenditure on education prior to the school leaving age is distributed equally; but expenditure on all forms of education after that age accrues largely to the better off. The subsidies that accrue to owner-occupiers through their various tax reliefs also dramatically favour the well off, with the richest group receiving nearly seven times as much on average as the poorest group. Much of public transport spending too is pro-rich. Indeed, the subsidies to rail travel are the most unequal of those listed.

The picture is one that many may find surprising. Of all current expenditure on social services listed here, it can be estimated that only about one fifth is directed primarily at the poor. All of the rest is either distributed equally, or, more disturbingly, towards the better off.

Now, a number of qualifications are needed to these figures. First, they show only the distribution of public expenditure in each area; they do not give the distribution of 'benefits' from that expenditure. However, it seems unlikely that the distribution of the latter would differ in any systematic way from that of the former. Second, they take no account of the taxes paid by the different groups. This was discussed in more detail in Chapter 2, but one point should be made here.

It is often argued that the social services are redistributive because the better off pay more in taxes than they receive in services. But this proposition is incorrect. It may be true that the rich pay more in taxes for all the different forms of public expenditure from which they derive benefits, including defence, police and social security. But we cannot deduce from this that the social services as such are redistributive. To do so would require identifying that part of the tax system which funds the social services – an impossible task. It seems preferable to treat the overall tax system as an instrument of redistribution separate from the social services, and hence – as here – to consider the distributive effect of social service provision independently.

Third, most of the estimates date from the 1970s, and so are now rather elderly. However, it is unlikely that, were more up-to-date figures available, the estimates would change significantly. General subsidies to council housing have been cut sharply since 1977 (Atkinson, Hills and Le Grand, 1986, p. 35) and the rent rebate and allowance system has been replaced by housing benefit. Since the general subsidy is not means tested, but housing benefit is, those changes, if anything, are likely to increase the pro-poor nature of these housing subsidies. There has been a limited expansion of private education and the introduction of a (means-tested) assisted places scheme by which local governments support pupils at private schools. Both of these factors might render the primary and second-ary education systems a little more pro-poor. There has been some redistribution of medical facilities under the RAWP process; this is discussed further below. The decline in the value of the student grant and cuts in higher education have probably made it yet more difficult for working-class individuals to obtain higher education. Mortgage interest tax relief has expanded since 1977 (*ibid*, p. 41); we do not know the exact distributional consequences but they are unlikely to have changed significantly. And the most recent evidence on public transport subsidies (UK Central Statistical Office, 1985 p. 107, Table 3) suggests that they still sharply favour the better off.

Is it possible to reform the social services so as to increase their redistributive impact, while preserving their essential character? The answers vary from service to service. We shall deal with each separately.

Health Care

The evidence concerning the distribution of public expenditure on the National Health Service suggests that the poor do not use the service, relative to need, as much as their middle-class counterparts. The reasons for this can only be summarized here (they are discussed at greater length in Le Grand, 1982b, ch. 3). They include: the absence of good medical facilities in poorer areas; the poor having worse access to such facilities as do exist, due to their possessing fewer cars and telephones; manual workers, unlike the salaried middle class, losing money when they take time off to go to the doctor; and failures of communication between middle-class medical staff and working-class patients.

On the first of these, it is possible to make some progress.

Following the report of the Resources Allocation Working Party (RAWP: UK Department of Health and Social Security, 1976), creditable attempts have been made to relocate health service facilities away from the medically over-endowed and wealthy Southeast to the underendowed rest of the country. Partly because the increment to distribute is so small in a barely growing service, partly because of the impassioned protests of the losers in the South, this process has encountered severe difficulties. But it could be revived; any government should make doing so one of its top priorities.

However, it is difficult to be optimistic about the potential for more extensive reforms. All the other factors listed are beyond the control of the National Health Service; they are all part of wider social economic inequalities about which there is little the NHS can do on its own. Inequality in health care largely reflects overall inequality in society; there is little that can be done about the former without doing something about the latter. In education, housing and transport, however, there is more scope for improving matters, as we shall now see.

Education

Education expenditure is broadly equally distributed prior to the school leaving age but subsequently it becomes highly unequal. One way to redress the balance would be to redirect education expenditure further towards schools. To some extent this has happened in the past decade. At the same time it is obviously desirable to preserve, so far as possible, the poor's access to education past the school leaving age and not to undermine university standards. The question is how best this can be done. One proposal is to expand state nursery education. Perhaps surprisingly, nursery schools and nursery classes in primary schools are already used broadly equally by different social groups (see note 1). If this pattern were maintained following an expansion (and there seems little reason to expect it not to be), then the proportion of education expenditure that was equalizing would be increased. Moreover, since the difference between the home and the school environments is likely to be greater for working-class than middle-class children, the academic and social gains for the former would be greater.

Expanding nursery provision need not be very expensive. Primary schools are already suffering from substantial over-capacity, capacity that it would be relatively easy to convert for nursery use. In 1983/4, to provide nursery classes in primary schools on a part-time basis for all children aged 3 to 4 who were not then receiving any pre-school education would have cost about £417 million, or just over 3 per cent of the total education and science budget for the year.[2]

A more controversial proposal is to raise the school leaving age. This would reduce the overall inequality in public expenditure, since it would expand the period of compulsory education which is equally spread between income groups. Quite apart from this 'statistical' gain it might also contribute to reducing inequality in access to post-compulsory education, and it might even contribute to greater equality in later earnings. A group of London University economists has estimated that the raising of the school leaving age in 1972 reduced the dispersion of earnings by as much as 15 per cent in the younger age group (Blaug, Dougherty and Psacharopoulos, 1982).

To be sure, the proposal has unattractive features. It would be expensive. For instance, if the leaving age had been raised by one year in 1983/4, and if the same amount per person had been spent on each of the extra people staying on as was spent on those who did in fact stay on, the cost would have been £1,280 million.[3] There would also be costs to the economy to take into account. Raising the leaving age by a year would withdraw over one million people from the labour force, with a possible loss in production, though that assumes full employment which is far from being the case in the present or medium-term prospect. Many poor households' incomes would be reduced, due to the loss of earnings from children who would have been in work (or the loss of social security payments from those who would have been unemployed). Some children and their teachers already regard the year from 15 to 16 as a waste of time educationally. For them, raising the leaving age might simply prolong the agony. Finally, the proposal involves an erosion of civil liberties, to which many (not least those primarily affected) might take objection.

Yet the force of these points can be exaggerated. The overcapacity already apparent in primary schools is also appearing in secondary schools. As a result, the marginal resource cost of taking on extra children is likely to fall substantially below the present cost. Hence the cost to the education budget will almost certainly be less than the 1983/4 calculations suggest. Moreover, that cost is not much above that of the total for the government's Youth Training Scheme and is considerably less on a per person basis.[4] With three million people already unemployed (many of them school leavers), the loss to the economy of withdrawing even a million from the potential labour force is unlikely to be great.

The cost to poor families is a more significant problem. But this could be alleviated by an expansion of child benefit: a reform that might be desirable for other reasons as well. It could be financed at least in part by the savings in social security due to the reduction in payments to unemployed school leavers. More vocationally oriented curricula with work experience could be introduced. Comprehensive tertiary educational institutions could make the extra period both useful educationally and more attractive to students.

An alternative which would yield some of the benefits of raising the school leaving age and impose fewer of the costs in terms of educational motivation, civil liberties and reduction in family income is the extension of grants to 16- to 18-year-olds. Already, local authorities provide minimal grants to students who stay on at school after 16. Many have advocated that these be made much more generous, and given a wider national coverage. They do have serious shortcomings nevertheless. First, in order to overcome all the financial pressures on working-class children to drop out of school, they would have to be extremely generous. Second, to ensure that they did not simply help the middle classes to extract even more financial resources out of the system, they would have to be subject to a strict means test. Third, they would only have a major impact on the numbers of poor children staying on at school if the main reason why poor children did not stay on was the cost. For many, and possibly most, the reasons are more complex – lack of relevant information, parental distrust of the educational system and peer group pressure. None of these are likely to be affected by a system of student grants. All in all, therefore, it is a less effective option in redistributive terms than raising the school leaving age or extending industrial training combined with an increase in child benefit.

In the post-18 education sector, major redistributive gains could be achieved by raising fees and switching from student grants to student loans. If all higher and further education students were charged the marginal cost of their education and if they had to finance this, not from government grants, but via loan repayments out of their subsequent earnings, then the principal source of financial inequality in the education system would be eliminated. The consequent savings in public expenditure could be used to finance the extensions in pre-school leaving age education discussed earlier. In the absence of information on the marginal costs of students' education in different institutions, it is difficult to quantify these savings; but if the result were to cut the bill for higher and further education by only half (and it might well be considerably more than that), then nearly enough would have been saved in 1983/4 to finance an increase in the school leaving age for one year.

There are, and have been, many objections to this proposal. First, it is argued that higher education generates what are called 'social' or 'external' benefits. That is, over and above the rewards that university education offers to the individual student, it also confers benefits on the nation as a whole. Some of these are cultural. The nation needs educated individuals to promote moral, political and cultural values. Other benefits are more directly economic. The nation needs scientists, engineers, doctors and the like. If university students were not subsidized, so the argument runs, many qualified people would not be able to meet the cost of university. There would be a shortage of graduates, and we would all be worse off as a result.

However, this view is in turn open to challenge. The cultural benefits from university education can be exaggerated: most of these benefits stem from home and class background. So far as the economic needs of the nation are concerned, if the nation needs doctors, engineers or scientists, this will be reflected in the incomes those individuals command. If people have their productivity increased by university education, then, other things being equal, their employers will pay them higher wages. There is little here by way of external benefit; insofar as the nation benefits from graduates, it will be through the normal process of market exchange (income for skills). So long as people can borrow on the strength of their future earnings, no one whose potential skills the nation 'needs' will be deterred from acquiring those skills; hence there is no need to subsidize them. Universities exist and more students attend them in countries where students are financed by loans than in Britain. Indeed, it could be argued that the public expense of the British system, and the accompanying Treasury controls, have restricted entry, not expanded it.

Now these arguments are over-simplified. The absence of security makes the private sector reluctant to provide loans, even to prospective undergraduates with potentially high earnings. There are many

occupations where graduates perform activities where their education is socially valuable, but which are not appropriately rewarded
in the market – not the least of these is bringing up children. On these
grounds, therefore, there may be a case for some form of government
subsidy.

A more powerful argument against raising fees and abolishing
grants is that it would reduce the poor's access to the system.
Children from working-class families would undoubtedly find it
more difficult than middle-class children to find sources of finance for
their education; their parents could help less and the banking system,
if it offered them loans at all, would probably do so on more
expensive terms. The result could be that their participation in higher
education – already small – might fall yet further. Yet this is not
inevitable. It will depend in part on what use is made of the money
saved. If it is used to expand pre-school education and financial
incentives to stay on at 16, the demand for higher education by
working-class children might increase. Raising the cost of higher
education would, other things being equal, reduce the number of
aspirants relative to the number of places available. Entrance to
higher education would become less competitive. This would
actually improve the chances of a working-class candidate relative to
a middle-class one. The reduction in subsidy to higher education,
therefore, although it increases the cost to working-class students by
raising their fees, simultaneously reduces the other barriers such
students face. Nevertheless the possibility has to be faced that, on its
own, such a policy would reduce working-class access to the system.
There are also the problems of the absence of security for private
sector loans and of graduates with low-paying but socially valuable
jobs. Are there any alternatives?

One possibility is for the government itself either to guarantee
private bank loans to students or to offer loans itself. This is what
happens in North America and in the countries of Western Europe.
Loan guarantees cost little. But such systems can be complex to
administer; and there can be difficulties about preventing default.
Even if loans are subsidized, they will present repayment problems
for graduates in socially valuable but low-paying jobs.

Loans by government bring no immediate gain to the Exchequer,
either. In the short run, they can do the reverse. If a government
simply replaces the existing means-tested grant by a loan, the sum
expended is the same. Government has to wait at least three years

before any revenue comes back in repayments – or longer, if Sweden's example of a period of grace is followed. The revenue may help the next government, but not the one that incurs the odium of moving to a loans scheme.

A Graduate Tax

In many ways a more attractive idea is that of a 'graduate tax', first advanced by Howard Glennerster (Glennerster, Merrett and Wilson, 1968) and recently advocated in the context of the current debate in Britain concerning student support (Glennerster and Le Grand, 1986). Under this scheme every student would receive a flat-rate (not means-tested) grant that covered both maintenance and tuition. The cost, or part of it, would be recouped by a proportional tax which was levied on subsequent earnings. The tax would be administered by the Inland Revenue as part of the income tax collection system. By deciding to take a place on a designated course, and to accept a maintenance grant, students would accept a future specified tax obligation over and above the standard rate.

The choice is the student's. The obligation to pay is his or hers, not the parents'. This has the attractive feature of not requiring the student initially to lay out any money, and would therefore be less likely to deter students from poor families. Linking repayments to people's incomes means that those with low or no earnings would pay less or nothing. This would overcome the problem of under-rewarded activities like childcare. The scheme would be relatively easy to administer and to enforce.

Another attractive feature is that it could be extended to people of all ages. It would give adults a repayable entitlement to paid educational leave, or to training after childcare. The tax could be assessed to achieve rough justice in a fairly simple way. Those who opted to receive free tuition and a full maintenance grant would agree to pay a flat x per cent on top of the standard rate of tax for, say, fifteen years after graduation. The level of tax would be essentially a political judgement.

A more complex system would involve the standard fee being related to the cost of the subject taken. The tax rate would vary accordingly. Though superior in economic logic, this version could run into administrative and political difficulties. A major difficulty is that, as with loans, the scheme could cost the government more in the short run, before the revenue comes in. But if better-off parents could buy their children out of future tax liabilities by paying their maintenance and tution costs now, this could reduce the additional cost to public funds, or even cancel it out. That may seem unfair, but children of rich parents will always be better off. Moreover, in the longer run, revenue would build up. Also, as higher education expanded, so would the eventual revenue base. This might help to relax some of the constraints on the higher education budget.

Any proposal to reduce the subsidy to higher education will be politically unpopular. Hence it is important to consider these proposals only in conjunction with those for extending pre-school and post-school-leaving-age education. If all the reforms are introduced as a package, then the purpose of the whole could be better appreciated.

Housing

Housing policies are of two kinds: those designed to help owner-occupiers and those aimed at tenants (council or private). The first mostly consist of tax exemptions of one kind or another and favour the better off; the second take the form of direct grants or rebates and favour the worse off. An obvious way of improving the overall redistributive impact of housing policy is therefore to switch public expenditure from the first to the second.

By now it is commonplace among social reformers to argue for the abolition of tax subsidies to owner-occupiers. There is less agreement concerning the way in which this might be done. Some argue for the abolition of the tax relief on mortgage interest payments. Others advocate the reintroduction of taxation of the 'imputed income' on housing (imputed income, roughly, is the rent that an owner-occupied house would fetch if it were rented – and which the owner-occupier, by virtue of his ownership, can avoid paying). The two are mutually exclusive: for, if imputed income is taxed, then mortgage interest payments – as part of the cost of obtaining that income – should be allowable as a deduction.

Of the two possibilities, taxing imputed income is theoretically superior, but practically and politically inferior. It would be difficult to explain to taxpayers; it would be difficult to assess imputed income accurately in every case; and it would have unfortunate transition costs (most of the initial burden would fall on the elderly, who have paid off their mortgages and hence have high imputed incomes).

Mortgage interest relief on the other hand is already widely perceived as an anomaly. The people most affected by its withdrawal are on the whole those best able to pay: the better off with larger mortgages. Although the savings to the Exchequer might not be as great as if imputed income were taxed, they would nonetheless be sizable: £4,750 million in 1985/6 (UK Treasury, 1986 II, p. 30).

The savings made from closing this tax loophole could be used – in whole or in part – to raise the general subsidy to council housing, and to increase the generosity of the housing benefit schemes. If they were all used for this purpose they could have a considerable impact. If, for instance, in 1985/6, mortgage interest tax relief had been abolished, this would have permitted a more than 50 per cent increase in housing benefit without any net increase in public expenditure.

Before we finish this discussion of housing, we should comment on the redistributive effect of one controversial aspect of current British housing policy: the sale of council houses. Prospective purchasers, although certain to be among the better-off council tenants, are still likely to have below average income. Hence council house sales could temporarily improve the redistributive impact of housing policy – so long as the tax subsidy to the new owner-occupiers plus any capital gain made through purchasing the house at a discount was greater than the subsidy they received as a council tenant. If the reforms just discussed were carried out, then there would be little or no tax subsidy; hence the question would depend on whether any capital gain outweighed the value of the tenant subsidy, summed appropriately over the remaining years of the tenancy. Since under our proposals this subsidy would be substantially increased, the outcome is by no means certain. One calculation suggests that the average council tenant in 1982 would have received a larger public subsidy through remaining a tenant for twenty-five years than by buying his house at a discount of £5,000.[5]

Public Transport

Public subsidies to rail users (British Rail and the London Underground) massively favour the better off. The subsidies to bus travellers are more equally distributed, but even they do not benefit the poor as much as they do the rest of the population. A major reason for this is the existence of commuter services. Generally, the higher the income or occupational status, the further is the distance travelled to work. The very poor, the old, the unemployed and many single parents do not go to work at all. Manual workers often live close to their work. Professionals, employers and managers, on the other hand, usually live in the suburbs and travel into central city offices by rail, or a combination of rail and bus. Commuter services are expensive to run. To cope effectively with the morning and evening peak periods, they need massive amounts of rolling stock and (in the case of the railways) a complex infrastructure of track and signalling. But all this capital equipment is only used intensively for about five hours out of the twenty-four; for the rest of the day, much of it lies idle. Commuter services are therefore substantial loss-makers.

An obvious way to improve redistribution, therefore, would be not to increase the subsidy to commuters (as did the Greater London Council in 1981), but substantially to reduce it. Indeed, the only way to correct the pro-rich distribution of public transport subsidies would be to eliminate them entirely, and to run public transport on a break-even basis. However, redistribution is not the only aim of social policy. The promotion of social and economic efficiency is another; and there are two important reasons why, on efficiency grounds, a break-even policy would be undesirable. The first of these is that many forms of public transport have high fixed costs (for instance, railways have high costs of installation and maintenance of track); and it is a standard proposition within economics that the efficient pricing policy for an industry with high fixed costs will be one that requires a subsidy. Secondly, the existence of public transport reduces road-use, particularly in peak hours. Eliminating the subsidy would therefore mean greater congestion and greater costs for the community as a whole.

A proposal that would reduce the need for a public transport subsidy because of the costs of congestion, and would be desirable on redistributive grounds, is the introduction of some form of pricing for road use. The reason why there is excessive congestion on the roads is because road travel, as well as public transport, is also heavily subsidized. In particular, motorists travelling in the rush hour do not have to pay directly for the costs they inflict on other travellers at that time through their contribution to traffic congestion. They will tend to over-use the road system, particularly at peak hours. An obvious remedy therefore is to levy a charge that is directly related to their use of the system. This would discourage road use, reduce congestion, increase the use (and hence the revenues) of public transport and hence reduce the need for public transport subsidies. Moreover, the cost would be borne primarily by the better off; for car ownership and use (particularly in central cities) is still far more widespread among the wealthier parts of the community than it is among the poorer.

Nor is such an idea, as many might think, quite impractical. In Singapore, a charge is levied on cars entering the central area during the morning rush hour. Its initial effects were dramatic. Following its introduction, there was a 50 per cent decline in total traffic during the charge period: the volume of passenger cars alone declined by nearly three-quarters. Car pools nearly doubled, and bus ridership increased by 10 to 15 per cent. The system generated revenue at the rate of £1 million per year (Anderson *et al.*, 1978).

Singapore is somewhat exceptional in that it is geographically compact and with relatively few entrances to the central area. But similar schemes could be – and have been – devised for larger, more spread-out cities. An elaborate, multi-price system has been proposed for Los Angeles. In 1974, the Greater London Council (GLC) produced an investigation into a proposed 'Supplementary Licensing Scheme' for London (GLC, 1974). Motorists planning to drive within an area of about eight square miles in the city centre between 9am and 6pm would have to buy a licence, to be displayed on the windscreen, at a cost (then) of approximately £1 per day. There would be special treatment for residents, commercial vehicles and disadvantaged groups such as the disabled. Enforcement would be undertaken by the police or traffic wardens in the ordinary course of their duties. Again, the likely outcome was impressive. It was predicted that the scheme would reduce traffic in central London by one third, substantially increase public transport revenues and generate considerable revenue on its own. The revenue raised by such a scheme would go to subsidize capital expenditure on public transport. This would overcome the problem that an efficient pricing policy might not cover the fixed costs of a public transport system, and allow the public transport operator to break-even on its operating costs.

Conclusion

Any review of the figures showing the distributional impact of the social services leaves at least one clear impression. Policies involving subsidies whose distribution is dependent upon people's decision to consume the good or use the service concerned favour the better off. Public transport, health care, continuing education and owner-occupied housing, all are subsidized, all are distributed in whole or in part according to people's decisions to use or consume them, and all have a distribution that is pro-rich.

The reasons for this are not hard to find. Unless it is one of those rare commodities whose consumption falls as income rises, the better off will always purchase more of a commodity than the worse off, and hence, if it is subsidized, obtain more of the subsidy. This will be true even of goods provided free of charge, such as continuing education or health care under the National Health Service. There is always some private expenditure involved in using even a free service, if only in the form of income foregone during the period of use: expenditure that will weigh more heavily on the poor than the rich. Moreover, the better off, being generally better educated, more articulate and more confident, will be more able to manipulate even those parts of the system ostensibly not under their control, more able to ensure that the GP refers them to the specialist, that the hospital provides them with the appropriate facilities, that their children go to the right schools and the right universities.

Hence, any reforms designed to improve the redistributive power of the welfare state should not involve any increase in the subsidies for these services, and may well involve a decrease. Instead, they should concentrate scarce fiscal resources upon those areas of policy whose distribution is determined not simply by the individual's decision whether or not to consume, but by other criteria.

As can be seen from the evidence of other chapters, it will be difficult to implement such reforms. Moreover, even if they were successfully introduced, not too much should be expected of them. In particular, they should not be seen to have much impact on poverty or on overall social and economic inequalities. There is too much evidence from too many sources that inequality in health care and education is created by inequality in the wider society, rather than the other way around. Nor will altering the housing subsidy system eliminate inequalities in housing itself. The squalor and decay in poor areas arises not so much from deficiencies in subsidy policy, but rather from the poverty of their inhabitants. Since the poor travel relatively little, either by car or public transport, changes in the system of subsidizing transport will have little impact on their lives. Rather it is only by the direct redistribution of private income that poverty can be eliminated and overall inequality significantly reduced. That is where new spending and innovations in social policy should be primarily addressed.

Finally, nothing in this chapter implies that the welfare state should be dismantled and its key institutions handed back to private enterprise. There are excellent reasons for maintaining state owner-ship and control of health services, institutions of higher education, council houses and public transport. Such control prevents exploita-tion by private monopolies; it permits and facilitates social and economic planning; and, by reducing that area where the profit motive is king, it helps moderate the baleful influence of greed and self-interest. But the preservation of state control does not necessarily imply the preservation of existing systems of state subsidy. It is perfectly feasible to have one without the other. The state does not have to provide its services free or at subsidized prices. What is being argued here, essentially, is that redistribution policy should concern itself less with subsidizing services and more with 'subsidizing' the poor – or, rather, acknowledging the poor's legitimate claims on a greater share of the nation's income and wealth.

Notes

An earlier version of some of this material was published under the title of 'Making Redistribution Work: The Social Services' in a Fabian Society book *The Future of the Welfare State* (London: Heinemann, 1982) edited by Howard Glennerster. I am grateful to Howard Glennerster, the Fabian Society and the publisher for permission to make use of the material here. I would also like to thank Howard Glennerster for allowing me to include material in this chapter from a joint article on the graduate tax (Glennerster and Le Grand, 1986).

1   The figures in Table 5.1 are from Le Grand (1982b). Specific references are: council housing and tax subsidies to owner-occupiers, pp. 88–9; National Health Service, p. 26; primary, secondary, non–university higher, and university education, p. 58; public transport subsidies, p. 109. There were no estimates for the distribution of public expenditure on

rent allowances and nursery education. However, the former (now part of housing benefit) are means tested and must favour the poor; and evidence from the General Household Survey suggests that the proportion of children under 5 at nursery or primary school in each socioeconomic group was broadly the same (UK Office of Population Consensuses and Surveys, 1981, Table 6.14, p. 108).

2 In 1983/4 there were 490,000 children under 5 attending full- or part-time maintained nursery education in England. The participation rate was 41.6 per cent, implying that 688,000 were not attending (UK Treasury, 1986, p. 191, Table 3.12.5). The net unit cost per full-time equivalent pupil at nursery school in 1983/4 was £1,211 (Chartered Institute of Public Finance and Accounting – CIPFA – 1985, p. 3, Table 5). To provide half-time nursery education to those not attending would therefore cost £416.6 million. The total education and science budget for 1983/4 in England was £13,433 million (UK Treasury, 1986, p. 187).

3 Calculated from the same sources and in a similar manner as the equivalent figures for nursery schools (see note 2). It was assumed that half the numbers between 16 and 18 not attending school would attend.

4 In 1983/4 the Youth Training Scheme cost £700 million, providing training for 350,000 young people. The cost per full year place was £2,370. This compares with cost per full-time pupil in Secondary School in the same year of £1,059. Sources: UK Treasury, 1985 II, p. 84 and 1986 II, p. 114; CIPFA, 1985, p. 3, Table 5.

5 Robinson (1981) estimated the average subsidy to council tenants in 1977 as £353. In terms of 1982 prices this would be about £550. The net present value of a stream of subsidies of £550 p.a. over a period of twenty-five years at a discount rate of 10 per cent is approximately £5,500.

Chapter 6

Creeping Universalism in the Australian Welfare State

ROBERT E. GOODIN and JULIAN LE GRAND

It is a commonplace in the study of regulatory policy that, over time, watchdog agencies are 'captured' by the very groups they are meant to control, and end up serving interests very different from those originally intended. Here we shall be making – tentatively – a similar claim about some areas of social welfare policy. Programmes which were at their inception tightly targeted on the poor are, over time, increasingly 'invaded' by the non-poor.[1] Hence they can end up defeating, or at least defusing, their own redistributive aims.

In saying that these programmes were 'targeted on the poor', we mean merely to say that their receipt was conditioned upon their recipients passing a 'means test', expressed as a limit on either (or both) the maximum permissible income or maximum permissible assets that recipients could have and still be eligible for benefits under the programme. Why, historically, such limits were imposed in the first place is an open question. But, whatever its original intent, targeting benefits on the poor in this way can be justified *post hoc* as a mechanism for enhancing the redistributive effects of the programme. Our claim here is that such programmes are increasingly 'universalized' over time. That is, they move from being tightly targeted on the poor towards being more nearly indiscriminately available for all. As they do, their redistributive effects are severely weakened, as has been demonstrated in the case of the British universal social services (Le Grand, 1982b and Chapter 5 above).

Of course, redistribution is not the only value to which such programmes might appeal. Some of those other goals, such as social integration, might actually be well served by the increasing universalization of social welfare programmes. But if our speculation about the life cycle of these programmes is correct, at least this one centrally important goal is systematically thwarted – and increasingly so as time goes by.

The argument is developed in two stages. First we offer theoretical arguments to explain why this creeping universalism might occur. Then we turn to empirical evidence from Australia to suggest that it is indeed occurring, even in one of the more vigorously means-tested social security systems in the developed world.

The Theory

There are four quite distinct reasons for expecting that social welfare programmes originally targeted on the poor will increasingly become universal over time. One is relatively innocent, the others somewhat more sinister.

BOUNDARY PROBLEMS

These are of two kinds. The first concerns eligibility requirements: there seems to be no good reason to grant a benefit to one group of people but to withhold it from others who are in much the same situation. Once a pension is granted to deserted wives, for instance, it is hard to justify denying it to deserted long-term cohabitees. Or, as the United States Social Security Administration found, once you have started paying disability benefits to those incapable of work, it proves very difficult to deny them to those theoretically capable of performing certain sorts of tasks 'if no reasonable opportunity for this is available' in the local economy (Stone, 1984, p. 153; Liebman, 1976, pp. 860–4). In the end, we are driven to expansive notions of 'group eligibility, whereby residents of low-income neighbourhoods and other groups such as those in institutional settings become eligible' whether or not they are themselves poor (Gilbert, 1977, p. 626; 1982). Of course, extensions of this kind do not necessarily contribute to the infiltration of the service by the non-poor. That would only be true if the extended category contained a greater proportion of the non-poor than the original one. However, this is quite likely, since the original category is usually picked out for a specific benefit because the people in that category are particularly needy.

The second sort of boundary problem is directly concerned with the poor/non-poor distinction. It concerns the means tests that are an integral part of most selective programmes. These tests always have some cut-off point in terms of income or income-plus-asset holdings, above which people cease to be eligible for the benefits concerned. But this point is necessarily arbitrary. It is never clear why people earning x deserve benefits and those earning $x + e$ deserve none. Nor is it clear in social security systems with 'tapered' benefits why people earning x deserve, say, only half as much benefit as those earning $x - e$.

All those judgements appear arbitrary because the boundary between the needy and the non-needy is fuzzy. There simply is no obvious point at which we can naturally justify cutting off benefits. In such situations the bias is typically (Wildavsky, 1979, ch. 4), but not invariably (Chambers, 1985, p. 13), towards granting benefits to too many people rather than too few. This is as it should be, given that in denying truly needy people social security would inflict far more harm on them than richer taxpayers would suffer from the marginally higher tax rates required to pay for these errors of generosity (Goodin, 1985a).

These boundaries are in some sense always problematic. But the point is that, given the bias towards errors of generosity, the pressure is always in the one direction. Consequently, policies that start out being focused tightly upon the poor become increasingly universal with repeated relaxations of eligibility requirements and means tests. Furthermore, this bias towards generosity might itself actually increase over time. Programmes that began as tightly targeted on the poor encouraged, at their outset, those who were charged with their administration to police rigorously the means test. Over time, however, more and more exceptions are made, and more and more expansions of the eligibility requirements are granted. The administrative ethos naturally alters in consequence. Even in the absence of formal relaxations in the rules, those charged with administering them slacken in their efforts to enforce them and still more universalization ensures.

BUREAUCRATIC EMPIRE–BUILDING

Another explanation for universalization is in terms of bureaucratic expansionism. Bureaucrats are said to be notorious empire-builders because they are self-interestedly trying to maximize budgets, personal perks or power (Niskanen, 1971; Marris, 1964); or it may be because they are committed to their agency's mission and are trying to further it (Goodin, 1982b). Whatever the cause, the consequence is always the same. Bureaucracies' staffs, budgets and responsibilities would all tend to grow over time.

That, too, would lead to creeping universalism in social welfare programmes. Suppose we start with a programme that is tightly targeted to serve the poor and only the poor. If bureaucrats want to expand their operations an obvious direction in which to grow is by bringing in more and more less needy clients. (If they were solely interested in maximizing their budgets, then they could also achieve this aim by getting higher benefits paid to existing clients. But politically it is tricky to increase expenditures dramatically without simultaneously expanding the programme's constituency; so even in this situation they would want to expand the number of beneficiaries. Since sheer budget maximization does not necessarily enhance the utilities of top-level bureaucrats (Dunleavy, 1985), expanding their programme to cover new client groups is more likely to affect the factors that really matter in bureaucrats' utility functions than expanding the size of payments to existing clients.) Thus, the tendency for bureaucracies to grow, combined with the fact that all the growth has to be in one direction, provides another explanation for the increasing universalism of social welfare programmes as the years go by.

BEHAVIOURAL RESPONSES

A third explanation focuses on the behaviour of applicants for welfare benefits. Even without any changes in eligibility criteria or means tests, there is always some scope for people initially ineligible for benefits to arrange their affairs so as to qualify for them. On this account, more and more non-poor people are receiving welfare benefits because, as a direct result of the programme, more and more of the non-poor are becoming (or, in some cases, masquerading as) 'poor' within the terms of the programme's means test.

People seeking benefits and denied them because of a means test may respond in any of three ways. They may reduce their actual means by reducing their work effort or their savings. They may engage in 'test avoidance' by rearranging their affairs so as to take advantage of any loop-holes in the means test, that is, reducing their 'means' as defined for the purpose of the test, while retaining the same overall command over resources. Or they may engage in direct evasion, illegally reporting their means as less than they really are.[2]

There are several reasons to expect such phenomena to increase over the life of a programme. Due to the combined effects of private inertia and social custom, it takes time for people to change their work or savings habits. There may be a bandwagon effect operating, whereby reduction, avoidance and evasion become increasingly respectable the more people that are already engaged in them. An avoidance industry takes time to develop; and there may be scale economies at work, whereby the more people who arrange to fiddle their affairs appropriately, the lower the marginal costs to the next person to do so.

A question arises concerning the exact status of the people who respond in the first of the ways mentioned above: those who reduce their means via reducing their work effort or savings. If poverty is defined strictly in terms of income or assets at the point when the means test is applied, such people cease to be non-poor and become poor. However, in a wider sense it is legitimate to regard them as being part of the non-poor, for they are simply taking part of their higher real incomes in the form of leisure (if they reduce work effort) or consumption expenditure (if they reduce savings).

POLITICAL PRESSURE

There are two ways in which political pressures might be thought to lead to the non-poor's infiltration of social welfare programmes. One explanation emphasizes the power of the median voter to determine electoral outcomes (Mueller, 1979, pp. 106–11). According to the well-known argument of Downs (1957), whichever party wins the support of the median voter is certain of election in a two-party system, just so long as electors vote for the party nearest them in some well-behaved ideological or policy space. Analogously in multi-party systems, the party representing the median voter is sure of a position (and probably a very powerful one) in the governing coalition, just so long as parties coalesce similarly with other parties nearer them in the ideological/policy space in preference to ones further away.

One way to attract the electoral support of median voters is by promising expenditure programmes that benefit them. If the median voter is not poor, this requires easing means tests for programmes. If parties adopt this strategy, the consequences of the median voters' electoral clout will be 'excessive' government spending and, more to our present point, spending that is concentrated disproportionately on median voters. They will try to capture those benefits for themselves, insofar as it is politically possible to do so and retain their position of power as median voters. But even if forced to share those benefits, they will insist that they must enjoy those benefits if anyone does as the price of their all-important electoral support for the party sponsoring the programme. Hence the tendency for the non-poor to benefit from social welfare programmes (Stigler, 1970).

However, this explanation does not account for any tendency towards increasing universalism in such programmes over time. The same median-voter logic should operate from the outset. Occasional extensions of the suffrage apart, nothing happens with the passage of time to increase the power or to shift the interests of the median voter. If we are looking for an explanation of changes over time – of creeping universalism in social welfare programmes – we must look elsewhere. The median voter model is a static one in this crucial respect.

Notice, furthermore, that the analysis described so far depicts a curiously one-eyed voter who perceives only profits and not losses. Promising to cut median voters' taxes should in principle prove just as effective an electoral strategy as promising to increase expenditures benefiting them. Indeed, certain considerations suggest that the median voter should be more responsive to promises of tax cuts than to promises of increased social benefits (Downs, 1960). Thus, the median-voter analysis is indeterminate as well as static: it tells us to expect that the median voter will back either increased expenditures or tax reductions, but it does not tell us which or when.

A second and more satisfactory analysis of the political pressures leading to creeping universalism in social welfare programmes focuses upon legislatures and lobbies.[3] The basic point here is that there are certain costs (fixed and variable) associated with organizing and operating an effective pressure group. Given that, two things follow. With fixed costs and diminishing marginal utility of income, richer people will find it easier to organize themselves into pressure groups than will poorer ones; and, assuming the variable costs are at least in part a function of how many members the group has, it will be easier to organize pressure groups where interests are concentrated among a few people than it is to organize larger groups where interests are more diffuse (Olson, 1965; Goodin, 1982b; Becker, 1983). These two factors combine to suggest that groups of non-poor citizens will be in a better position to press for marginal expansions of social welfare programmes benefiting themselves. And assuming pressure pays off, that explains the constantly increasing universalism of social welfare programmes.

Indeed, whereas the median-voter model leaves this dynamic tendency unexplained, the pressure group model offers a strong explanation. Constant pressure would itself lead to constant change, and when the pressure is predominantly in one direction then so too is the change. However, pressure is not just constant but increasing. The high start-up costs associated with organizing a pressure group mean, firstly, that the number of such groups will increase slowly but steadily over time (producing the increasing 'institutional sclerosis' that Olson, 1982, observes) and, secondly, that the political lobby will be a curious market place characterized by entry barriers that make entry easier for those who can produce the requisite cash up front. The former factor leads to an increasing number of pressure groups over time, the latter guarantees that they will be speaking predominantly for the non-poor.

However, it is important to note that this process will be selective. The non-poor will not push for universalizing a programme from which they perceive themselves as unlikely to benefit. For instance, they will press for the relaxation of any means test applied to old age or widow's pensions, since the chances of their receiving those pensions are high, or for a national health service, because they perceive themselves as likely to need services that could not be satisfactorily covered by private insurance (see Chapter 3). But they will not push for an expansion of the eligibility criteria for, say, safety-net cash transfers to the poor or for public housing, since they do not see themselves as likely to need those benefits. In such cases, the pressure is likely either to operate in reverse, pushing the programme concerned into being ever more heavily targeted on the poor, and thus reducing its expense, or to be directed at increasing subsidies to parallel programmes that do benefit the better off (such as increasing personal tax allowances or tax loop-holes for owner-occupiers), or both, as the Thatcher Government in Britain has done (Atkinson, Hills and Le Grand, 1986).

THE BASIC HYPOTHESIS

In summary, our hypothesis is this. There are three forces at work that might impel *any* programme initially targeted on the poor to expand its coverage over time to include an increasing proportion of the non-poor. These are the difficulties of defining boundaries, the expansionist tendencies of the bureaucracies, and behavioural responses by the non-poor to render themselves eligible for the programme. For *some* programmes, there might also be an important political force operating in the same direction: the non-poor perceiving themselves as likely to need the benefit in question, and hence using pressure groups to ensure that the eligibility criteria are relaxed. For programmes where they perceive no such benefit but only a tax burden, pressure from the non-poor will operate in the opposite direction; and it is unclear *a priori* what the net effect will be.

The thesis is a limited one. We are not attempting to predict the initial coverage of the programme. We merely predict that, whatever proportion of the relevant group originally got benefits, under certain circumstances it will increase with the increasing age of the programme. Nor are we making any statement about programmes that are universal from the outset (although we believe that many of the same forces are at work in such programmes, particularly in *maintaining* their universal nature: see Chapter 8). Nor do we offer any definite prediction about programmes from which the non-poor do not perceive themselves as likely to receive any direct benefit. However, the thesis does lead to highly specific predictions about social welfare programmes that do not fall into either of these categories, predictions that are supported by empirical evidence from Australia, as we shall now go on to demonstrate.

Evidence from Australia

In some countries, universalism has existed for so long that it is difficult to find readily available data with which to test our hypothesis. Australia, by contrast, still tries (officially at least) to restrict the number of welfare beneficiaries by imposing strict eligibility conditions and means tests. That makes it an excellent laboratory for our purposes.

DEMONSTRATING CREEPING UNIVERSALISM

In order to explore creeping universalism in Australian social welfare programmes, we examine the growth over time in the percentage of people in the 'relevant group' that is in fact receiving welfare benefits.[4] This relevant group is composed of those persons in the population as a whole who would seem to meet the basic categorical requirements of the programme. Thus, for old age pensions, the relevant group is the aged population; for invalid pensions the relevant group is invalids old enough to qualify for the pension; etc.[5]

The difficulty is getting good data on relevant groups that go back far enough in time. There are three Australian programmes for which we can find such data: old age pensions, widow's pensions (Class B), and invalid pensions. All these programmes are means-tested, and have been since their inception. The tests have varied in form over time. But they have always involved some assessment of the relevant individual's income and, in some cases, their assets as well.

Old age pensions are only available to males aged 65 years and over, and females aged 60 years and over. That is the 'relevant group' for this programme. Data on the size of this group and on the proportion of the group receiving a pension in full or in part are available from the Census, the Treasury and the Department of Social Security (Goodin and Le Grand, 1986, Table 1). Class B widow's pensions are paid, *inter alia*, to widows between 50 and 60 and without dependent children.[6] Data on the size of the relevant group are available for selected years from the Census, and on the numbers actually receiving the benefit from the Treasury and the Department of Social Security (*ibid*, Table 3).

The situation with respect to the invalid pension is more complicated. Data are available over time on the numbers of persons of invalid-pensionable age: males aged 16 to 64 years and females aged 16 to 59 years. However, these are not strictly the relevant group, since the pension is awarded only to those persons of pensionable age who are '85 per cent incapacitated for work'. Not surprisingly, there are no data directly available on the numbers of persons who are 85 per cent incapacitated. However, the Australian Bureau of Statistics undertook a survey of handicapped persons during February to May 1981 classifying them according to various levels of handicap (Commonwealth of Australia ABS, 1982), and this was used to obtain the necessary estimates as follows.

Of those handicapped persons not working at the time of the survey, people categorized as 'permanently unable to work' seemed most likely to qualify for the pension as 85 per cent incapacitated for work. The remaining categories – 'would have difficulty getting or keeping a job', 'would need to have special working arrangements' and 'would be restricted in numbers of hours could work' – implied less than 85 per cent incapacity for work. Hence the total number of persons in the first category was taken as the total eligible population for the year 1981. In that year they constituted 2.74 per cent of the total population of invalid pensionable age (i.e., 16 and over but too young to qualify for the old age pension). To obtain the necessary estimates for other years, this proportion was applied to the total population of invalid-pensionable age for those years. It seems unlikely there would have been massive changes in the proportion over time. In any case, the results are sufficiently striking that they are unlikely to be wholly accounted for by any error in this assumption alone.

There is, we should emphasize, substantial uncertainty surrounding the pre-1940 figures for numbers of old age and invalid pensioners. Formally, the rule had always been that, upon becoming old enough to qualify for the old age pension, invalids should be shifted over to it. But in practice a great many invalids continued being carried on invalid-pension rolls even though they should, by that rule, have been regarded as old age pensioners.[7] So far as the pensioners themselves were concerned it was a matter of indifference: benefit levels for the two pensions were identical. The effects on the statistical series is rather more serious, however (Kewley, 1973, p. 122). We have compensated as best we can by making suitable adjustments to the definition of what would constitute the effective pensionable age in each period. (We assume that prior to 1940 any invalid aged 16 years or over was *de facto* in this category, but that from 1940 onwards they also had to be too young to qualify for the old age pension). This is, however, only a rough-and-ready accommodation to a serious data problem, and we would therefore place less faith in the pre-1940 age and invalid pension series than on the data for subsequent years.

The trends over time in the proportion of the relevant group receiving benefits are summarized for all three programmes in Goodin and Le Grand (1986) in Figure 6.1 below. Old age pensioners rose from 32 per cent of the population of pensionable age in 1911 to nearly 76 per cent in 1981. Prior to the Second World War there was no clear trend; there was a slight fall in 1921, a rise of 10 per cent by

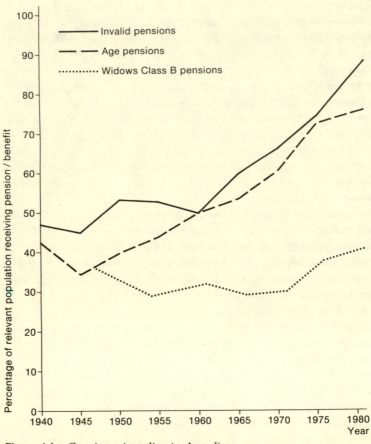

Figure 6.1   *Creeping universalism in Australia*

Source: Goodin and Le Grand (1986), Tables 1, 2 and 3

1940, followed by a fall almost back to the 1911 level in 1945. Since the Second World War there has been a steady increase, with the percentage more than doubling between 1945 and 1981. For invalid pensions, the percentage of the relevant group receiving a pension has increased even more dramatically since the programme's inception, from just over 9 per cent in 1911 to over 88 per cent in 1981. As noted above, less emphasis should be placed on the pre-1945 figures; but since the Second World War the percentage has nearly doubled. The trend for widow's pensions also shows an increase, after an initial fall, with the percentage of the relevant population receiving the pension rising by 11 points from 1954 to 1981.

These three programmes therefore provide evidence that the universalization predicted by our theory has occurred, especially since the Second World War. The growth has not always been steady, and has at times gone into reverse. The overall pattern, however, is clear.

The pattern of universalization, though, is not absolutely conclusive evidence of non-poor infiltration. To infer the one from the other, we need to assume that pensions/benefits are given to the neediest people first. Then (and only then) would expansions of the programmes necessarily benefit progressively less needy recipients. We know that such an assumption would not be completely accurate. The poorest of the poor often very belatedly hear about and take advantage of programmes, even when they desperately need such assistance. Consequently, some of the expansion – especially in the first years of the programmes – might represent more poor people being brought into the programme rather than non-poor people infiltrating it. But the dramatic expansion we have observed, especially in the later years of the older programmes, almost certainly is not of this type.

The increasing proportion of claimants may just reflect increasing take-up of benefits among those who were qualified for them all along, as participation in the programme becomes increasingly 'respectable'. But, again, we have no particular reason to suppose that late-comers are on average any poorer than early arrivals to the programmes. In general, sensitivity to stigma seems likely to be constant across all classes. Only in the case of the lower classes being much more sensitive to stigma than the upper classes would our conclusions about increasing non-poor infiltration of the programmes be undermined.

TESTING ALTERNATIVE THEORIES

Our general hypothesis, that a variety of forces will tend to universalize previously selective programmes, is broadly supported by the evidence presented so far. However, that evidence does not give us any indication as to the relative importance of the different forces. So far we are lacking any indication as to whether it is boundary problems, bureaucratic expansions, political pressures or behavioural responses that are the cause.

Some insight into this can be obtained from the development of the relevant means tests during the period. Three of the four factors in the universalization process listed above would all imply that these tests would gradually be relaxed over time.[8] The difficulty of distinguishing the needy from the non-needy provides a continuous incentive to increase the size of the needy group by relaxing the means test. Bureaucratic empire-builders want to increase the number of their clients; again, the way to do this is to relax the means test continuously. Pressures from the non-poor will encourage an easing of the means test so that more of their members can become eligible for the programme. Only one factor – behavioural responses – does not have this implication. That explanation posits individuals responding to a *given* means test by 'reducing' their means in one way or another, rather than any change in the means test itself.

Hence, if for any particular programme we observe that the means test has *not* relaxed over time, we can conclude that it is behavioural responses rather than any of the other factors that has been instrumental in the programme's 'universalization'. An indication of the severity of a particular means test is the maximum permissible income (MPI) that individuals are allowed to receive and still remain eligible for the benefit concerned, expressed as a percentage of average income.[9] *Ceteris paribus*, the higher the MPI relative to the average, the less severe the means test. Accordingly we calculated the MPI as a percentage of *per capita* GDP for our three test programmes which have always been subject to the same means test.

The results are shown in Figure 6.2. The interesting aspect of this figure is not the saw-tooth pattern but the flatness of the long-term trend. It is apparent that there has been no systematic relaxation of the means test. Indeed, despite erratic bursts of generosity, in general it has got, if anything, *more* rather than less severe.[10] Hence it seems that for these programmes, at least, the principal determinant of

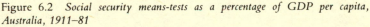

Figure 6.2 *Social security means-tests as a percentage of GDP per capita, Australia, 1911–81*

Source: Goodin and Le Grand (1986), Table 4

universalization has been behavioural responses by individuals to means tests, rather than boundary problems, bureaucratic expansion or political pressure.

A MORE FORMAL TEST

We can undertake a more systematic test of this proposition. If the true explanation for the creeping universalism that we have observed concerns boundary problems then we might expect the means test to be eased during periods of economic growth (when errors of generosity can be more easily afforded) but to be tightened in periods of economic stagnation or decline (when errors of harshness become more acceptable). That is, we would expect the severity of the means test to be *positively correlated* with GNP. If the correct explanation involved bureaucratic empire-building there would be a *continuous relaxation* of the means test over time, regardless of changes in GNP. If the explanation concerned political pressures we might expect a relaxation in severity during periods of economic decline (more people, including the median voter, are closer to needing the benefit concerned), and an increase in severity during the period of growth. In that case, the severity of the means test would be *negatively correlated* with GNP. Finally, if the explanation involved individual responses, there would be *no necessary correlation* in the severity of the means test with GNP.

To explore these possibilities, a simple multiple regression exercise was undertaken, relating MPI as a percentage of GNP to money GNP, to prices and a constant term. The dependent variable lagged by one year was also included. The basic equation was thus of the following form:

$$M = \beta_0 + \beta_1 M_{-1} + \beta_2 G + \beta_3 P$$

where the βs are the estimated coefficients, $M = \text{MPI}/G$, $G = \text{GNP}$ per head and P is a price index. The predictions concerning this equation that follow from our four possible hypotheses are as follows:

Hypothesis	*Predicted Effect*
H_1 Boundary problems	β_2 significant and > 0
H_2 Bureaucratic empire building	β_1 significant and > 1
H_3 Political pressures	β_2 significant and < 0
H_4 Individual responses	β_2 not significant

The data were yearly from 1909 to 1981. To capture the possibility of delays in the hypothesized mechanisms, several different lag structures were tried, including no lags, a lag of one year and a lag of two years. The most 'satisfactory' structure was that for a one-year lag. The estimated equation was:

$$M = 4.9449 + 0.7576M_{-1} - 0.0083G + 0.0085G_{-1} - 0.1004P + 0.1102P_{-1}$$

$$(1.66) \quad (9.59) \quad (-1.26) \quad (1.14) \quad (-1.13) \quad (1.22)$$

$$R^2 = 0.648 \quad \bar{R}^2 = 0.6209 \quad \hat{\sigma} = 3.448 \quad DW = 1.871$$

where M = MPI/GNP
G = GNP
P = Price Index (1900 = 100)

and the -1 subscript indicates a one-year lag. The t-ratios are in brackets.

The Durbin-Watson (DW) statistic is close to two, suggesting no significant autocorrelation. However, when the lagged dependent variable is included as one of the independent variables, the Durbin-Watson procedure is not appropriate; instead, it is necessary to calculate Durbin's h statistic (Durbin, 1970). This was done for the coefficient of the lagged dependent variable, giving a value for the statistic of 0.747, well below the value that would reject the null hypothesis of no significant autocorrelation at the 5 per cent level. Hence there does not appear to be significant first-order autocorrelation.

The only significant variable is the lagged dependent variable. This suggests that the other independent variables cannot satisfactorily explain the variation in the dependent variable; there are important omitted variables whose influence is being picked up by the lagged dependent variable. Precisely what those are is an interesting topic for future research. However, for our purposes here, it is important to note that none of the predictions concerning H_1 to H_3 are borne out. The coefficients for GNP are not significant; that for the lagged dependent variable is significant, but less than 1. The findings are consistent only with H_4, the individual response model.

This support is negative in form, so our conclusions about it must be cautious. The estimated equation is unsatisfactory in many respects, particularly with respect to omitted variables. But in the absence of a further hypothesis, the individual response model, by default, appears to be the most satisfactory explanation of the phenomenon.

Conclusion

In this chapter we have suggested that there are good reasons to suppose that the non-poor will invade some programmes originally targeted on the poor. We have provided evidence from three Australian programmes that this has actually occurred. We also suggested that the principal reason in each case was that the non-poor responded to the imposition of a means test by rearranging their affairs, legitimately or illegitimately, so as to pass the test.

Our conclusions must be tentative. We have settled upon the behavioural response explanation, not because we have found a way of securing positive evidence of its existence, but merely because we have found evidence to discredit all alternative hypotheses presently available. Still, the behavioural response model has substantial surface plausibility. Australian policy-makers have long known that some such process was at work among claimants, and they have long suspected that it was of major proportions. A 1980 Report of the Social Welfare Policy Secretariat expresses the fear that 'the tendency for people to circumvent the income test by rearranging their assets to ensure that any income produced has minimal effects on pension eligibility may mean that a growing percentage of income support expenditure is going to persons in relatively comfortable financial circumstances' (Commonwealth of Australia, SWPS, 1980, p. 39). An in-house report of 121 examples of 'Service Pensioners with Large Assets' prepared by the Department of Veterans' Affairs in November 1983 reveals the mechanisms by which this (perfectly legal) avoidance of the means test is typically effected: investing in life insurance policies, low-interest-bearing bank accounts on debentures, building society accounts, low dividend shares, and quite commonly, very large ($A100,000 or more) chequing accounts bearing no interest at all; interest-free loans or gifts to children were also popular.

Of course, all of these strategies take advantage of loop-holes in means tests that could in principle be closed. Indeed, the means tests for all these programmes did take account of the value of peoples' property, as well as the level of their income, until a 1976 reform (Commonwealth of Australia, DSS, 1983, pp. 47, 82); and an asset test was restored after the period of our study.) Our point here is not that any particular loop-hole is inevitable. It is merely that individuals will inevitably find some way of adapting to any set of rules imposed through a means test so as to fail – to some greater or lesser degree – the intent of that test.

Notes

This study was originally published as 'Creeping universalism in the welfare state: evidence from Australia', *Journal of Public Policy*, vol. 6, no. 3 (1986), pp. 255–74. We are grateful to the publishers and the editor, Richard Rose, for permission to reprint it here.

A large part of the research was undertaken during our tenure as Visiting Research Fellows in the Social Justice Project at the Research School of Social Sciences, Australian National University. At the time, Le Grand was also being funded by the Nuffield Foundation on a Research Fellowship. Subsequent work was supported by the Welfare State Programme at the Suntory–Toyota International Centre for Economics and Related Disciplines, London School of Economics. We are most grateful to all these institutions for their generous support.

We are greatly indebted to Chris Davies and, especially, to Janette Ryan for research assistance. Valuable comments and criticisms of earlier versions of this argument have come from A. B. Atkinson, John Braithwaite, J. P. Cox, Meredith Edwards, Fred Gruen, Richard Musgrave, Andrew Podger, Richard Rose, Peter Self, Ralph Smith, David Stanton, Patricia Tulloch and David Winter. Jenny Newton of the Department of Social Security in Canberra was most helpful in assisting us in revising and adjusting the basic data. Of course, we exonerate all of these individuals from any responsibility for the final product.

1   The phenomenon of the 'expanding target' is associated with a parallel tendency of 'rules and principles of law [to] become more and more uncertain in context and in application' over time (D'Amato, 1983). Note that our theme is that programmes which were originally tightly targeted on the poor have expanded their coverage over time. This is distinct from the proposition, popularized in Britain by Titmuss (1958) and within Australia by Jones (1983, pp. 88, 310–11) and Jamrozick (1983), that on balance (and over time increasingly) middle-class people benefit from the 'division of welfare' which is socially-determined and state-subsidized.

2   Parallel phenomena are discussed by Atiyah (1980, pp. 421–3), Schorr (1980, p. 30), Commonwealth of Australia, Social Welfare Policy Secretariat (1980, pp. 39), and D'Amato (1983, p. 5).

3   This is the point emphasized in the speculations of both D'Amato (1983, pp. 4–5) and Peltzman (1980). The latter marshalls econometric evidence in support of the proposition that 'the growth of the middle class has in fact been a major source of the growth of government in the developed world over the last fifty years' (Peltzman, 1980, p. 285). He

hypothesizes that the key factor is that the middle classes are better 'capable of articulating demands' (i.e., bringing political pressure to bear), but he offers no evidence in support of this hypothesis.

4   The alternative is to use cross-sectional evidence to compare the proportion of the relevant population receiving benefits under different programmes with the ages of the programmes. Our hypothesis would predict that the older the programme, the larger the proportion of the relevant population receiving benefit, *ceteris paribus*. But, among the other things that must be equal for that prediction to hold is the initial coverage of all the various programmes. In fact, this varies substantially, and for this reason we eschew cross-sectional evidence.

5   One major reason for the growth of the absolute numbers of beneficiaries is that there are more and more people in the relevant groups. There are more old age pensioners if, *inter alia*, there are more people surviving to pensionable age, etc. This increase in absolute numbers of beneficiaries is of prime importance to policy-makers (Commonwealth of Australia, Social Welfare Policy Secretariat, 1980; Jones, 1983, ch. 5) but it is the changing *proportion* of the relevant group that gets the pension/benefit that interests us here.

6   Widows over the age of 60 are eligible for both (i.e. may receive either) this pension and the old age pension. It proved impossible to determine the degree of overlap necessary to define the relevant group for the over-60s; hence we have confined our analysis to the 50–60 age group.

It should be noted that both sets of data include only those women who become eligible for the pension because of widowhood or divorce; it does not include women who claimed the pension under the categories of dependent female, deserted wife or husband in mental hospital or prison. In 1980/81 the number of women who received the pension due to widowhood and divorce represented 84.9 per cent of total recipients.

7   In 1940, some 38,351 invalid pensioners (out of a total of 91,047) were shifted to the old age pension in an effort to regularize the statistics.

8   Strictly speaking, they would imply *either* a relaxation in the means test *or* a relaxation in the administration of eligibility requirements. The latter is harder to measure; judging from the legislative history presented in Commonwealth of Australia, DSS (1983), this seems unlikely to be the explanation for the expansions in recipients.

9   We are adopting here a 'relativist' measure of severity. An 'absolutist' alternative would be to ignore economic growth and simply examine changes in the absolute level of MPI over time (suitably adjusted for prices). However, we believe that 'severity' is better interpreted in relative rather than absolute terms.

10   In passing, it might be noted from Figure 6.2 just how severe the Australian means test is. By way of comparison, the (per capita) MPI for a family of three under the British Family Income Supplement in November 1984 was 32 per cent of 1984 *per capita* GDP.

Chapter 7

Distributional Biases in Social Service Delivery Systems

ROBERT E. GOODIN,
JULIAN LE GRAND and D. M. GIBSON

In examining patterns of utilization of medical and paramedical services by the Australian elderly, Gibson (1983) made an interesting, counterintuitive discovery. While it is only to be expected that a person's income should constitute a barrier to service utilization, it was somewhat surprising to find that barrier persisting even when services were publicly funded. Even more surprisingly, that barrier seemed to persist for publicly-funded, publicly-provided services but to disappear for services which were publicly funded but privately provided.

That finding runs counter to our ordinary expectations. After all, it is the private market in which income has the most direct role in rendering people's desires into 'effective demand'. Whatever impact income has on the delivery of goods and services from the public sector must surely be less direct, and therefore presumably less strong. Yet paradoxically, where service utilization is concerned, low income seems to be a hindrance in the public sector but not in the publicly-funded private sector.

This chapter is devoted to attempting to dissolve that paradox. While it is essentially a theoretical exercise, our analysis does turn crucially at several points on empirical speculations that will ultimately require far more testing in far more countries and far more policy contexts. The empirical evidence we offer here is intended to be suggestive and illustrative, but certainly not conclusive.

The crucial variable in our theory will be the distance people have to travel to the point of service provision. For various reasons discussed below, publicly-provided services will ordinarily be centralized whereas publicly-funded, privately-provided services will be decentralized. And distance, in turn, introduces well-known distributional biases in resource utilization.

Up to that point, our analysis might seem to argue, on grounds of equity, for privatization of social services. But we go on to suggest that the tendency toward geographical centralization in publicly-provided service delivery systems can be overcome. When it is, publicly-provided services tend to be even more decentralized than privately-provided ones and, hence, low income less of a barrier to utilization. What we are offering, then, is not a brief for the privatization of social services but rather for the decentralization of publicly provided ones.

The Puzzle

This essay is devoted to developing a theoretical response to a puzzle that emerged in the course of analysing data collected for somewhat different purposes. We are under no illusion that such data can constitute a 'proof' of our hypotheses, or even a proper 'test' of them. Still, a brief description of the results is important in helping to motivate our hypotheses.

The background is this. In 1981, a stratified, random sample of 1,050 persons aged 60 or over and living in private dwellings in Sydney was quizzed on use of medical and paramedical services (Gibson and Aitkenhead, 1983; Rowland, Kendig and Jones, 1984). The results indicated that the poorer aged were not significantly less likely than those on higher incomes to use medical, optical or aural services; in fact medical consultation rates were higher amongst poorer groups, given similar levels of health status. Yet, poorer old people were less likely to use dental and podiatry services than the wealthy, suggesting that inadequate income may well prevent the use of these services for a significant number of older people (Gibson, 1983). Why the difference?

Arguably, one major factor is the system of public provision. In Australia, existing government programmes providing medical (general and specialist), optical and aural services to old age pen-

sioners essentially involve the public payment of private practitioners. Geographic accessibility is thus likely to be high, particularly
in urban centres like Sydney whence this study sample was drawn. In
order to obtain free or subsidized dental and podiatry services, on the
other hand, one must attend specific government service centres. Free
dental services are available to eligible pensioners only at the Sydney
dental hospital, and in the outpatients' sections of certain public
hospitals. Remedial podiatry services are provided free of charge to
eligible pensioners only at public hospitals and some community
health centres. For both services, geographic accessibility is a major
problem, with services not being locally available in many areas.
Hence our hypothesis: where the system of public provision is
directly via public agencies, poorer people use less than their wealthier counterparts; where the system of public provision is through
the public funding of private practitioners, no such disparity occurs.

Alas, our data bear only very imperfectly upon this *post hoc*
explanation. Indeed, location data are available only for dental
utilization, so at best we can only hope for very partial confirmation
of our hypothesis. Still, such limited analysis as can be performed on
these data does lend tentative support to that hypothesis.

Since the aim of the analysis was to examine the effect of location
on dental-service use amongst those eligible for publicly provided
services, only eligible persons (those with an annual income of less
than $6,000, or $10,000 for a married couple) were included. The
analysis was also limited to those respondents with only natural teeth,
as earlier analyses (Gibson, Broom and Duncan-Jones, 1984) suggested that patterns of dental service use were quite distinctive for
those with false teeth. (There tends to be a long period between
consultations, yet little discretion in consulting behaviour when it
does occur, because people with false teeth consult dentists only when
a lost, damaged or ill-fitting denture requires replacement.) Location
was measured in straight-line distance to the nearest public dental
service, dichotomized at the 5 kilometre point. The indicator of
dental utilization was the period elapsed since most recent consultation. For a number of technical reasons, ordinary linear regression
was inappropriate and an extension of logit analysis was used instead.
(For details of the analysis, see Gibson, Goodin and Le Grand, 1985,
Appendix I.)

To illustrate the effect of location on service use, probabilities can
be calculated at each of the three levels of utilization (see Table 7.1).

Table 7.1   *Effect of Distance on Utilization*

	Probability of consultation during		
	last year	last 2 years	last 5 years
Distance			
≤5 kilometres	.25	.47	.56
>5 kilometres	.14	.30	.38

Note: Effect significant at the 0.01 level. Probabilities calculated for those with a school leaving age of 15 or 16.

Thus, the probability of consulting within the last year decreases from 0.25 for those living within 5 kilometres of a dental clinic to 0.14 for those living outside that distance. Similar effects are observed for the other consultation intervals. These effects remained constant and significant when other variables found to be significant in earlier analyses (disability and living arrangement) were added to the equation.

These results indicate that the distance which respondents had to travel to reach public agencies supplying free dental care was indeed a significant determinant of dental service use, at least for those respondents with natural teeth. This finding thus lends some credence to our hypothesis that location is a key explanatory factor in the comparatively low service use by the poor of publicly-provided as distinct from privately-provided social services. Here our aim is to develop a theoretical explanation for this apparent anomaly. First we explore why distance should matter so much to the poor; and next we explore why publicly-provided services should be so much more distant than privately-provided ones.

The Role of Distance

Users of a social service incur three types of cost. First, there is the charge, if any, levied by the suppliers of the service. Second, there is the (financial) cost of travelling to the facility providing the service. Finally, there is the cost of the time involved: time spent travelling to the facility, time spent queueing upon arrival and time spent actually using the service. Time used in any of these ways has costs in terms of the activities thereby forgone: these include paid work, unpaid work, such as child-care and housework, and leisure activities.

Distance is an important determinant of the last two types of cost. The financial costs of travel, by whatever mode, are directly related to distance. Time spent travelling is usually (although not invariably) a direct function of distance, as therefore are the costs associated with it. Even time spent queueing can be longer for those who live further away, for the larger periods of time involved overall mean that they are less able to 'fine-tune' their activities so as to minimize waiting time. As costs affect use, and distance affects costs, distance will affect use. This proposition, tentatively established in the previous section, has also been confirmed in several studies of health service use (Acton, 1975; Aday, 1975; Phelps and Newhouse, 1974; Riessman, 1974; Shannon, Bashshur and Metzner, 1969; cf. Smith and Ames, 1976, pp. 44–9).

Standard consumer theory suggests that, even if the poor and the non-poor face exactly the same distance to travel to utilize a service, that distance will cause the poor to use less of that service than the non-poor. There are a number of reasons why this might be so. First, diminishing marginal utility of income implies that even if rich and poor faced the same financial costs of travelling a particular distance, the actual sacrifice involved for the rich would be less than for the poor. Second, some of the very factors that thrust people into poverty in the first place raise the costs of their travel: disability, single parenthood, etc. Third, the fact that the rich generally have easier access to private transport than the poor means that they face lower travel costs, both financial (the marginal cost of using a car for an extra trip generally being lower than using public transport) and in terms of time (car travel generally being quicker). Fourth, the opportunity cost of each unit of time to the poor may be greater than to the rich; in that case the same travel (or queueing) time would involve greater costs for the former than the latter.

This last point needs some amplification. At first sight, it appears to conflict with one of the principal results obtained from the economic theory of the allocation of time (Becker, 1965; Sharp, 1981). If individuals can vary their hours of work without constraint, they will work up to the point at which the marginal gain from working an extra hour is equal to the marginal loss (in terms of other activities forgone, such as leisure or unpaid domestic work). If there are no non-monetary advantages associated with work, then the marginal gain from working an extra hour equals the wage rate, which therefore also equals the marginal value of the other activities foregone. Hence the value of an hour taken in, for instance, travelling to a service facility equals the hourly wage, whether that hour comes out of work or non-work time. Since the rich generally face higher wage rates than the poor, the opportunity cost of a wealthy individual's time is therefore greater than that of a poorer individual's.

In practice, there are a number of reasons why this result may not hold (or, if it does, why the actual difference may not be very significant), of which two are of immediate relevance to this paper. First, the salaried workers that form a large proportion of high income groups can often vary their hours at the margin without loss of pay; hence the cost to them of a marginal hour would be less than the hourly equivalent of their salary. In particular, if the work goes away when the individual is not there, or if it is covered by colleagues on a non-reciprocal basis, then the cost is effectively zero. Second, many of the poor are prevented from entering the work force at all, because the wage they would require to compensate them for the costs they would incur is greater than the wages they can command. For example, for single parents, the costs (monetary and non-monetary) of employing someone to undertake the necessary child-care may be greater than the wages they would receive if they were at work; for an elderly person, it may be the costs of lost pensions and associated fringe benefits that are too great. Since poor people are likely to face lower wage rates, this is more likely to occur among the poorer sections of the community; hence to use actual or potential wage rates may (seriously) under-estimate the value of their time relative to that of the better off.

In general, therefore, there are a number of grounds for supposing that the cost of time to the poor (in utility terms at least) may be greater than the cost to the rich. When to this is added the fact that the poor will generally take longer to travel, and that their financial and other costs are likely to be greater (creating even larger disparities in utility terms), this means that there is good reason to expect that the same geographical distance will act as a more effective deterrent to the use of a service for the poor than the rich.

The Logic of Location: The Basic Model

PRIVATE PROVIDERS

A priori, we would expect to find some tendency towards geographical dispersion in the service delivery points of a privately-provided service, whether or not it was publicly subsidized. Perhaps this can be most easily appreciated in the context of a simple model of service location.

Following standard location theory (Losch, 1954; Lloyd and Dicken, 1972; Heilbrun, 1974), assume the potential users of a service are evenly distributed throughout a region, have identical resources and demand characteristics, and are perfectly informed. Assume also that the resource inputs for the service are also evenly distributed, and that each supplier of the service has one delivery point to which potential users travel to obtain the service. A single profit-maximizing supplier would then command a market that was in the shape of a perfect circle, beyond which the cost to potential users of providing the service themselves or of going without it altogether was less than the combined cost of travel and the profit-maximizing price. To maximize profits, other suppliers would then locate outside this supplier's market so that they too could act as monopolists.

If the whole space filled up with such suppliers, it would consist of a set of tangential circular areas, each with the same radius. Such a situation would not be stable, however, since each supplier would be earning monopoly profits; hence, in the absence of any entry restrictions, new suppliers would enter the market and reduce the market areas of the former monopolists. Long-run equilibrium will be achieved where any further shrinkage of market areas will push the sales of individual suppliers below the minimum necessary to ensure normal profits. At this point, suppliers will be evenly dispersed through the region, each equidistant from its nearest neighbours. 'Perfect' geographical dispersal would have been achieved, with the distance for each user from the nearest service delivery point being at the minimum consistent with each supplier's survival.

The main effect of the introduction of a system of public subsidy to suppliers is to underwrite one of the crucial assumptions underlying this model – it goes some way towards equalizing all users' resources. Publicly-subsidized suppliers will disperse as this model predicts just so long as the amount of the subsidy is directly related to the number of units of service use. Suppliers will still have the same incentive to maximize the number of units of use (for any given cost), and hence to maximize the distance from other suppliers which, in turn, minimizes the distance from consumers. Only in the unlikely event that the subsidy were in some way inversely related to units of use would the basic result not hold.

This model is, of course, highly unrealistic. Still, it is not unreasonable to suppose that the tendency towards dispersion that it predicts will be observed in the real world. Almost whatever the conditions, private suppliers of social services will usually have a tendency to locate as far as possible from their competitors and as close as possible to their customers.[1]

PUBLIC PROVIDERS

Whereas private market provision of publicly-funded social services tends towards geographical dispersion, public-sector provision tends towards geographical concentration. There might be various reasons for this. Some are fiscal in nature, relating to savings (real or imagined) that would be made through centralizing service delivery systems. Another reason – and the one we shall focus upon here – has to do with notions of control. Whatever the particular objective in view, control is a prime imperative in the public sector, and concentration facilitates control. This emphasis upon control in the public sector follows ultimately from the logic of organization, and most immediately from the reward structure facing public-sector managers.

Focus first upon the logic of organization, and upon the firm as the paradigm case of an organization. The central question is why a firm should internalize some particular portion of the production process within itself, rather than buying the outputs of that process on the open market. As Hayek (1945) says, under ideal market conditions there would be no firms at all: every productive unit would consist of a single individual, coordinated with other units through price signals.

Firms arise because markets fall short of the ideal in various respects. One, emphasized by institutional economists, is that contracting itself is not costless, so it may be cheaper to sign one big contract employing people rather than lots of little ones purchasing their products (Coase, 1937; Williamson, 1975; 1981). Mainstream economists also point to a bundle of other factors: externalities, especially in the form of complementarities between component parts of the productive process (Alchian and Demsetz, 1972); the specificity of certain assets to certain productive uses (Williamson, 1981, pp. 1546–9); and uncertainty, especially as it relates to the impossibility of organizing futures markets in certain commodities (Meade, 1971, pp. 66ff.; Arrow, 1964). All these factors lead to the needed components being produced internally within the firm, rather than being acquired externally through the market.

What is important to notice for present purposes is that most of the reasons why markets are replaced by formal organizations (i.e. firms) pertain to the need for *control*. Producers organize a firm to guarantee control over resources which they require but which, for one reason or another, they could not be sure of securing on the open market.

The logic of organization in the public sector is much the same. There we face the analogous question of why formal public bureau-cracies are set up to perform certain tasks, rather than contracting those tasks out to private agencies. And the answer is once again couched in terms of the failure of 'price signals' to convey all the needed information, and of the need to exercise control over suppliers in ways that ordinary market arrangements cannot guaran-tee.[2]

One of the most important reasons is that there are few good 'output' measures for most of the things that governments do. When it is impossible to monitor the quality of the goods adequately, it is difficult for the government concerned to contract with private firms to supply them. It simply does not know whether or not it is getting what it is paying for. Perhaps the most famous tale, which turns out to be apocryphal but nonetheless telling in the basic point it makes, concerns the first US experiment with performance contracting in education: when contractors were getting paid according to how much better their students performed on certain standardized tests, they allegedly leaked the questions to their students the day before the test was officially administered (Rivlin, 1971, p. 107). Further investigation shows that particular story to be untrue. But the basic point remains: output measures are remarkably poor for a great many services that are presently provided by public agencies. We can measure some outputs but not others; and we can get only the most indirect measures of some of the outputs that matter most to us (US

DHEW, 1969; Rivlin, 1971; Hatry, 1972; Rose–Ackerman, 1983). Given this, it would be folly to contract these services out to private agencies.[3]

This provides a useful criterion for deciding what functions to 'contract out' to the private sector. We can safely contract out only when product quality can be monitored easily, as for example in the case of munitions (Hood, 1976, ch. 3; Sharkansky, 1980). Similarly in regulation policy, 'command-and-control' techniques are required where output measures are inadequate; quasi-market solutions internalizing social costs through taxes and fees are feasible only where we can effectively measure the outputs (pollutants, work injuries, etc.) we want to control (Schultze, 1977; Nichols and Zeckhauser, 1977; Ackerman and Hassler, 1981).

We assume that the state is a service-provider of last resort. We assume that it will contract out wherever possible. Where outputs can be monitored, that is possible. Where they cannot, it is not possible – or, anyway, not desirable. The advantage of internalizing such activities within a bureaucracy is that, even though output cannot be monitored effectively, at least input and behaviour within the productive process can then be monitored. Indeed, that is the essence of the supervisory function within a formal organization, be it public or private (Arrow, 1964, p. 400; Ouchi and Maguire, 1975; Stiglitz, 1975). Through organizations, control is secured over uncontrollable outputs by controlling inputs, most especially the behaviour of agents within the bureaucracy responsible for performing the task. That is the whole point of public bureaucracies (Massam, 1975, ch. 8; van Gunsteren, 1976).

Of course, it is also difficult to monitor *inputs* effectively unless we know the production function, which in turn requires that we know what the outputs are. But there is a difference between knowing the particular outputs of particular inputs, on the one hand, and what sorts of outputs generally flow from what sorts of inputs, on the other. It is the former, more demanding requirement that needs to be satisfied for governments to contract out to private suppliers; it is the latter, less demanding one that needs to be satisfied for governments to be effective in internal monitoring inputs in publicly-provided services. Of course, private agencies can monitor inputs, too. But that constitutes no reassurance for the ultimate purchaser (here, the public) of products of unascertainable quality. Presumably the private profiteer, when producing such a product, strives to minimize costs, and that alone; if the user of the product were to produce it himself, he would strive to maximize on a function combining both costs and quality. Therein lies the logic of providing social services through the not-for-profit sector (Hansmann, 1980; Gilbert, 1984).

So far we have been talking almost exclusively in terms of systemic imperatives. These are reflected, however, in the reward structures facing public-sector administrators and in the management styles which they are thereby forced to adopt. Where outputs can be monitored directly and managers' rewards varied accordingly, Theory *Z* (Japanese-style) management techniques have much to recommend them: delegating authority to the lowest levels and letting subordinates get on with the job probably is then the most productive strategy (Gold, 1982). But where outputs cannot be monitored, or can be monitored only very imperfectly, managers cannot be rewarded according to the outputs of their agencies; nor can they count upon output measures to provide them with automatic evidence as to how well their own subordinates are doing. In these circumstances, managers will be expected to monitor and control the activities of their subordinates directly, and will be rewarded or penalized according to how well they perform these classically supervisory tasks (Breton and Wintrobe, 1982).

In emphasizing the reward structure facing public-sector administrators, we are not meaning to imply that they are necessarily seeking narrowly economic or materialistic rewards. They may be; and if so, they will certainly behave as we have suggested. Alternatively, they might actually care about the content of the policies they are implementing. Bureaucrats might be 'mission-committed' (Downs, 1967, ch. 19; Margolis, 1975; Goodin, 1982b). Perhaps they have gone into the public service with the aim of advancing certain causes, and want to make the most difference they possibly can to promoting those desired outcomes. That, too, will lead them to want to maximize their control over policy; and where output-monitoring is impossible, that means maximizing control over the activities of their subordinates.

Many factors might contribute to the weakening of this control of subordinates. The one that is of particular concern here is *location*. Other things being equal, it is easier to monitor and control the activities of subordinates when they are working in close proximity to you than when they work at some distance (Friedkin, 1983).[4] 'Street-level bureaucrats', as Lipsky (1980) calls them, inevitably have considerably more discretionary power than those who work in the central office.

In conclusion, if a publicly-funded service is privately-supplied, there will be an incentive to disperse the service-delivery points. If it is publicly supplied, there will be an incentive to concentrate service-delivery to a small number of points – perhaps even just one. This centralization necessarily imposes upon users higher travel costs, which differentially disadvantage poor users. Even if the centralized facilities are more often located in poor neighbourhoods poor people on average will still have to travel further to reach some centralized service point than they would if service centres were dispersed to a number of delivery points. Whereas private suppliers have an incentive to maximize the distance between delivery points, public suppliers have an incentive to minimize it. That means, in turn, that private suppliers have an incentive to minimize the distance to clients, whereas the incentive to public suppliers is to maximize it. And from the discussion above we know that distance disadvantages – indeed, differentially disadvantages – poor users.

Towards a Refined Logic of Location

Previous sections might seem to constitute a powerful indictment of publicly-provided services. There it was argued that the basic logic of location decisions is such that private services tend to be geographically dispersed while public services tend to be geographically concentrated. And distance, in turn, differentially disadvantages poor users.

A refined version of that same basic model, however, turns into a brief in support of publicly-supplied services. Two particular refinements are required. First, there are circumstances under which we would expect the decentralization of public service provision. Second, a decentralized publicly-provided service will reduce the distance to (and hence the bias against) poor users more effectively than will a decentralized service in the private sector.

PUBLIC PROVIDERS CAN BE MADE TO DECENTRALIZE

The rationale for centralization of publicly-provided services offered above was couched in terms of the logic of organization and the control imperative implicit within it. But there are limits of organization, defined in the self-same terms of control (Arrow, 1974; Hood, 1976; van Gunsteren, 1976; Breton and Wintrobe, 1982). Some subordinates, by the very nature of their task, are uncontrollable. Police officers, for example, must necessarily act largely at their own initiative far from supervisors' watchful eyes (Lipsky, 1980). In other cases 'control loss' inevitably follows from the nature of the task: the size of the organization, the number of layers of managers, the degree of specialization of tasks within it, and the complexity of those tasks all affect the degree of control superiors can exercise over subordinates (Arrow, 1964; Monsen and Downs, 1965; Downs, 1967, chs 11–12; Ouchi and Dowling, 1974; Marris and Mueller, 1980; Breton and Wintrobe, 1982).

Whatever the cause, the consequence of this control loss is that project sponsors might rationally prefer to get the task done externally instead of internally. This will be the case just so long as their output measures (imperfect though they may be) allow for better control of outputs than can be achieved by trying to monitor and control activities of subordinates within the organization. Contracting the job out is the most dramatic form this might take (Sharkansky, 1980). Allowing the task to be performed at some site distant from the central office is only a slightly less dramatic manifestation of the same basic logic. Thus, where internal mechanisms of control are so imperfect as to make external ones comparatively advantageous, decentralization is to be expected.

In both the private and the public sectors, failure to meet consumers' demands can lead to penalties being imposed on senior management. In the case of private firms, market pressures are reflected primarily in unsatisfactory profit-and-loss statement, leading owners to pressure senior managers for better performance, and senior managers in turn to rethink their preferred strategies for controlling their juniors.

In the case of public bureaucracies, these take the form of political pressures. Client dissatisfaction is reflected in low levels of client contacts and the absence of satisfactory case closures; and an underused or ill-serving programme is a prime target for budgetary cuts.[5] There is thus a strong incentive for senior management (if not street-level professionals; see Smith and Ames, 1976, pp. 49–52) to reformulate the programme to maximize use by, and praise from, the client population. (Maximizing praise and maximizing use might sometimes be incompatible goals; but this is unlikely to be true insofar as it is just the question of location that is at issue, since both praise and use are presumably inversely related to the distance users have to travel to receive the service.)

Decentralization has been one popular strategy for producing this effect as evidenced by the proliferation of community, neighbourhood and outreach programmes in Australia, the United Kingdom and the United States over the last two decades (Kahn, 1976; Ouchi, 1977). Such strategies are an especially appropriate response where the failure of the programme consists essentially in a failure on the part of intended (usually impoverished) beneficiaries to come and get the services when they were located more centrally.

DECENTRALIZED PUBLIC PROVIDERS LOCATE NEARER THE POOR

When public providers of social services decentralize, they do so more thoroughly than private providers. There are various reasons for expecting this to be so. One has to do with motivational differences between personnel in the public and private sectors. Were social-service bureaucrats personally committed to redistributive goals, as surely they *must* be in some instances, they might actually prefer serving the poor than the rich. In that case, public-sector providers would strive to maximize access for the poor, whereas private-sector providers maximize a payoff function that consists partially (perhaps largely) in payments from relatively rich private clients (Kahn, 1976).

Then there is the matter of political pressures, once again. The whole point of personal social services, from the point of view of programme sponsors (in the first instance, the legislature; ultimately, the electorate), is to help the poor. Presumably this objective is reflected – however imperfectly – in the reward structure facing senior bureaucrats. The better their programmes serve the target population, the more credit (in whatever currency) they get. One way supervisors can make sure their programmes are achieving their objectives is to stand over subordinates – *ergo* the tendency towards centralization. But against that they must offset the disincentive effect of distance. If bureaucrats are rewarded according to how many people they serve, and if fewer poor will come to be served the further they have to travel, then it is clearly in the bureaucratic interest to decentralize the services and locate them nearer the poor.

In short, one good way for senior bureaucrats to influence *what* their subordinates do is to control *where* they do it.

There is, however, one last argument which is at once both simpler and even more decisive. *Ex hypothesi*, private providers do not work permanently and exclusively for the state. (Their designation as 'private' would be inappropriate if they did.) They are, therefore, looking both to the state and to the private market for clients. And most prefer to attract at least some private clients as well – both the pay and the company of private clients are usually deemed preferable. Given this desire to attract private as well as (or, indeed, in preference to) publicly-funded clients, private service providers will tend to be more heavily clustered in rich neighbourhoods than in poor ones. The poor will have to travel further to a provider, and will use less (indeed, disproportionately less) of the service in consequence. No such logic is at work for public-sector providers of the service. They are explicitly prohibited from accepting side-payments over and above their ordinary salaries, so 'private' clients are out of the question for them. Thus, private providers have an incentive to locate nearer the rich, while public producers have no such incentive. That in itself guarantees that a privately-provided service, even if it is publicly-subsidized, will be relatively pro-rich compared to a decentralized publicly-provided one.

Conclusion

The strategy of telling clients to 'come and get it', like the cognate strategy of having them queue for services, might be thought to be a reasonable way to ration social services. *Ceteris paribus*, those who need the service most should be expected to come first to queue up, and to be prepared to wait longest in that queue. However, the 'other things' – in particular, the costs of physically getting to the queue – might not be equal. In that case, the rule of 'come and get it' would be distributively biased against poor users. We have found good theoretical reasons for believing this might be so. What is now needed is more empirical evidence. Do take-up rates decay with distance, and indeed more sharply for the poor than the non-poor? Are private suppliers more dispersed than ordinary public suppliers? And when public providers decentralize, do they locate still nearer the poor? Theoretical considerations lead us to expect affirmative answers, but the empirical evidence is not yet in. If it turns out as we expect, however, then the conclusion is clear. If we want to get social services to those who need them most, we should be prepared to take the service to them instead of waiting for them to come and get it.

Notes

This chapter draws on research undertaken by Gibson partly funded by a grant from the Australian Department of Health. It was written at the Research School of Social Sciences, Australian National University, while Gibson was attached to the Ageing and the Family Project and Goodin and Le Grand to the Social Justice Project. Le Grand was also being funded by the Nuffield Foundation on a Research Fellowship. We thank those institutions for their generous support, and exonerate them from any responsibility for the final product. We are grateful for the assistance of Gina Roach in the preparation of this paper, and for comments on earlier drafts from Glen Bramley, Geoff Brennan, Max Neutze, Patricia Tulloch and Stephen Uttley. The paper was originally published in *Policy and Politics*, vol. 13 (1985), pp. 109–25. We are grateful to the editors and publishers, Sage, for permission to reprint it here.

1   A classic piece by Hotelling (1929) has shown that where there are only two competitors and the market can be represented by a straight line, both suppliers will locate next to one another in the middle of the line; however, the conditions for this are even more extreme than the dispersal model.

   If users have different incomes, and if publicly-subsidized suppliers can augment their incomes by selling extra services, then suppliers will have an incentive to locate closer to wealthier areas than to poorer ones. Or, again, if users are clustered, then suppliers will want to locate close to the clusters. However, in both cases, suppliers will still have an incentive to keep their distance from their competitors; and while location may not be 'perfectly' dispersed, it will tend in that direction. Only when resources are clustered, are expensive to convey, and/or there are significant economies of scale in production will supply be concentrated. It is rare that any of these conditions are found in the social services.

2   This logic explains why they *should* be provided through the public sector. Various other logics (of e.g. political pressure) might be required to explain why, in any particular case, services *are* provided publicly or privately. In the case of Australian medical services, for example, the reason general medical services are provided through private contractors but dental ones are not may well have more to do with the relative power of the relevant professional associations.

3   Notice that problems of variable, non-monitorable product quality vitiate proposals for 'proxy shopping' for social services as well. The argument for allowing private suppliers to charge the government the

same price for services delivered to public clients as is paid by private ones crucially presupposes that the same quality of service is delivered to both (Rose-Ackerman, 1983). If that can vary, but the government cannot monitor how it varies, then the logic of the proposal collapses.

4 Other things might not be equal. There is some evidence, for example, that those who have to work in close proximity to their subordinates will treat them more gently, on the grounds that they 'have to live with those people'. But that seems to work both ways: subordinates also anticipate and adapt to supervisors' demands, obviating any need for formal orders to be given (Blau, 1963, ch. 11).

5 Of course, the poor are relatively inactive politically. That means that there will be fewer protests per unit of real dissatisfaction from poor people than richer ones. But it also means that any given sign of dissatisfaction from them before an election should be taken *more* seriously by vote-maximizing politicians as a forewarning of a real electoral backlash. One poor person writing to complain might be thought to speak for thousands of poor voters who cannot be bothered to write, but who may well vote politicians out of office for just such grievances; with rich people, politicians can feel pretty confident that all those with a serious complaint will speak up for themselves.

PART FOUR

The Challenge to the Welfare State

Chapter 8

The Middle Classes
and the Defence of the
British Welfare State

JULIAN LE GRAND and DAVID WINTER

Hell hath no fury like that of the middle class when its subsidies are at issue
George Will[1]

The election of a new Conservative Government in 1979 was widely
thought to represent a watershed in British politics. For almost the
first time since the Second World War,[2] an administration was in
power that had the avowed intention of breaking with the 'Butskell'
consensus concerning the role of the state in promoting economic
growth and social welfare.[3] In her introduction to her party's election
manifesto in 1979, Margaret Thatcher wrote that 'no one . . . can fail
to be aware of how the balance of our society has been increasingly
tilted in favour of the state'. Later in the manifesto, previous Labour
governments were blamed for 'enlarging the role of the state' and
'diminishing the role of the individual', thereby crippling 'the
enterprise and effort on which a prosperous country with improving
social services depends'. The Conservatives were to reverse that
process 'and thereby to restore the balance of power in favour of the
people'.

Nowhere was this emphasis more apparent than in the area of
social policy and the welfare state. Many supporters of the new
government viewed the welfare state as among the principal causes of
Britain's economic decline, imposing a burden on the tax side that
stifled incentives to work and to save and, on the benefits side,

undermining individual initiative and self-reliance. The welfare burden was to be lifted off the backs of the tax-payer; social expenditures were to be reduced, public assets were to be sold, and public services contracted out to the private sector.

Yet, as has been remarked by several commentators (for example, O'Higgins, 1983; Robinson, 1986), the outcome was rather different. As we shall see, far from being reduced, during the first five years of the new administration public expenditure increased in real terms in most areas of welfare provision; moreover, with the important exception of the sale of council houses, other forms of privatization were minimal.

Why is this? Why, despite facing the most serious ideological assault it had encountered since its inception, did the welfare state prove so remarkably resilient? One of the present authors has suggested (Le Grand, 1984) that the key lay in the role of the middle classes; that as both users and employees of important parts of the welfare state, the middle classes had significant interests in its preservation, interests that neither politicians nor civil servants could safely ignore. Elsewhere (Le Grand and Winter, 1987) we have developed a theoretical framework for analysing this proposition and have attempted to use it to test systematically a number of hypotheses relating to it. This chapter summarizes our arguments and conclusions.

The Hypothesis

The new philosophy represented by the government of Mrs Thatcher was in some respects not new at all. During the period of the previous Labour government (from March 1974 to May 1979), there was increasing pressure to reduce public spending: a pressure that became acute after 1976. The immediate agents of this pressure were usually the Prime Minister and the Chancellor of the Exchequer; they in turn were reflecting pressure from other agencies, such as the Treasury and, notoriously, the International Monetary Fund, where there was a widespread perception that public expenditure was 'out of control' (Pliatzky, 1984). But all the individuals involved in the policy-making process were, to a greater or lesser extent, influenced by a pronounced ideological shift: a shift away from a generalized belief in the virtues of public intervention in the operations of the economy to a widespread perception that such intervention was, more often than not, actually harmful. This shift was both reflected in, and partly generated by, the development of economic theories of the 'crowding out' consequences of public expenditure (Bacon and Eltis, 1976). It was also fuelled by a general perception that the mixed economy had, literally, failed to deliver the goods: that neither the public sector, nor the private sector nor the economy as a whole was providing the quantity and quality of goods and services that people expected.

In some ways, the election of the Conservative Government can be viewed as an extension of this process. The rhetoric of the election on the Conservative side constantly emphasized the evils of 'excessive' public spending, an attack to which the incumbent Labour administration, given its own ambivalence on the subject, found it difficult to reply. After the election, the Government consistently reiterated its commitment to the goal of reducing public spending, a commitment that it retained despite the difficulties to which we shall be alluding shortly.

We thus have a picture of continuous, and continuously increasing, pressure to reduce public expenditure at least from 1976 onwards. From 1979 onwards, there was also pressure to engage in a more explicit form of privatization. This was to reduce not only state *subsidy*, as financed by public expenditure, but also to cut state *provision* – to sell state-owned assets, or to replace direct public provision of certain services by 'contracting out' the services concerned to private firms.

What happened in practice? Table 8.1 shows the percentage changes in the real value of public expenditure on various areas of welfare, and in some other areas as well, in the period of Labour government and in the first five years of the Conservative government. It also shows changes in 'needs' for the services concerned. These will be discussed in more detail in the next section. However, it is clear from Table 8.1 that, in most areas of government expenditure (housing being the principal exception), the pressure to reduce public spending in both periods largely failed. Moreover, the other form of privatization advocated during the Conservative period, the reduction in state provision, was not notably successful either – again with the significant exception of housing – being largely confined to the contracting out of some hospital catering and cleaning services (Atkinson, Hills and Le Grand, 1986).

Table 8.1   *UK: Percentage Changes in Public Expenditures and Needs*

	Expenditures[a]		Needs	
	Lab.[b]	Con.[b]	Lab.	Con.
National Health Service				
Hospital (diagnosis and treatment)	34.20	10.34	1.41	4.23
Hospital (support services)	17.69	−3.71	1.41	4.23
Family practitioner services	8.68	10.51	1.41	4.23
Personal social services				
Residential	43.29	4.13	19.71	63.64
Field	31.77	16.63	19.71	63.64
Community care for the elderly	34.23	2.77	4.04	3.70
Education				
Nursery	62.77	14.40	−21.16	5.63
Primary	5.81	−6.45	−5.90	−17.91
Secondary	18.02	5.20	21.47	2.68
Higher and Further	−3.72	4.21	13.00	12.47
Social Security				
Child benefit	79.20	32.11	−8.45	−9.28
Age-related benefits	25.48	17.54	4.04	3.70
Income-related benefits	36.19	97.24	19.71	63.64
Unemployment benefits	80.00	45.14	125.21	115.84
Housing				
Capital	−3.69	−61.36	6.05	4.68
Current	70.38	−71.20	11.46	−7.47
Other Government Services				
British Rail	49.56	18.53	2.50	2.61
Roads	−35.56	7.68	4.46	13.75
Arts and Libraries	34.31	1.44	2.50	2.61
Labour-market services	262.08	52.70	125.21	115.84
Police	19.00	22.25	54.52	26.76
Defence	−2.37	17.96	−9.98	37.33
Tax Expenditures				
Age allowance	283.76	13.73	4.04	3.70
Tax exemption of social security	−11.12	−58.82	19.71	63.64
Mortgage interest tax relief	−0.71	48.73	−9.45	32.15
Retirement annuity and pension scheme relief	—	102.14	—	3.70
Mean growth[c]	45.57	13.23	16.26	23.63
Standard deviation	74.22	39.19	35.88	36.14

Notes
[a] Changes in expenditure at constant prices.
[b] Lab. refers to the period 1973/4–1978/9. Con. refers to the period 1978/9–1983/4.
[c] Note that the means given here and discussed throughout the chapter are unweighted means and are not necessarily an accurate guide to the overall growth in total expenditure even of the services considered in the sample.

How can such a pattern be explained? The hypothesis put forward in Le Grand (1984) was that the key lay in the role of the professional and managerial classes: the middle classes. Here we outline the basic argument.

First, who are the middle classes? They are professionals (architects, clergymen, doctors, administrative grade civil servants, lawyers, teachers, nurses, accountants, engineers, scientists, etc.), employers and managers plus the immediate members of their families. In terms of the Registrar-General's Classifications of Occupations, the middle classes correspond most closely to Social Classes 1 and 2 (Professional and Intermediate); in terms of the collapsed Socio-Economic Group (SEG) classification used by the General Household Survey, to SEGs 1 and 2 (Professionals, Employers and Managers) plus teachers and nurses from SEG 3 (Intermediate and Junior Non-Manual).

Now important groups within the middle classes have various interests in a number of different areas of the welfare state. As *taxpayers*, the middle classes perceive themselves as contributing heavily to the funding of the welfare state. This perception is often exaggerated; but it is the perception, rather than the reality, that is relevant here. They thus perceive an interest in reducing welfare state activities. More specifically, they will obviously have a direct interest in cutting state subsidies. They may have an interest in diminishing state provision, too, if this is thought to lead to inefficiency and waste. They may also exert pressure to *shift* the tax burden, as well as to reduce it overall. This can be achieved by promoting specific tax reliefs from which they particularly benefit, such as mortgage interest tax relief.

Many members of the middle classes are *suppliers of services* from the welfare state. Doctors, nurses, teachers, lecturers, social workers and office managers form an important – and disproportionately powerful – part of the personnel supplying many welfare services and benefits. As suppliers of state-provided services, these members of the middle classes will have an interest in protecting their own employment, and also in either promoting the expansion of the sector in which they work or, at least, in opposing any cuts in either expenditure or subsidy in order to protect the demand for their services. They may also tend to oppose the replacement of state by private provision, as this may undermine the powerful and entrenched positions that they have managed to secure within the existing structures. Thus it would appear that middle-class employees of the welfare state have a major stake in the government continuing to provide and to subsidize the service they work for.

Thirdly, the middle classes are *beneficiaries* of the welfare state. The families of professionals, employers and managers use the National Health Service (NHS) and the education system (particularly after the age of 16) more than their numbers in the relevant populations would justify. Although there are no estimates of the distribution of social security benefits by social class, on average the middle class live longer than the working class and have similar-sized families. So they have a considerable stake in the old age pension and child benefit. Users of a service, or recipients of a benefit, have no particular interest in whether it is state or privately provided (unless they think they will get a better service under one than the other). But they do have a strong interest in the size of the subsidy, for this affects their real income. Any subsidy to a welfare programme which has a significant proportion of middle-class beneficiaries is likely to have a strong supporting lobby.

Table 8.2 shows the degree of involvement in different programmes. It divides programmes into four categories: those with relatively high proportions of middle-class beneficiaries and suppliers; those with relatively low proportions of each; and those with relatively high proportions of one and relatively low of the other. We have categorized the proportion as 'relatively high' where it is at least as great as the proportion of social classes 1 and 2 in the general

Table 8.2   *UK: The Middle Classes and the Welfare State*

		Proportion of middle-class beneficiaries	
		High	*Low*
	High	NHS medical services Education	Personal social services (field)
Proportion of middle-class suppliers	*Low*	NHS support services Child benefit Age-related benefits All tax expenditures except tax exemption of social security	Housing Unemployment and income-related benefits Personal social services (residential workers and community care) Tax exemption of social security

population (22 per cent in the 1971 census). 'Relatively low' means the proportion falls below this. The allocation of programmes in the Table is based on data detailed in Le Grand and Winter (1987, Appendix) and discussed in the next section.

To establish that the middle class has interests in public spending is not sufficient to establish it as an effective agent in determining public spending, however. To do that it is necessary to show that it has the means to exercise power over public decisions. We can isolate three possible routes. The first is electoral. Politicians may fear they will lose more votes if they tamper with a middle-class programme than with a working-class one. The middle classes are more effective than the working classes at portraying their programmes as in the 'national interest', e.g. the arts, universities etc. Hence a cut in a middle-class programme may lose working-class votes as well as middle-class ones; but cuts in working-class programmes will only lose working-class votes (indeed, if the middle classes can successfully portray those cuts as being in the 'national interest', perhaps not even those).

The next route is through the values of the politicians and civil servants themselves. Politicians from all the major parties are disproportionately drawn from the ranks of the middle classes; so are high-ranking civil servants. However dispassionate they may be, or however much they may perceive their interests as lying outside those of the middle classes, it is unlikely that they will be able completely to overcome the effects of their background or of their current social status.

Finally, the middle classes, if they dislike a policy, are better placed than the working classes to let policy-makers know. They are more articulate, have better access to the media and, where necessary, have the resources to set up campaigning pressure groups. Also, they are more likely to try to influence policy-makers; for they have a greater faith in their own power to change aspects of their environment with which they feel uncomfortable.

The middle classes thus have both an interest in maintaining parts of the welfare state and the power to further that interest. How this will affect proposals to cut or privatize a specific programme can be predicted from the position of the programme concerned in Table 8.2. Proposals that mean less state *provision* will meet with less resistance if they concern programmes in the lower row of the table than if they concern those in the upper row. Proposals for a reduction in *subsidy* will meet with less resistance if they concern programmes in the second column of the table than if they concern programmes in the first column. More specifically, programmes in the top left-hand corner of the table are likely to be almost immune from privatization of either kind. Those in the bottom left-hand corner are relatively protected from cuts in state subsidy, while those in the top right-hand corner are relatively protected from cuts in state provision. Those in the bottom right-hand corner will bear the brunt of both types of attack.

This pattern is in some respects close to what happened under the Conservative government from 1979 to 1983. The privatization schemes involving a reduction in state provision that succeeded – that is, where any resistance apparently failed – include: the contracting out of NHS ancillary services (like laundry and catering), the selling of council houses, the closing of residential homes, and cuts in the home help services. All these are programmes in the vulnerable lower row of the Table.

Proposals to reduce state provision for the programmes in the top row, on the other hand, did not emerge. The medical part of the NHS remained firmly in place. Education vouchers – the only serious proposal to privatize education, and one supported in the past by both Margaret Thatcher and Sir Keith Joseph – did not appear. And no proposals were put forward to privatize field social workers' activities.

The predictions for cuts in public expenditure are less satisfactory, however, as can be seen from Table 8.1. Some fit the predicted pattern: NHS expenditures, secondary education, old age pensions, child benefit and housing. But others do not: income-related benefits, unemployment benefit, primary education. The three last were, of course, all affected by considerable changes in the number of their potential clients (increases for the first two, falls for the second); this suggests that simply to focus on the role of the middle class is insufficient and that a more sophisticated theory, incorporating indicators of need and other factors is required.

Le Grand and Winter (1987) put forward a model of government behaviour that tries to account for some of the principal influences on public policy. In addition to the middle-class 'effect', it draws attention to three other factors. First, the overall resource constraint. The annual series of negotiations between the Treasury and the spending departments strongly suggests that most recent governments have had strong views as to the appropriate overall change in government expenditure (Pliatzky, 1984). This overall budget constraint will not vary between services; but it is likely to vary over time and across governments.

Second, it is reasonable to suppose that the size of any client group to which a particular service is directed may also influence changes in expenditure. If the number of children of school age rise in the population, we would expect, other things being equal, that expenditure on education will also rise – though not necessarily by a proportionate amount. The same would be true for most other kinds of service. Accordingly an indicator of the change in needs was included in the model as an independent variable. Third, price or cost variables were also included. Any model of government decision making based on the theory of optimal choice will include prices (see Dunne *et al.*, 1984). If one kind of service becomes relatively more expensive to deliver, then other things being equal, we would expect the government to substitute resources away from that service towards others which have become relatively cheaper to deliver. Thus changes in expenditure will be related to changes in needs and changes in relative prices. The degree to which any government will respond to such changes will depend on the users and suppliers of a particular service. Thus if the need, defined in terms of the total number of users, for a particular service rises, but the users are not largely from the middle classes, then we would expect the government to respond less in terms of increases in expenditure than if the users were from the middle classes. The same argument applies to the effect of relative price changes.

The possible differential response of government to different groups in the population was modelled with 0–1 shift variables. These had the advantage that they allowed the data to determine whether the effect of different client groups works through the needs or price elements; or whether some governments may wish to increase (or decrease) expenditure to all services predominantly used (or supplied) by the middle classes across the board. The precise specification of these effects will be described below, following a brief description of the data.

Statistical Analysis

Data were assembled for a variety of different areas of public expenditure for two periods: 1973/4 to 1978/9, to cover the period of Labour government, and 1978/9 to 1983/4, to cover the first five years of the Conservative Government. Twenty-two services involving direct public expenditures, and four tax-expenditures, were selected, and are listed in Table 8.1. Our main interest was in welfare state services and these provide the bulk of the data. To the sixteen welfare state services we added six more general kinds of service, which are nevertheless categories of government expenditure which we judged benefit consumers directly. The total expenditure on these twenty-two services in 1978/9 consisted of about 57 per cent of the 'Planning Total' for that year given in the White Paper on Government Expenditure in 1984 (UK Treasury, 1984). The data set was completed by four categories of tax expenditure (three for Labour). These kinds of expenditures have become increasingly important in recent years (see Willis and Hardwick, 1978), and it is of interest to see whether changes in their levels can be explained in the same way as for other kinds of expenditure.

The dependent variable in the analysis was the proportional five-year change in expenditure at constant prices. The main independent variables were indicators of needs and prices. A relative price variable was constructed by taking the ratio of the price variable for each service to the GDP price deflator. A needs indicator was constructed for each service. They are listed in Table 8.3. A number of services have a fairly straightforward demographic indicator of needs. For any service which is provided for a part of the population that is entirely defined by its age, e.g. primary schools, age-related benefits, community care for the elderly etc., a needs indicator could reasonably be constructed from the numbers in the population of that particular age group. For other services the appropriate needs indicator was less obvious. The criteria adopted was to try to select the variable that most closely reflects needs as they might be perceived in Whitehall. Thus the indicator for Income Related Benefits was the number of households receiving such benefits, rather than a variable that attempted to measure the number of households facing some level of relative deprivation or poverty. The NHS services were each related to a measure of the change in demographic structure that reflects the use of the NHS by different age groups. This is the variable used by the Department of Health and Social Security in its own planning. For defence, we adopted a different procedure and, following the work of Smith (1980), used the growth in defence expenditure at constant prices in the United States.

It was also necessary to classify services in terms of middle-class

Table 8.3   *UK: Needs Indicators*

National Health Service
  Hospitals (diagnosis and
    treatment)
  Hospital (support services)
  Family Practitioner Services
	Changes in demand due to changes
	in demographic structure of the
	population

Personal Social Services
  Residential
  Field
	No. of recipients of income-related
	benefits

Community care for elderly	No. of men over 65 and women over 60

Education
  Nursery
  Primary
  Secondary
  Higher and Further
	No. of under fives
	No. of 5–11-year-olds
	No. of pupils
	No. of pupils leaving school
	with suitable qualifications

Social Security
  Child benefit
  Age-related benefits
	No. of children under 15
	No. of men over 65 and women
	over 60

Income-related benefits Unemployment benefit	No. of recipients No. of registered unemployed

Housing
  Capital
  Current
	Stock of dwellings
	No. of council houses

Other Government Services
  British Rail
  Roads
  Arts and Libraries
  Labour-market services
  Police
	Growth in GDP
	No. of licensed vehicles
	Growth in GDP
	No. of registered unemployed
	Notifiable offences recorded by the
	police

Defence	Growth in US defence expenditure at constant prices
Tax Expenditures Age allowance	No. of men over 65 and women over 60

Tax exemption of social
    security
  Mortgage interest tax relief
  Retirement annuity and pension
    scheme relief
	No. of recipients of income-related
	benefits
	Burden of mortgage debt
	No. of men over 65 and women
	over 60

'supply' and 'use'. So far as the former is concerned, there is little detailed evidence concerning the class or income composition of the employees of the public services that we are investigating. Accordingly, services were allocated to the middle-class category if their employees contained members of one or more of the professions (doctors, nurses, teachers or social workers). Although other services clearly have middle-class employees of managerial status, we considered that managers generally formed a sufficiently small proportion of the relevant labour force that these services could not be classified as middle class in terms of supply.

There is more evidence concerning the distribution of benefits from the use of services. However, the evidence is eclectic in both origin and form. Where the evidence existed, the procedure followed was to allocate a service to the middle-class category, if its benefits were distributed either equally per household or individual, or favouring the better off, where better off is defined either in terms of income or occupation. More details follow.

As was discussed in Chapter 5, it has been calculated (Le Grand, 1982b, p. 26) that the Socio-Economic Groups (SEGs) 1 and 2 (Professionals, Employers and Managers) received an amount of public expenditure on health care (of all kinds) per person reporting illness equal to 120 per cent of the mean. They also received 90 per cent of mean public expenditure per person in the relevant age range on primary education, 88 per cent of that on secondary education (pupils of 16 and under), 165 per cent of that on secondary education (pupils over 16), 149 per cent of that on higher and further (non-university) education and 272 per cent of that on university education (*ibid.*, p. 58). All these services were therefore classified as middle class. On public housing, it has been estimated that the top 27 per cent of the household income distribution received an amount of public subsidy per household equal to 54 per cent of the mean subsidy per household, compared with 170 per cent received by the bottom 21 per cent (*ibid.*, p. 88); all public housing was therefore categorized as non-middle class. On transport, one calculation (*ibid.*, p. 109) suggests that the top 22 per cent of the household income distribution received an amount of public subsidy per household to rail travel equal to 244 per cent of the mean compared with an amount equal to 25 per cent of the mean received by the bottom 18 per cent; the equivalent estimates for road travel were 204 per cent and 12 per cent. Although these are probably partly distorted by life-cycle factors, the scale of the uncorrected differences seem such as to justify the classification of the relevant services as middle class. There is no evidence concerning the distribution of benefits from the personal social services; it seems unlikely, however, that these could plausibly be described as middle class in terms of their use.

On social security, Central Statistical Office (CSO) estimates show, unsurprisingly, that the distribution of unemployment and income-related benefits clearly favours the worse-off (see, e.g., UK CSO, 1985, Table 3, p. 107). These are therefore non-middle class benefits. Child benefit, on the other hand, is broadly equally distributed across the income distribution; hence this is a middle-class benefit.

The situation is more complicated with respect to old-age pensions. The CSO estimates show that these favour the worst-off, when worst-off is defined in terms of current 'original' income (income before taxes and the receipt of state benefits). Yet the value of original income for the elderly is clearly dependent in part on the fact that they receive a state pension; hence this evidence tells us little about the actual distribution of this benefit. However, Victor and Evandrou (1986), using General Household Survey data, have shown that over 97 per cent of all elderly, regardless of social class, were in receipt of the state pension. Moreover, the higher the social class the longer the average life expectancy for both males and females (Black, 1980); hence the greater the value of state pension received over the lifetime by members of the higher social classes. Hence this, too, can be classified as middle-class use.

Police and defence benefits are traditionally allocated either on a per head basis (on the grounds that they are public goods) or according to the distribution of income or wealth (on the grounds that those with a greater stake in the existing social order derive a greater benefit from its protection). Although neither of these procedures is wholly uncontroversial (Le Grand, 1982b, pp. 158–9), they are sufficiently plausible to justify allocating these as middle-class use. There is little empirical evidence concerning the distribution of public expenditure on the arts; such as there is (*ibid.*, p. 158) supports the reasonable view that this, too, is middle class. Labour-market services and regional aid, on the other hand, were classified as non-middle class use. All tax-expenditures except the tax exemption of social security benefits were classified as middle-class use.

Before summarizing the econometric results, it is of interest to look at the data on the proportional changes in expenditure at constant prices and the proportional changes in the relevant needs indicator. These are given for each service in Table 8.1; they are aggregated in Table 8.4. The (unweighted) mean growth in expenditure for the Labour period was 46 per cent. For the Conservative period it was considerably lower – 13 per cent. On the other hand, the needs indicators grew on average by less for Labour than for the Conservatives. It would appear therefore that the Conservatives at least succeeded in the aim of reducing the growth of public expenditure, if not in that of reducing its absolute level.

Table 8.4 also shows the mean growth rates of welfare state services, those services that have a relatively high proportion of middle-class users and those that have a relatively high proportion of middle-class suppliers. For both governments the growth rate in welfare state services is less than for the total, as is the growth in needs. For the Labour period, mean expenditure growth for the middle-class-user services was 37 per cent, while their needs grew on average by only 3.5 per cent. For the middle-class-supplier services expenditure grew by 24 per cent while needs increased by 4.06 per cent. So while expenditure grew for the former group at a rate of about 80 per cent of the growth rate for the total, needs grew only by approximately a fifth of the average growth for all services in the sample. There is a similar, but less pronounced, tendency among the middle-class-supplier services.

Turning to the Conservative period, we find that the middle-class-user services grew on average by 19 per cent while their needs grew by only 7.5 per cent. Again comparing these mean growth rates to the overall mean appears to confirm an even more pronounced bias towards the middle classes than under the Labour governments. For middle-class-supplier services on the other hand, expenditure grew

Table 8.4   *UK: Mean Growth Rates of Expenditure and Needs (per cent)*

	Expenditure		Needs	
	Lab.	*Con.*	*Lab.*	*Con.*
All services	45.57	13.23	16.26	23.63
Welfare state	33.77	7.34	13.83	19.52
Middle-class (use) services	37.26	18.63	3.49	7.48
Middle-class (supply) services	23.98	7.04	4.06	9.02

Notes: Lab. refers to the period 1973/4–1978/9; Con. refers to the period 1978/9–1983/4. The means are unweighted: see note C to Table 8.1.

by only 7 per cent, while needs grew by 9 per cent, suggesting no strong bias towards these services. These preliminary estimates suggest that our data do not reject the hypothesis that the middle class have been favoured in the growth of government expenditure. The effect appears to be stronger for middle-class use rather than supply and for the Conservatives rather than for Labour.

We now turn to the econometric analysis. The basic equation that was estimated in Le Grand and Winter (1987) was of the following form:

$$DX_i = a_o + a_1 MDU_i + a_2 MDS_i + a_3 DN_i + a_4 DNMDU_i$$
$$+ a_5 DNMDS_i + a_6 DP_i + a_7 DPMDU_i + a_8 DPMDS_i + e_i$$

where:

DX_i is the proportional change in expenditure at constant prices.
MDU_i is a shift variable, 1 if a middle-class-user service, 0 if not.
MDS_i is a shift variable, 1 if a middle-class-supplier service, 0 if not.
DN_i is the proportional change in needs.
DP_i is the proportional change in relative prices.
$DNMDU_i = DN_i \times MDU_i$
$DNMDS_i = DN_i \times MDS_i$
$DPMDU_i = DP_i \times MDU_i$
$DPMDS_i = DP_i \times MDS_i$

$E(e_i) = 0,\ E(e_i e_j) = 0 \quad i \neq j$
$$= \sigma^2 \quad i = j$$

It should be noted that the two middle-class shift variables entered into the specification so that the constant term, the coefficient on the needs variable and the coefficient on the relative price variable can vary with middle-class use or provision.

This equation was estimated, in a variety of forms, for both the Labour and Conservative periods. The detailed results given in Table 8.6, may be thus summarized. Neither the relative price variables nor the middle-class supply shift variables were significant in either period. This suggests that changes in expenditure were not affected by changes in relative prices; and, in opposition to one component of the thesis outlined earlier, there was no significant difference between services with a large proportion of middle-class suppliers and those without. However, while the estimates for the constant term were small and insignificant for Labour, they were negative and significant for the Conservatives. Moreover, the changes in needs variable were significant and positive in each period.

Of particular interest for our hypothesis, the results indicated that each government treats middle-class-user services differently from other services. However, the way in which they did so varied. For Labour, the estimate of the coefficient for *DNMDU* was significant and negative, implying that the Labour Government penalized those services used by the middle classes as their needs for services grew. For the Conservative period, on the other hand, *MDU* was significant and positive, indicating an across-the-board increase in expenditure on middle-class services, independent of any changes in expenditure due to changes in needs.

The implications of these results can be perhaps most easily assimilated by means of the diagrams in Figures 8.1 and 8.2. These plot changes in expenditure against changes in need, and show the regression lines for services with a relatively high middle-class use and those with relatively low middle-class use. The Labour diagram, Figure 8.1, shows that for both types of service there would have been a constant increase in expenditure of about 20 per cent, even without any change in need. However, Labour governments apparently respond differently to changes in needs, depending on whether the users of the service concerned are middle class or not. If they are not middle-class, then expenditure increases proportionately with needs (a unitary needs-elasticity); but if there is a relatively high proportion of middle-class users, expenditure will *fall* as needs increase, as illustrated by the negatively sloped line. If correct, this is inconsistent with the middle-class effect hypothesis, at least so far as that effect is supposed to apply to all governments, regardless of political allegiance.

However, for Conservatives, the picture is rather different (Figure 8.2). In the absence of any changes in needs, there would have been a cut in non-middle-class-user services of nearly 40 per cent. In contrast, there is an across-the-board increase of around 10 per cent for all those services which are used by the middle classes. Also, there is an increase in expenditure due to increases in needs for all services with an elasticity of around 0.8. Thus the results suggest that, *ceteris paribus*, Conservative policy was sharply to cut all non-middle-class

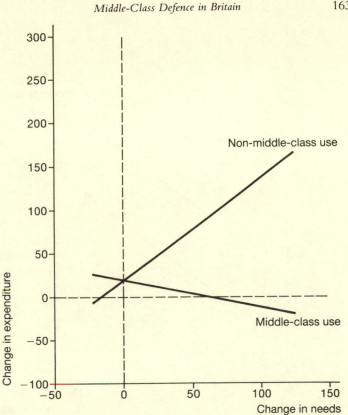

Figure 8.1   *UK: Changes in needs and expenditures, 1973/4–1978/9 (Labour)*

services, slightly (but not significantly) to increase expenditure on middle-class services but to respond similarly to changes in needs for both middle-class and non–middle-class services.

Tests were undertaken to determine how far these results were dependent on the inclusion or exclusion of out-lying observations. These suggested that, while the Conservative results were not sensitive to the exclusion of out-liers, the Labour results broke down when the principal out-liers were excluded. This, coupled with other tests, suggests that the Labour equation may be misspecified.[4] Any conclusions drawn from the results about the Labour period must, therefore, be heavily qualified.

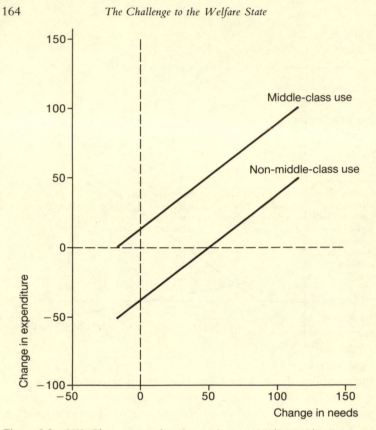

Figure 8.2   *UK: Changes in needs and expenditures, 1978/9–1983/4 (Conservative)*

The estimates were used to perform some counterfactual experiments. First, estimates were obtained of how expenditure would have changed during the Conservative period, if the government had not had the bias in favour of middle-class users. The resulting mean 'growth' in service expenditures is given in Table 8.5 (the second row); in effect, there would have been a cut of 21 per cent in all services, and 24 per cent in welfare state services. Second, the growth rate in service expenditures that would have occurred in the 1980s, if Labour had been in power, was calculated, and is provided in the third row of Table 8.5. It shows that there would have been a mean increase in expenditure of 40 per cent in all services and 37 per cent in welfare state services (compared with actual increases of 13 per cent and 7 per cent respectively).

Table 8.5   *UK: Estimates of Mean Percentage Growth in Expenditure Under Different Counterfactual Assumptions*

	All Services	*Welfare State Services*
Actual Growth	13.23	7.34
No *MDU* effect	− 20.04	− 23.04
	(13.27)	(12.73)
Labour	39.68	36.69
	(8.33)	(6.44)

Note: Standard errors, conditional on the observed mean of *DN*, in brackets. The second row – no *MDU* effect – gives the estimated mean growth rate if the Conservative Government had not favoured middle-class users. The third row – Labour – gives the estimated mean growth if the Conservative Government had behaved according to our estimates for the Labour Governments 1973/4–1978/9. Since these means are not weighted by size of service, care needs to be taken in extrapolating these rates of growth to total government expenditure.

The results given in Table 8.5 should be treated with caution. The fit of none of the estimated equations is very good, so that there is a fair amount of variation in spending on different services that our model does not explain. The standard errors of the mean growth figures are fairly high. Thus the statistics in Table 8.5 do not rule out the possibility that had the Conservatives not favoured middle-class users, the growth in both the all service category and the welfare state services might have been zero. The appearance of greater precision for the Labour estimates in Table 8.5 is misleading since we suspect that the estimated relationships on which they are based are misspecified.

Conclusion

To sum up, the statistical results confirm our view that the Conservative Government was hampered in its policy of reducing state expenditure and state involvement in the economy by its willingness to favour state-provided services that were predominately used by members of the middle classes, and it should be added by the increases in needs during the period. However, the middle–class–supplier effect did not appear to be present in any significant form.

The results for the Labour period are much weaker. We were surprised to discover some evidence for a negative middle-class-user effect for those services where the growth in needs was positive. However, there also seemed to be evidence of misspecification of the model when estimated over the whole Labour sample. Although this largely disappeared when the estimates were confined to the welfare state services, the results did depend on the inclusion of a small number of outlying observations. We feel therefore that we have to be extremely cautious in making inferences from our analysis concerning Labour preferences and policy.

Our results, in other words, suggest two rather different conclusions. First we can assert with a certain amount of confidence that the Conservative Government of 1979–83 favoured government services which were extensively used by the middle classes. This bias conflicted with, and in practice strongly attenuated, other policy goals. To that extent, the basic middle-class hypothesis is supported. Second we find that our analysis leaves tantalizingly open the question of whether the middle classes are sufficiently influential to affect government policy of *both* the major political parties in this period, or whether each political party changed government expenditure to favour those groups in society which might be described as their traditional sources of support. Attempts to provide a resolution of this second problem must await further study.

Appendix

Table 8.6   *Regression Results*

	Labour		Conservative	
	(1)	*(2)*	*(3)*	*(4)*
C	0.147	0.191	−0.481	−0.379
	(0.319)	(0.090)	(0.195)	(0.170)
MDU	0.632	—	0.886	0.509
	(0.474)		(0.253)	(0.176)
MDS	−0.476	—	−0.397	—
	(4.614)		(0.355)	
DN	1.136	1.180	0.759	0.756
	(0.525)	(0.238)	(0.273)	(0.237)
DNMDU	−0.652	−1.492	−0.495	—
	(1.494)	(0.638)	(0.775)	—
DNMDS	−1.634	—	−0.001	—
	(2.370)		(0.685)	—
DP	6.424	—	2.218	—
	(5.841)		(2.432)	—
DPNDU	−17.022	—	−5.226	—
	(10.947)		(3.161)	—
DPMDS	9.395	—	3.441	—
	(90.013)		(3.567)	
n	25	24	26	26
R^2	0.381	0.545	0.486	0.333
s.e.	0.715	0.398	0.341	0.334

Source: Le Grand and Winter (1987). Column (1) gives estimates of the full specification for the Labour sample. Column (2) gives estimates for the Labour sample with the age allowance omitted, and with the indicated coefficients restricted to zero. Column (3) gives estimates for the full Conservative sample; column (4) for the same sample with the indicated coefficients restricted to zero.

Notes

This chapter reports on research undertaken as part of the Welfare State Programme at the Suntory-Toyota International Centre for Economics and Related Disciplines, London School of Economics. We are grateful for comments from A. B. Atkinson, Howard Glennerster, Ray Robinson, Ron Smith and members of the Welfare State Programme Discussion Group.

1 George Will was commenting on the response to the plans by Sir Keith Joseph, then Secretary of State for Education and Science in the Thatcher Government, to reduce grants for students in higher education, in the *International Herald Tribune* of 11 December 1984.

2 'Almost' the first time, because the Conservative government, elected in 1970 under Edward Heath, arguably had intentions that were similar in some respects to, if less extreme than, the 1979 administration.

3 Named after the 1950s Labour leader, Hugh Gaitskell, and the prominent Conservative politician of the same period, R. A. Butler, this 'consensus' consisted of a broad commitment to Keynesian economic policies and to social policies involving both state finance and state provision of social services.

4 In particular, the estimated Labour equations suggested that the error term was heteroscedastic. See Le Grand and Winter (1986) for details.

Chapter 9

The Expansion and Contraction of the American Welfare State

RUSSELL L. HANSON

The American welfare state is exceptional in many respects. Social welfare policies were enacted much later in the US than in other industralized democracies, and on a much smaller scale. Moreover, the American welfare state was, and still is, characterized by the assignment of most social insurance functions to the national government, and the joint provision of public assistance by national, state and local governments. Indeed, the strongly bifurcated organization of the American welfare state may be its most distinguishing feature.

This differentiation reflects the distinctive purposes of social insurance and public assistance, respectively. Insurance programmes are not means tested; they are broadly-based entitlement programmes that benefit all classes, though not equally. Assistance programmes, on the other hand, are means tested, and as such they are targeted on those whose ability to support themselves has been impaired for some reason, and who are impoverished by resulting loss of income. As such, assistance programmes benefit lower classes; even those of modest means are generally not eligible for aid under them.

Thus, social insurance and public assistance serve distinctly different constituencies, and in quite different ways. This manifests itself in the American public's understanding of and attitudes toward social welfare policy. National insurance programmes are held in high esteem, and are politically sacrosanct, as President Reagan discovered after suggesting that it might be necessary to curtail increased spending for Old Age, Survivors, Disability and Health Insurance

(OASDHI) in order to reduce the deficit of the national government. On the other hand, public assistance programmes have long been viewed with suspicion by the general public, and Reagan has successfully aroused public concern over waste, fraud and ineffectiveness in public assistance and translated it into reduced growth in spending for such programmes.[1]

In so doing, Reagan has exploited a chronic weakness of public assistance programmes in the United States. The federal organization of welfare in America makes it especially vulnerable to underfunding by subnational governments. Upon occasion the national government has succeeded in stimulating greater effort by state and local governments, but recent administrations have not shown a strong commitment to income redistribution. As a result, subnational governments, freed from national political pressure and faced with taxpayers' revolts and rising concern over regional economic development, have restricted the scope of public assistance programmes and limited their effectiveness in combating poverty.

At the same time, the national government has expanded social insurance programmes. This combination of expanding insurance and contracting assistance has produced a welfare state that is highly lopsided in favour of middle-class interests. Programmes that benefit the 'haves' are sustained at a high level, while those that redistribute income from 'haves' to 'have-nots' are underfunded. The opposing political dynamics that underlie this development are the subject of this chapter.[2]

The Relative Size of Insurance and Assistance Programmes in the US

As a point of departure, let us compare the budgetary significance of social insurance and public assistance in the United States. Figure 9.1 describes the trends in government expenditures, expressed as a proportion of Gross National Product, for these two kinds of policy over the period 1929–83.[3]

Figure 9.1 illustrates the continuous expansion of so-called 'uncontrollable spending' for entitlement programmes in the US during the postwar era.[4] By 1983, total government outlays for social insurance and public assistance represented 12.6 per cent of Gross National

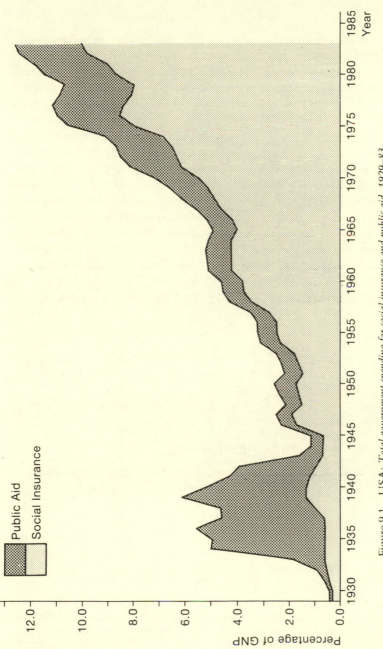

Figure 9.1 USA: *Total government spending for social insurance and public aid, 1929–83*

Public Aid

Social Insurance

Product, and the welfare state had become firmly established in the United States.[5]

Indeed, as of March 1984, fully 46.7 per cent of all families and unrelated individuals received some form of government transfer.[6] The breakdown by type of transfer can be seen from Table 9.1. As this Table clearly shows, the largest proportion of households that receive benefits obtain them from non-means-tested programmes, principally social security (OASDHI). However, nearly one-fifth of all households receive benefits from means-tested programmes (especially Medicaid), and nearly two-thirds of all single-parent, female-headed households do so. This, of course, is precisely that portion of the population most likely to experience poverty.

The most interesting development portrayed in Figure 9.1 concerns the very different fortunes of social insurance and public assistance during the rise of the welfare state in America, particularly

Table 9.1   *USA: Percentage of Households Receiving Benefits, by Source of Benefit*[a]

	All households (%)	*Female households, no husband present, own children under 18 (%)*
Benefits from:		
one or more programmes	46.7	69.8
one or more non-means-tested programme[b]	36.6	21.6
OASDHI or Railroad Pension	28.1	12.4
Unemployment Insurance	3.2	3.1
one or more means-tested programme	19.2	61.7
AFDC	4.6	33.3
SSI	3.4	3.7
Food Stamps	7.7	39.5
School Meals	7.0	39.6
Medicaid	9.1	37.7
Housing Assistance	4.3	17.5

Notes:

[a] Monthly average; First Quarter, 1984.

[b] Includes Social Security, railroad retirement, Medicare, unemployment compensation, workers' compensation, Veterans Administration compensation, Black Lung benefits, state temporary sickness or disability benefits, foster child care and educational assistance.

Source: US Department of Commerce, Bureau of the Census (1985, p. 4).

during the postwar era. Before the war, public assistance was highly significant, partly because of the great need generated by the Depression, and partly because social insurance for the aged was just getting underway. After the war, however, social insurance quickly dwarfed public assistance, at least in fiscal terms, and its subsequent growth is largely responsible for the expansion of the welfare state in America. This reversal in importance bears further scrutiny.

Where social insurance and public assistance are concerned, three distinct comparisons must be noted. The first concerns the *level* of public commitment toward the two kinds of welfare. In fiscal year 1983 all governments spent about $350 billion on social insurance, and about $85 billion on public assistance (including SSI, Food Stamps, AFDC, Medicaid, etc.). Thus, for every dollar spent on assistance for needy families and individuals, four dollars were spent on pensioners and the unemployed. Since the end of the Second World War this ratio has never been closer than 1:2, and since 1960 (when it reached nearly 1:5) it has never been closer than 1:3. In the postwar era social insurance, particularly for retired workers, has alway been substantially more costly than public assistance, though it is almost always the latter that is the target of those who would reduce assistance in order to help balance budgets.

The second comparison involves the *rate of growth* in spending for social insurance and public assistance, respectively. During the 1950s insurance spending grew twice as rapidly as did assistance expenditures, but during most of the 1960s their growth rates were equivalent. By the late 1960s and early 1970s, however, assistance spending increased twice as rapidly as insurance outlays, though this has been nearly reversed again in the 1980s. This quite clearly reflects the budgetary consequences of the so-called 'welfare explosion' of the mid-1960s to early 1970s, which saw rapidly expanding case-loads in public assistance. As we shall see in a later section, this explosion was eventually contained by subnational governments' refusal to make cost-of-living adjustments to means tests and benefit payments, even as insurance payments were indexed to the Consumer Price Index by Congress. Hence the reversal of trends in assistance and insurance in recent years.

The third point of comparison is related to this, as it concerns the *pattern of change* in social welfare spending. Spending for social insurance has expanded more or less continuously over time, although recently the rate of expansion has accelerated as a larger proportion of the population becomes older, and a larger proportion of the elderly population becomes eligible for social security. By contrast, spending for public assistance follows a cyclical pattern, responding both to fluctuations in the business cycle and to larger changes in the underlying bias of the national economy, e.g. the mechanization of agriculture and the subsequent dislocation of the workforce. This suggests that national and federal programmes have quite different dynamic tendencies as a result of their different constituencies and forms of organization. In particular, it may be that federal assistance programmes will not show uniformly expansive tendencies, but will alternately expand and contract as they respond to the underlying rhythms of sociopolitical change.

Not surprisingly, these differences in spending patterns have produced remarkably different results. The sustained commitment of a fairly large proportion of the national product to social insurance has made social security an effective antipoverty programme, as Table 9.2 shows.

Social insurance cash transfers had the greatest impact on poverty, reducing the number of pre-transfer poor by 33.8 per cent in 1982. In

Table 9.2   *USA: Relative Anti-Poverty Effectiveness of Various Transfer Programmes*

| Year | Percentage of pre-transfer poor removed by: | | | |
	Cash social insurance[a]	Cash public assistance[b]	In-kind transfers[c]	All transfers
1965	23.5	3.3	16.4	43.2
1976	37.6	6.2	28.1	71.9
1978	37.6	5.9	NA	NA
1980	35.2	8.5	NA	NA
1982	33.8	3.8	25.8[d]	63.3[d]

Notes:
   [a] Includes Social Security, railroad retirement, unemployment compensation, workers' compensation, government employee pensions and veterans' pensions and compensation.
   [b] Includes AFDC, SSI (OAA, APTD and AB in 1965) and general assistance.
   [c] Includes Medicare, Medicaid, Food Stamps and, for 1976, school lunch and public housing; this figure also adjusts for direct taxes and the underreporting of cash transfers.
   [d] Based on estimate for adjusted income poverty for 1982.
   NA = not available
Source: Danziger *et al.* (1984, p. 8).

fact, this understates the true impact of social insurance, insofar as in-kind transfers associated with insurance, chiefly Medicare, further reduced the poverty rate. It is difficult to estimate this latter impact; column four in Table 9.2 aggregates in-kind transfers from insurance and assistance programmes. However, in 1982 the national government spent over one-and-a-half times as much on Medicare as national, state and local governments together spent on Medicaid. It therefore seems reasonable to attribute much of the reduction in poverty associated with in-kind transfers to social insurance pro-grammes, since medical services comprise the bulk of the value of in-kind transfers.

That is not to say that social security is an efficient way of attacking poverty. In 1982 about half of all Social Security payments went to 'pretransfer nonpoor', i.e., those whose incomes before transfer payments were taken into account was greater than the poverty level. The half that went to pre-transfer poor reduced the poverty rate among the aged by 71.2 per cent (from 50.7 to 14.6) by lifting some 9.3 million of them out of poverty. Furthermore, aged recipients who remained poor after transfers saw the poverty gap substantially reduced (US Congress, House of Representatives, Committee on Ways and Means, 1983).

Thus, social insurance in the United States has enlarged the lower middle-class by raising incomes above the poverty level for a large segment of the population – and a segment of the population that is growing in size and electoral importance. The effectiveness of social insurance in preventing further poverty is remarkable when com-pared to the ineffectiveness of public assistance programmes explicitly intended to address the impoverishment of certain categories of the deserving poor. As Table 9.2 demonstrates, cash public assistance transfers reduced the number of pre-transfer poor by only about 4 per cent in 1982. (It is quite possible that poverty might have been much more common – or much more severe – if assistance pro-grammes had *not* been in place; cf. Harrington, 1984 on this point.)

Of course, the number of poor people eligible for public assistance is much smaller than the number who are covered by social insurance. For that reason alone, we ought to expect public assistance programmes to achieve only modest reductions in aggregate poverty rates; they simply do not reach enough poor people to have the same sort of impact that insurance does. However, even if we restrict our attention to poor people who are the intended beneficiaries of public assistance, the ineffectiveness of these programmes in combating poverty is evident.

Consider Table 9.3, which charts the recent performance of means-tested programmes (including food stamps and housing assistance, but not – unfortunately – Medicaid). The rows in Table 9.3 report the effectiveness of public assistance in elevating poor individuals in families with related children under 18 years of age, and reducing the overall poverty gap for this group. (The poverty gap is simply the amount by which this group's earned income falls short of the poverty line income for the group.)

Quite clearly, means-tested programmes have not removed many

Table 9.3   *USA: Relative Anti-Poverty Effectiveness of Selected Means-Tested Transfers for Pre-Transfer Poor Persons in Families with Children Under 18*

| | Year | | | | | |
	1979	1980	1981	1982	1983	1984
Percentage of pre-transfer poor[a] removed by:						
Cash insurance	13.5	13.1	12.6	12.9	12.7	10.5
Cash assistance (means-tested)	8.3	6.6	5.9	4.3	3.5	4.1
Food and housing assistance (means-tested)	16.5	13.9	11.7	10.1	8.7	9.8
Total for means-tested programmes	24.8	20.5	17.6	14.4	12.2	13.9
Percentage reduction[b] in poverty gap by:						
Cash insurance	19.7	19.7	19.0	17.9	18.2	15.9
Cash assistance (means-tested)	28.7	27.0	25.1	23.5	23.8	25.0
Food and housing assistance (means-tested)	16.9	17.2	16.2	17.2	17.1	17.7
Total for means-tested programmes	45.5	44.2	41.4	40.7	40.8	42.7

Notes:
[a] Calculated on a population that includes pretransfer poor individuals living in families with children under 18, who are the 'targets' of the survivors component of OASDHI, AFDC, portions of SSI, etc.
[b] All based on constant dollar figures, with 1984 as the reference year.
Source: Adapted from US Congress, House of Representatives, Committee on Ways and Means, Staff (1986).

in the target population from poverty, and they are becoming even less proficient at doing so. In 1979, all means-tested transfers raised almost 25 per cent of the pre-transfer poor above the poverty line, but only five years later they were only half as effective. Partly this was because the number of pre-transfer poor increased rapidly during this period, 'swamping' the assistance programme. And partly it was because these programmes were removing absolutely fewer people in later years, as their benefit provisions lagged. The degree to which these programmes fell short of their goal is evident in the fact that the combined efforts of means-tested programmes reduced the poverty gap by less than 50 per cent for the pre-transfer poor, and this percentage, too, was declining.

The ineffectiveness of assistance in combating poverty is almost certainly *not* a result of poor or improper targeting. In 1982, 85.5 per cent of all cash benefits paid under AFDC, SSI and general assistance went to individuals or families whose pre-transfer incomes were below the poverty level. Most of these poor recipients remained poor even after receiving assistance; fully 68 per cent of all such benefits accrued to those whose post-transfer incomes fell below the official poverty line (US Congress House of Representatives, Committee on Ways and Means, 1983).

Of course, this reflects the different histories of benefits for insurance and assistance in the US, particularly insofar as cost-of-living adjustments (COLAs) are concerned. Beginning in 1975 social security benefits were tied by Congress to the Consumer Price Index. Whenever that index shows a 3 per cent or larger increase in the cost of living since the last increase in benefits, a concomitant adjustment of benefits is 'triggered' three months later (although Congress did delay the June 1983 increase until January 1984 amidst concern over the apparent insolvency of the trust fund). As a result, real average monthly benefits for retired workers in the United States are now much higher than they used to be, and the rate of poverty among social security recipients is substantially lower than it would have been in the absence of indexing (Baum and Sjogren, 1983).

Not surprisingly, public assistance payments have not been indexed for inflation, although Congress did consider doing so in 1967 (Rabin, 1970), and a handful of states (e.g. California, Vermont, Washington and Utah) experimented with cost-of-living adjustments from time to time. Most states have not done so, however, and as a result inflation has seriously eroded the purchasing power of those on assistance, so much so that many remain substantially below the poverty threshold even when their transfer payments are taken into account.

Figure 9.2 charts the average benefits per recipient, in real terms, of selected insurance and assistance programmes in the United States.[7] As can be seen, recipients of public assistance do not fare nearly as well as those who receive social security payments. In 1968, OASDHI benefits were increased by 13 per cent, and in 1970 they were increased by another 15 per cent. There then followed increases of 10 per cent in 1971, 20 per cent in 1972 and 11 per cent in 1974, all of which exceeded increases necessary to offset the effects of inflation (Baum and Sjogren, 1983). This accounts for the sharp upturn in average real monthly benefits for retired workers, and when automatic COLAs were implemented in 1975, the gap between OASDHI benefits and those of other transfer programmes continued to widen.[8]

In every respect, then, the expansion of the American welfare state

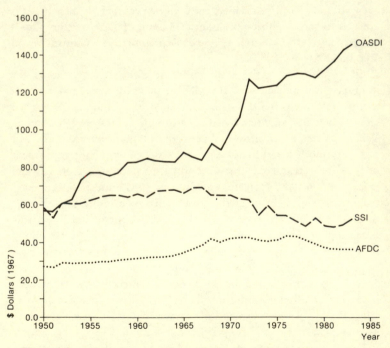

Figure 9.2   USA: Average real monthly benefits in four transfer programmes, 1950–84

has been quite lopsided. Social insurance has increased in scope and generosity, while public assistance has grown sporadically and without substantially reducing the poverty toward which it is directed.

Targeting the Poor

As I noted in the preceding section, social insurance has lifted a sizable number of persons out of poverty, effectively enlarging the size of the middle class. In addition, social insurance has extended benefits to a great many who do not need them; hence it is relatively inefficient, by contrast with programmes explicitly designed to target assistance on the poor.[9]

The enlargement of the lower middle class by social insurance has been augmented, albeit in a minor way, by recent developments in public assistance. As Bawden and Palmer (1984, p. 184) observe, during the past two decades or more 'means-tested programs were broadening their coverage to encompass new population groups. More and more people were receiving multiple benefits, and liberalization of eligibility requirements – in particular, the treatment of earned income – meant that benefits were extending up the income scale toward the middle class.'

To some extent this is the result of extending public assistance to individuals and families not previously eligible for aid. For example, in 1962 Congress added the unemployed parent (UP) programme to AFDC, which gave states the option of extending assistance to intact families in which children were deprived of support because the chief breadwinner was unemployed. By 1983, twenty-three states operated AFDC-UP programmes, including all of the 'big programme' states that together account for the vast majority of all national AFDC cases.[10] However, AFDC-UP cases account for a very small proportion of AFDC caseloads (about 8.5 per cent in the second quarter of 1984), in part because rates of participation by eligible families are extremely low (Hosek, 1978).

In addition, during the mid-1960s access to welfare improved with the relaxation of administrative practices that previously restricted access to public assistance.[11] Piven and Cloward (1971; 1977; 1981) believe that this must be attributed to the mobilizing effects of nationally sponsored antipoverty programmes, which encouraged welfare rights organizations to demand the assistance to which they were entitled. 'Poor people's movements' challenged local elites' use of various gatekeeping rules and regulations, and their success in doing so helped ignite the so-called 'welfare explosion' of the late 1960s (Bell, 1965).

At the same time, benefits were being improved, not so much by increasing cash assistance, as by supplementing cash transfers with in-kind benefits. Taking AFDC as an example again, the 1962 amendments to the Social Security Act made a host of social services available to recipients on the theory that an integrated attack on the culture of poverty was needed. In 1964 the Food Stamp programme was created, and in 1965 Medicaid was established, so that the total value of assistance increased substantially during this period. Albritton (1979a; 1979b) suggests that these expansions better account for the welfare explosion, than the electoral instability and civil disorder emphasized by Piven and Cloward (1979).

With respect to cash benefits only, those receiving AFDC assistance have seen a very modest growth in benefits since 1969, when the well-known 'thirty and one-third' rule for disregarding earned income was implemented. This rule requires administrators to disregard the first thirty dollars of monthly earned income, plus one-third of the remainder, when determining the extent to which a family's own resources are able to satisfy its financial needs. Prior to this time, all income was typically regarded as available, and benefits were reduced accordingly. In effect this levied a dollar for dollar 'tax' on earnings. The thirty and one-third rule was designed to reduce this tax, thereby creating stronger work incentives for those on AFDC.

The immediate effect of this change was to increase average benefits, but the disregard was not subsequently adjusted for inflation, nor could it be invoked by those not on AFDC seeking to become eligible for assistance. Moreover, state policy-makers, who enjoy virtually complete control over public assistance benefit levels, showed great reluctance to increase the standards that were employed to estimate families' financial needs. As Berkman and Hanson (1986) argue, such increases would have made means tests for AFDC much less stringent than they actually were, and would have doubled or even tripled caseloads. Faced with that prospect, policy-makers refused to make cost of living adjustments to the need standards, and thereby prevented a very large number of 'working poor' families from becoming eligible for assistance, cash or otherwise.

It was the working poor, after all, who were most affected by unadjusted means tests. Even those who worked part-time and for low pay were paid in inflated dollars, the nominal value of which easily exceeded means tests established at a time when inflation was low, and the purchasing power of the dollar was still intact. Indeed, because of the high inflation of the late 1970s, a family might see its nominal earnings double, its purchasing power fall, and its benefits terminated. Even more likely, such a family might never become eligible for AFDC in the first place, even though its real income fell dramatically. Not surprisingly, it became increasingly difficult to persuade people that it was in their financial interest to work.[12]

By keeping families off welfare, states and localities were in some cases able to liberalize benefits for those who remained on AFDC, many of whom had no outside income (Hanson, 1983). Even though need standards changed little during the high inflation years of the late 1970s, payments increased as states began to meet need more fully. In most states these increases were not sufficient to offset the effects of inflation, even when income disregards were taken into account, and this probably accounts for the relative ineffectiveness of cash pro-grammes in reducing poverty among groups in need of categorical assistance.

One way of seeing this more clearly is to compute 'entry' and 'exit' points for each state and year. The entry point represents the maximum permissible income *to qualify* for AFDC; a family 'enters' the programme when its income falls below this level (assuming the family satisfies other criteria of eligibility). The exit point is the maximum permissible income *to remain* on AFDC; a family 'exits' from the programme when its countable earned income exceeds this value. (Typically, the exit point is higher than the entry point, so that families on the rolls have an incentive to work.) Together, the entry and exit points define the means tests for a particular state at a given time. The trends for entry and exit points are shown in Figure 9.3, which covers the 1968–84 period.[13]

In 1968, the *average* entry point for all states was 80 per cent of the official poverty level, meaning that families had to be demonstrably poor before they were admitted to AFDC. Indeed, in some states, families did not become eligible until their incomes fell below 50 per cent of the poverty level. By 1981, the average entry point for all states had fallen to 57 per cent of the official poverty level, and in one state it was as low as 26 per cent. Only the decline in the rate of inflation prevented a further fall-off. This reflects the refusal of state

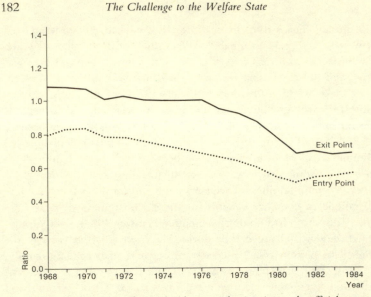

Figure 9.3 *USA: Ratio of annualized entry and exit points to the official poverty threshold, for family of four, 1968–84*

policy-makers to adjust need standards, which define entry points, for increases in the cost of living. The effect was to make means tests much more stringent, i.e. to target assistance ever more tightly on the desperately poor – those with little or no earned income.

On the other hand, in 1968 the *average* exit point for all states stood at 109 per cent of poverty level. It fell to 70 per cent by 1981, but the decline was less precipitous than that for entry points. Then the curve turns upward slightly, because state policy-makers were willing to improve benefits for the 'deserving poor', so long as others with marginally bigger incomes (but no medical benefits) were kept off welfare. At the same time it explains the relative ineffectiveness of AFDC in reducing poverty: because the target population had been red··ced to the desperately poor, it became harder to move them out of poverty without a very substantial commitment of resources.

Such a commitment would have required liberalizing need standards, which effectively 'capped' payments, but that in turn would have broadened the target population and increased caseloads. At the same time, precisely because this would have brought 'upper income' poor people onto public assistance, it might have increased the anti-poverty effectiveness of the programme. Such people were close to the poverty level, and with a little assistance might have climbed over the threshold; instead they lived below the poverty line and above the point of entry to AFDC.

Nor was AFDC the only programme in which means tests became more stringent in real terms. Table 9.4 documents this for other programmes as well.

As the first row of data in Table 9.4 shows, the proportion of population that met demographic criteria of eligibility for public assistance remained about the same throughout most of the 1970s, by which time the effects of statutory expansions of the eligible population had already registered. However, the rate of financial eligibility fell by nearly one-third. The decline was especially sharp for the elderly poor who did not qualify for social security benefits. At the same time, those who were eligible for assistance reported they were participating at higher rates than before. Apparently this offset the

Table 9.4   *USA: Changing Coverage of Public Assistance Programmes, 1970–77*

	Year				
Feature:	1970	1972	1974	1976	1977
Categorical eligibility rate[a]	36%	36%	37%	38%	37%
Financial eligibility rate[b]	47	40	39	34	33
SSI (OAA) only[c]	36	27	24	20	18
SSI (APTD) only	53	48	44	43	42
AFDC only	63	60	58	54	53
Reporting rates[d]	31	38	44	49	50
SSI (OAA) only	26	29	38	44	45
SSI (APTD) only	40	44	52	52	53
AFDC only	36	47	49	53	54

Notes:

[a] Measures the rate at which families or individuals qualify for assistance on the basis of relevant demographic characteristics.

[b] Measures the rate at which those who are categorically eligible pass the relevant means tests for various assistance programmes.

[c] The Supplemental Security Income (SSI) programme combined Old Age Assistance (OAA), Aid to the Blind (AB) and Aid to the Partially and Totally Disabled (APTD) assistance programmes.

[d] Measures the rate at which those who are financially (and hence categorically) eligible report receiving assistance; this measure typically understates the true rate of participation.

Source: Projector and Roen (1982, Tables 66–74).

effects of tighter financial eligibility requirements, since the number of cases on public assistance held fairly steady after 1975. Had means tests been adjusted for inflation, and rates of participation risen as they did, the 'welfare explosion' of the late 1960s and early 1970s might well have continued unabated into the late 1970s and early 1980s (Berkman and Hanson, 1986).

Thus, by not adjusting for inflation, state policy-makers let means tests become meaner over time, and this enabled them to contain the 'welfare explosion'. This did not require a direct assault on welfare, which might have mobilized resistance, and it was in any case necessary in order to satisfy the demands of larger and more active political constituencies. These constituencies were generally unsympathetic or even hostile toward welfare, sometimes because of latent racism (Wright, 1975).

By themselves, anti-welfare sentiments among the masses do not explain elites' reluctance to establish more generous programmes for the deserving poor, however. As we shall see in the next section, it is the federal organization of public assistance programmes that makes them particularly vulnerable to these and other sentiments and calculations. And it is their federal organization that makes funding for these programmes problematic when the economic basis of the welfare state is called into question. Hence the structural vulnerability of public assistance in the US.

Federalism and Welfare

Whereas social insurance programmes in the United States have consistently expanded over time, public assistance programmes have not. Instead, they have been alternately expanded and contracted in a fashion best described by Piven and Cloward (1971). The different dynamics that characterize these two kinds of social welfare policy reflect a number of underlying differences that account for the political invulnerability of social insurance, by comparison with public assistance and its acute susceptibility to policies that shrink or contract financial eligibility. One of the most important underlying differences, of course, is the vastly different constituencies served by each set of programmes.

The political invulnerability of social insurance programmes in general, and social security in particular, stems from the size and mobilization of their clientele. Social security has become nearly universal in scope as a result of amendments to the Social Security Act. Prior to 1954 self-employed persons were not compelled to participate in what was then OASDI, i.e. social security without health insurance, and as a result only about 60 per cent of all civilian jobs were insured under social security. The 1954 amendments included the self-employed, except for certain professionals, e.g. lawyers and physicians, who were eventually included (in 1956 and 1965, respectively). As a result of this and other expansions in coverage, nearly 90 per cent of all civilian jobs are now covered by Social Security, and have been for twenty years.

This, in conjunction with certain demographic trends, ensures a continuing source of beneficiaries for the foreseeable future. The age structure of the population is shifting in favour of seniority, and by the time today's 'baby boom' generation begins to collect social security, one in five Americans may be 65 or older. Furthermore, they can reasonably expect to live longer, and hence collect benefits for a longer period of time. Insofar as present and future beneficiaries have a significant stake in the social security programme they may be expected to defend it against political attack.[14] Senior citizens are to be found in large numbers in every constituency of Congress, and they participate at very high rates, and in difficult ways, e.g. lobbying. They are by all accounts a potent political force.

Finally, the national organization of social security gives political organization a single clear focal point: the Congress. It either makes basic policy decisions or oversees those who do, and it is therefore easy to target political action on key leaders and committee chairmen in Congress in order to influence policy.

In contrast, public assistance programmes are quite vulnerable. The number of affected families and individuals is comparatively small, and the beneficiaries of assistance are also highly concentrated. The five states with the largest AFDC caseloads together account for very nearly half of all national cases. This gives these states a strong interest in relatively liberal national policies; but other states do not share that concern, and in fact may chafe under programmes that consume federal tax revenues raised within their own jurisdictions, and which might be put to other uses.

Nor can poor people count on the support of the working class in defending public assistance programmes. As Korpi (1980, p. 305) argues, marginal social policies, of which public assistance is a prime example, 'split the working class and tend to generate coalitions between better-off workers and the middle class against the lower sections of the working class', because these programmes involve explicit transfers of workers' income to non-workers. 'Marginalistic social policies thus create a large constituency for a welfare backlash. In fact the "welfare backlash" becomes rational political activity for the majority of citizens'.

At a cross-national level, this implies that welfare states that depend primarily on public assistance to redistribute income are much more vulnerable to welfare backlash than are regimes that achieve redistribution through social insurance, which is a far less visible form of transfer connected, however tenuously, to prior contributions (Rosenberry, 1982). Korpi's argument also highlights the peculiar vulnerability of public assistance programmes in any welfare state that combines assistance and insurance programmes. Whereas social insurance encourages the formation of a broad coalition between the middle class and the working class on the basis of a common interest in work-related pensions, public assistance for the truly needy isolates the poor from other groups in society. It stigmatizes them, and it engenders the resentment of those who must pay the costs of these programmes. Hence, programmes that benefit non-contributors are at the mercy of those who contribute, but enjoy no benefits, and who cannot, therefore, be expected to err intuitively on the side of kindness in social welfare policy (Goodin, 1985a).

The specific conditions under which resentment is translated into a political assault on the welfare state in general, and public assistance in particular, are a matter of some dispute. Most agree that a welfare backlash is most likely to occur when economic stagnation makes it increasingly difficult to fund social welfare programmes without raising taxes or sacrificing other popular programmes. Usually, some connection is then drawn between macroeconomic developments and the waxing and waning of support for the welfare state. The United States is often cited as a prime example of this, with the Reagan administration usually being blamed (or credited) with making a successful attack on public assistance programmes in the name of downtrodden taxpayers, especially those in the middle class.

Unfortunately, this example suggests that the resentment of taxpayers toward public assistance is episodic, and only sometimes successful in curtailing this type of transfer. It also ignores the fact that the 'welfare backlash' associated with the Reagan revolution has been only partially successful in reducing entitlement spending. Bawden and Palmer (1984, p. 185) estimate that in fiscal year 1985, actions taken from fiscal year 1982 through fiscal year 1984 reduced outlays for AFDC by 14.3 per cent, whereas the Reagan administration sought reductions of 28.6 per cent. Similarly, the administration wanted to trim Food Stamp outlays by 51.7 per cent, but Congress would only do so by 13.8 per cent. Expenditures for housing assistance were trimmed by 11.4 per cent, whereas cuts of 19.5 per cent had been urged. Child Nutrition was pared by 28 per cent, but that was much less than the 46 per cent reduction proposed by Reagan. Only unemployment insurance was reduced by an amount (17.4 per cent) close to that desired by the President (19.1 per cent).

Hence the Reagan revolution is hardly a confirming instance of the argument initiated by Korpi and extended by Rosenberry, and it may even be a partially disconfirming one. Proponents of income main-tenance and social service programmes were able to deflect, if not defeat, the assault on the welfare state mounted by Ronald Reagan. This was due to the partial mobilization of the beneficiaries of these programmes, including not only the recipients of benefits, but also (and more importantly) non-profit organizations that provide ser-vices in exchange for government payments, as well as federal, state and local employees working in the affected programmes. Benefi-ciaries also enjoyed the support of state and local policymakers, who fear that reductions in national welfare spending will impose heavier, and politically unpopular, burdens on subnational units of govern-ment (Piven and Cloward, 1981).

This coalition of supporters demonstrated its strength in 1981, as its Congressional respresentatives responded to the Reagan administra-tion's deficit reduction proposals. Many of these recommendations aimed to reduce spending for entitlement programmes by narrowing eligibility provisions so as to better target assistance on the truly deserving poor. With respect to AFDC, for example, several pro-posed changes would have made working mothers on welfare ineligible for further assistance by lowering the entry and exit points for AFDC. Thus, the administration argued that no family with a *gross* income of more than 150 per cent should be eligible for AFDC. This meant that many mothers whose earnings were associated with substantial work-related expenses (including child care costs) would no longer be eligible, since their income would no longer be reduced by expenses before eligibility was determined. At the same time, the administration proposed that income disregards, i.e. the 'thirty and one-third rule' previously mentioned, be applied to *net* income, or income after allowable expenses were deducted, and limited to four months in a year. Under this policy, working mothers would begin to lose benefits as their earnings rose, effectively increasing the rate of taxation. The combined changes created a powerful set of work *dis*incentives by devaluing earnings, which were heavily taxed, and which led to an early exit from AFDC – and Medicaid.

Against these changes, the members of the House Ways and Means Committee moved precisely in the opposite direction. In particular, the members of the Public Assistance and Unemployment Insurance Subcommittee rejected the 150 per cent of gross income cap on eligibility, and the limitation of disregards to four months.[15] In fact, they proposed increasing the income disregard to fifty and one-third, which would have *raised* exit points for AFDC. These recommendations were ultimately undone by the machinations surrounding Gramm-Latta II and the passage of an Omnibus Budget Reconciliation Act (OBRA) which bypassed committees altogether, but that, too, demonstrates the dependence of the Reagan revolution upon extraordinary events even for its partial success.

The President's startling victory was implemented by state policy-makers, and only a handful of state legislatures made changes to counteract the effects of changes in AFDC eligibility policy that would exclude working mothers. For example, the legislature in North Carolina more than doubled its need standard so as to insure that working mothers would not be excluded by the new gross-income means test. At the same time, the legislature decided to pay only 50 per cent of its need standard, whereas it had previously met all unmet need, up to the need standard.[16] This produced a nominal $10 per month increase in the state's payment standard and prevented AFDC recipients in North Carolina from reaping a windfall as a result of state efforts to counteract the work disincentives created by OBRA. The annual net cost to the state of raising its need standard and keeping its payment standard nearly even was $615,000 (Joe and Rogers, 1985).

It is not surprising that North Carolina refused to raise AFDC payments by more than $10 per month. What is surprising is that policy-makers there and in seven other states were willing to enact legislation specifically designed to counteract Reagan administration policies for targeting benefits on the truly needy. The reaction of the other forty-two states, which did not specifically raise their need standards in response to the OBRA gross income limit, is far more typical and it is rooted in the very structure of public assistance programmes in the United States. That structure ensures a more or less constant pressure on welfare by taxpayers and their political representatives at a subnational level, where this coalition enjoys its greatest strength – and where the taxpayers' revolts that gave Reagan his electoral majority began.

The arrangement of financing for public assistance is the source of this pressure, as might be expected where taxpayer concerns are of paramount importance. Unlike national insurance programmes, *federal* public assistance programmes, e.g. AFDC, are jointly funded by national and subnational governments. The national government uses general revenues (raised mainly through a more-or-less progressive income tax), to reimburse subnational governments for a portion of the expenses they bear for providing public assistance. The rate of reimbursement by the national government varies from state to state; states with lower than average per capita personal incomes receive proportionately more than states with higher than average incomes.

The share of costs borne by subnational governments in most, but not all, cases falls exclusively on state governments. Some states require county governments to contribute toward the costs of public assistance not covered by the national government. In neither case have policymakers shown a strong inclination to tax citizens at a level that is necessary to support more generous welfare programmes. As a result, the occasional fiscal problems that are thought to underlie welfare backlashes at the national level become a *chronic* condition at the subnational level, a fact that is often overlooked by those who focus exclusively at the national level. When subnational politics are taken into account, however, the anti-tax sentiment that underlies all welfare backlashes comes clearly into view as an ever-present political constraint on public assistance in federal systems.

Evidence of this may be seen in state politicians' historical reluctance to pursue aggressive policies on redistribution, which undoubtedly reflects the political strength of taxpayers in state politics and the concomitant weakness of those who are the principal beneficiaries of transfer programmes. Indeed, the mere anticipation of political retribution by taxpayers is usually sufficient to deter policy-makers from vigorously pursuing redistribution, the more so because the political advantage that might be won by appealing to have-nots is both small and uncertain. Even in competitive two-party states have-nots do not usually participate in large numbers or at high rates in state politics, so that the pursuit of policies that appeal to have-nots may actually result in reduced levels of support for redistribution if it mobilises the haves, who are active in politics, in opposition to progressive taxes and larger social welfare expenditures.

The avoidance of taxation where possible, and the preference for regressive taxes where necessary, is typically justified by the need to improve a state's 'business climate'. All politicians can recite instances in which corporations left their state, or else refused to locate there in the first place, because the state's taxes were ostensibly too high. Furthermore, business groups explicitly link state tax structures and business climates in their lobbying efforts at the legislature – efforts which often include veiled threats of relocation, should tax increases or new taxes be approved. Business publications also rate states on various aspects of their business climates, including tax burdens, and state policy-makers are sensitive to the impact these publications may have on corporate decisions that will affect their state's economic vitality.

It does not seem to matter to state politicians that most studies of corporate location, relocation and investment decisions agree that state (and local) tax rates have only a marginal impact, in comparison to other factors that affect the cost of doing business (and hence the rate of profit) in a state (Vaughan, 1979). Labour costs, energy expenses, proximity to resources and markets, etc., all weigh much more heavily in corporate decisionmaking than considerations of taxes. Nevertheless, state officials *act* as if tax differences are crucial to business climates. In part this may reflect the fact that other, more important, factors are not very susceptible to manipulation by state policy-makers, especially over the politically important short-run. And those factors that might be manipulated are often politically explosive: labour costs can be reduced by state 'right to work' laws and restrictions on workmen's compensation, for example. However, that sort of action is not easily taken in states where high labour costs cloud the business climate, due to the fact that high labour costs are associated with the presence of strong unions. The existence of protective legislation in such states is testimony to the political power of such unions, and most politicians can easily anticipate the reaction from them if those past victories were called into question.

Opposition to redistribution stems not only from a desire to avoid taxes that would be needed to support transfer programmes, but also from the effects such policies have on the cost of an indispensable factor of production – labour. Income assistance programmes, along with unemployment insurance and workmen's compensation, all lead to a higher 'social wage' that increases the security of workers (Bluestone and Harrison, 1982, p. 133). This enables workers to extract higher wages from their employers, as well as greater involvement in corporate decision-making, because the existence of safety nets reduces the risks to workers should they lose a confrontation with management, or so the theory goes. Consequently, high social wages are associated with higher private wages, and that has a direct and significant impact on profit margins, especially where wage bills constitute a large share of production costs.

The concerns of the business community intersect neatly with those of taxpaying citizens, as far as many state and local policymakers are concerned. A sustained policy of low taxes provides the basis for a potent appeal for electoral support from influential constituencies, and even liberal policy-makers have been forced to follow suit in order to survive against conservative opponents and candidates from 'T Parties' – taxpayer parties.[17] However, a necessary result of this pervasive orientation is that state (and local) governments, which are required to balance their budgets, operate under severe revenue constraints: they simply cannot raise enough money to fund the broad array of public services that citizens have come to expect.

Under these circumstances, the unwillingness of state and local governments to support public assistance programmes is not difficult to understand. When resources are scarce, as they chronically are at the subnational level, policymakers first satisfy the demands of their largest and most insistent constituencies long before they concern themselves with the needs of unpopular and inactive constituencies like the poor and needy. This neglect of public assistance is easily carried out by simply not adjusting means tests for inflation; a simple non-decision, or failure to act, is all that is required in order to bring welfare expenditures under control. Neither the wrath of taxpayers nor the reaction of recipients to highly visible purges of the welfare rolls need be risked by any politician eager to follow the path of least political resistance.

That many state and local policymakers do so cannot be disputed. As I showed in the preceding section, means tests for public assistance programmes like AFDC have become much more stringent in the last decade, due to the failure to link public assistance payments to a price index. Substantial outlays for the needy have therefore been avoided at a time when taxpayer revolts and business climate considerations dominate state and local political agendas. The evidence therefore suggests that taxpaying citizens and corporations mounted a successful attack on public assistance long before Reagan assumed the Presidency, and that Reagan's own marginally successful efforts to dismantle the welfare state understate the extent to which the welfare backlash has become a structural feature of the American welfare state. The main channels by which taxpayer influence is translated into policies hostile toward public assistance are to be found at the subnational, not the national level of analysis.

The Efficiency and Effectiveness of Welfare Policy

The unwillingness of state and local policy-makers to commit a substantial share of resources to public assistance programmes seems to confirm the opinion of those who assert that redistribution must be accomplished by a central authority. Musgrave (1959), Musgrave and Musgrave (1977), and Oates (1968) claim that this function can be performed efficiently only by the national level of government because it is only at that level that the degree of economic immobility is sufficiently high as to eliminate the possibility of capital and taxpayer flight. When such policies are initiated at a subnational level, on the other hand, the mobility of taxpayers and recipients undermines their effectiveness.

Thus, the activities of subnational governments tend to be chronically underfunded, particularly in the area of social welfare policy. Means-tested programmes therefore tend to suffer from grossly inadequate means. They are simply unable to remove many people from poverty because they lack the resources that are necessary to close decisively or eliminate the poverty gap, the deficit between need and income. This occurs despite the fact that means-tested programmes are highly efficient, and have become more so over time. They devote few resources to those who are not poor, thereby concentrating their effect on the poorest of the poor.

Indeed, the efficiency of public assistance programmes in the United States has probably worked *against* their effectiveness, at least as measured by their success in removing people from poverty. That efficiency is a product of means tests that in real terms have actually grown more, not less, stringent over the past decade, thereby narrowing the target population deemed worthy of assistance. This has left a sizable number of people in limbo – their incomes are too high to qualify for assistance, but too low to escape from poverty. Under looser means tests these people would have become eligible for small amounts of assistance that might well have enabled them to cross the threshold of poverty, which in turn would have enhanced elite and mass perceptions of the effectiveness of antipoverty programmes.

These not-quite-desperately-poor people represent the 'easy' cases that might be aided by assistance programmes. Strict means tests exclude them from assistance, leaving the 'hard' cases of desperately poor people on the public rolls. The latter's needs are surely great, and probably ought to be met first, but at the same time their satisfaction demands an extraordinarily large commitment of public resources. That commitment has not been forthcoming, and as a result means-tested programmes have failed on two counts. They have not helped the marginally poor to escape from poverty, and they have only made slightly less desperate the plight of very poor people, without removing them from poverty.

Non-means-tested programmes, by contrast, have been effective, but inefficient. Since they do not explicitly target the needy, a good portion of their benefits go to those who are not in need of aid. However, simply by virtue of their extensive national funding, they succeed in rescuing many people from poverty. They succeed in spite of their inefficiency, while assistance programmes 'fail' despite their great efficiency.

Without adequate funding, not even efficient anti-poverty programmes can be effective. Yet the federal structure of public assistance in the United States virtually ensures that middle-class demands for efficiency and economy in the administration of welfare result in programmes that are only marginally effective in reducing poverty. The apparent failure of these programmes then invites new demands for efficiency and economy, further undermining the anti-poverty effectiveness of public assistance, and perpetuating a system that satisfies no one, but penalises only the poor. That is the irony of the American welfare state.

Notes

This research is part of a larger endeavour financed by the Ford Foundation's Project on Social Welfare Policy and the American Future. The interpretations presented herein are my own, although I draw on the findings of Berkman and Hanson (1986). I thank Julian Le Grand and Robert Goodin for their helpful editorial suggestions.

1   There is a further ambivalence concerning public assistance in the US. Public opinion polls have consistently shown that a majority of citizens favour assistance for the 'deserving poor', but they are highly critical of specific programmes that do just that. Ronald Reagan has successfully capitalized on this by emphasizing the ineffectiveness of these programmes.

2   The American welfare state is highly differentiated, and each aspect of it has its own political dynamic. The following cross-classification distinguishes the major social welfare programmes according to the type of transfer involved, and the nature and structure of the programme by which the transfer is effected:

Types of Transfer Policies

	Cash	In-Kind
Insurance		
National	OASDI	Medicare
Federal	UI	
Subnational	WC	
Assistance		
National	SSI, FAP	Food Stamps
Federal	AFDC	Medicaid
Subnational	GA	HCFI

Key: OASDI = Old Age, Survivors, Disability Insurance
       UI = Unemployment Insurance
       WC = Workman's Compensation (pre-1935)
       SSI = Supplemental Security Income
       AFDC = Aid to Families with Dependent Children
       GA = General Assistance
       HCFI = Health Care for Indigents
       FAP = Family Assistance Plan (proposed)

SSI was nationalized by 1972 amendments with effect from 1974. However, states may elect to supplement benefits beyond those established at the national level, and a number do so. Determination of eligibility and benefits, as well as actual payments, are made by the Social Security Administration, which is reimbursed by states paying supplementary benefits.

As will become evident, this chapter emphasizes the differences between national and federal cash transfer programmes. I neglect entirely social expenditures for education, transportation and local infrastructure, as well as national government involvement in primary and secondary mortgage markets, etc., which make it financially possible for a large segment of the middle class to move to the suburbs. Such programmes have clear redistributive consequences, but do not fall under the heading of transfer programmes. Neither do I consider private transfers; see Lampman (1984) for an accounting scheme that encompasses comprehensive changes in income transfers in the US from 1950–78.

3   The data on social welfare spending are from Merriam and Skolnick (1968, pp. 189–90), Skolnick and Dales, 1970, p. 5; 1977, p. 5), McMillan (1979, p. 4) and Bixby (1983, p. 10; 1986, p. 14). Data on GNP are from US Council of Economic Advisors (1985, p. 232).

'Social insurance' includes all governments' expenditures for Old-age, Survivors, Disability and Health insurance, railroad retirement, public employee retirement, unemployment insurance and workers' compensation. 'Aid' includes all governments' expenditures for Aid to Families with Dependent Children (Aid to Dependent Children in earlier years); Old Age Assistance, Aid to the Blind, Aid to the Partially and Totally Disabled (Supplemental Security Income in later years); Medicaid and Health Care for the Indigent; and General Assistance.

4   I have not included housing assistance in the expenditures on public assistance becasue there is no social insurance analogue, as there is for medical treatment. However, the following table compares expenditures for need-tested housing assistance programmes with an estimate of the costs of permitting homeowners (who are overwhelmingly middle class) to deduct mortgage interest and property taxes from their federal income taxes.

Relative Value of Various Housing Benefits

Year	Cost of public housing assistance ($ billion)	Amount of homeowner tax expenditure ($ billion)	Ratio
1975	2.1	9.9	.21
1976	2.5	8.9	.28
1977	3.0	8.7	.35
1978	3.7	13.1	.28
1979	4.4	17.5	.25
1980	5.5	22.2	.25
1981	6.9	28.1	.25
1982	(8.5)	(35.5)	(.24)
1983	(10.0)	(41.8)	(.24)
1984	(11.8)	(49.4)	(.24)
1985	(13.7)	(58.3)	(.24)
1986	(15.4)	(68.8)	(.22)

Source: Dolbeare (1981, p. 9). Figures in brackets are projections.

Of course, the middle class is not the only beneficiary of tax expenditures. As Witte (1983) demonstrates, almost all income classes receive some form of special tax treatment, though those who earn the most, and hence pay the most taxes, receive the most preferential treatment under any criterion of equity. Over all tax expenditures, the middle class is a net loser, i.e. it pays more than it gets, again under any criterion of equity. The poor receive more in value from tax expenditures than they pay in taxes, but get less than their share of income would otherwise entitle them to receive.

5   In 1983, half of all households received transfers. Transfers accounted for half of the gross income of recipient households, and about one-seventh of aggregate disposable personal income in the US in that year.

6   Despite the extensive reliance on transfers, the United States lagged behind other industrial democracies in terms of its commitment to social welfare spending, reflecting the relatively small size of its public sector. The overall size of the public sector in the US in 1983, measured by computing current expenditures for goods and services, plus transfer payments, represented about 36.9% per cent of GDP, less than the United Kingdom's 44.3 per cent, West Germany's 44.4 per cent, France's 48.6 per cent, and far less than Sweden's 61.3 per cent; see OECD (1985). The same basic pattern holds when only transfer payments are considered. They account for roughly half of the aforementioned expenditures, although the extent to which the United States lags is reduced somewhat when only transfers are considered.

7   The benefits charted in Figure 9.2 are, respectively, the averages for retired workers under OASDHI, aged recipients of SSI, AFDC recipients, and workers on unemployment compensation or insurance. The data for AFDC, OASDI retired workers and SSI are from the US Department of Health and Human Services (1984–5, p. 234), and for unemployment from various issues of the *Social Security Bulletin*.

8   The recent deterioration of SSI benefits may also reflect this. Critics of federal assistance have long argued that benefits would be equalized and enhanced under *national* programmes. However, the partial nationalization of SSI in 1974, which combined Old Age Assistance, Aid to the Blind, and Aid to the Partially and Totally Disabled into the Supplemental Security Income programme, has not produced better benefits, as Figure 9.2 plainly shows, although that may change now that SSI has been indexed for inflation.

9   According to the Census Bureau, almost a third of all social security benefits go to households with an annual income in excess of $30,000. Some 130,000 households with incomes greater than $75,000 receive benefits.

10   During the early years of the AFDC-UP programme, many states shifted cases from general assistance, which was wholly funded by state and local governments, to AFDC-UP, which was heavily subsidized by the national government (Piven and Cloward, 1971).

Steiner (1966; 1971; 1981) provides an excellent account of the broader political history of public assistance, of which the 1962 amendments are only a part. Oellerich and Garfinkel (1983) compare the merits of alternative child support systems, concluding that the present system (which relies heavily on AFDC and its support mechanisms) is nearly as bad as no system at all in reducing poverty, and would be only marginally better even if the collection of child support from absent parents was completely effective.

11   Of course, once this pressure from above weakened, as it did under Reagan, state and local administrators were once again free to practice what Lipsky (1984) and Brodkin and Lipsky (1983) call 'bureaucratic disentitlement'. On the general importance of administrative 'gatekeeping' in public welfare, see also Krefetz (1976), Nelson (1976), and Prottas (1979).

12   This is reflected in the declining number of AFDC families with outside earnings. As inflation rose, so did outside earnings, albeit at a slower rate. The number of families with outside earnings declined as those with modest earnings began to 'exit' under unadjusted means tests.

Workers on Welfare

| Year | Percentage of families in which mother had earnings | Mother's average monthly earnings[a] | |
		Nominal $	Real $[b]
1967	13.4	135.43	135.43
1969	13.7	175.86	155.77
1971	13.7	221.25	179.73
1973	14.4	257.78	186.12
1975	13.7	304.00	182.80
1977	12.3	332.04	178.42
1979	12.2	383.00	167.18
1982	5.3	261.00	87.58
1983	4.9	237.00	78.09

Notes:
[a] For mothers of families on AFDC.
[b] 1967 = 100.
Through 1979, data are from individual surveys designed to measure recipient characteristics from agency case files. For 1982 and 1983 data are drawn from quality control case samples, and some of the differences may reflect differences in these two kinds of samples.
Source: US DHEW Social and Rehabilitation Service (1970a, Tables 99 and 100; 1970b, Tables 61 and 62; 1972, Tables 56 and 57; 1975, Tables S–7 and 14; 1978, Tables 8 and 11), US DHHS Social Security Administration (1980, Tables 8 and 10; 1972, Tables 8 and 10) and US Congress House of Representatives, Committee on Ways and Means, Staff, (1986, Table 22).

13   For any state at a given time, the entry point is equal to its need standard; families with incomes larger than this ostensibly do not need assistance, and hence do not qualify for AFDC. The exit point is a function of a

state's payment standard; families with incomes that are (after disregards) larger than the payment standard exit from AFDC, that is, they receive no benefits. The payment standard is a proportion of the difference between need and income in some states, and in others it equals a proportion of need, less income. Maximum payment limitations also apply in many states. See Berkman and Hanson (1986) for other details.

14   The recent liberalization of tax laws *vis-à-vis* private pension annuities may reduce the overall importance of public pensions for retirement incomes. In the long run, that may have a dramatic impact on the degree of political support that is enjoyed by social security, since it is now estimated that roughly twenty-five million Americans have independent retirement annuities (IRAs) alone.

   Loyalty to social security may also be shaken in the future by the nature of the intergenerational transfer of income from young to old. Current retirees now receive far more than they contributed, mainly because current workers are forced to make increasingly large contributions. Upon their retirement, most of these same workers can also expect to receive benefits in excess of their contribution, but the difference will not be nearly as great as now, and it will decline over time. Furthermore, some workers, e.g. unmarried males and unmarried females with large incomes, will receive less than the taxes they paid into the system (Pellechio and Goodfellow, 1983). Fractures in the coalition that supports social insurance could conceivably emerge as this problem intensifies.

15   On the subcommittee, four Republicans (three from the Sunbelt) and one conservative Democrat (Ken Hance from west Texas) were overpowered by six liberal Democrats, four of them from urban industrial centres in the Frostbelt. The six were Fortney H. Stark, chairman of the subcommittee, from the Oakland Bay area; William Brodhead, from the northwest section of the Detroit metropolitan area; Marty Russo, from south Chicago and suburbs; Don Pease, from a district just west of Cleveland; Robert Matsui, from Sacramento; and Don Bailey, from east of Pittsburgh. Their respective Americans for Democratic Action (ADA) scores in 1980 were 94, 94, 50, 83, 94, 50 (100 is the most liberal). The conservatives included Hance; L. A. Bafalis, from south Florida; John Rousselot, San Marino and the John Birch Society; William Gradison, east Cincinnati; and W. Henson Moore, Baton Rouge. Their respective ADA scores were 11, 6, 11, 22 and 11.

   The liberal Democrats clearly represented constituencies in states with large and relatively generous AFDC programmes, while the conservatives came from states (or, in the cases of Rousselot and Gradison, Congressional districts within states) where anti-welfare sentiment has always been strong.

16   For a three-person family, the monthly need standard was raised from $192 to $404. Without that change, any family with a monthly gross income of more than $288 (i.e., 150 per cent of $192) would have been ineligible under OBRA; with the change, any family with an income

less than $607 (or 150 per cent of $404) passed this part of the means test. Under the old standard, the actual payment for a family with no outside income was 100 per cent of $192, or $192 per month. Under the new standard, the payment was 50% of $404, or $202 per month (Joe and Rogers, 1985).

17 In the late 1970s, when the Liberal Party in New York called for a 25 per cent increase in monthly public assistance grants, Mayor Koch called upon the state government to absorb the full cost of this change, so that the city of New York would not have to use its own resources to fund it. Democratic Governor Hugh Carey, in turn, agreed to support the measure only if the national government would pick up the entire cost. While affirming his commitment to the deserving poor, Carey explained that a welfare increase was not politically feasible, if borne by the state, because of the need to 'complete the revision of our personal income tax structure that has proven to be a disincentive for economic development'.

Thus, even would-be liberals have been forced to advocate economic development policies that inevitably squeeze public assistance spending by constraining revenues and intensifying the demands of powerful constituencies to be served best by a state's budget.

PART FIVE

Conclusion

Chapter 10

Not Only the Poor

ROBERT E. GOODIN and JULIAN LE GRAND

The broad outlines of the structure built in the preceding chapters should by now be unmistakable. They are:

- the non-poor benefit extensively from the welfare state;
- this has arisen in part because their interests were directly served by the setting up of certain 'universalist' programmes and in part because they have infiltrated programmes originally designed for the benefit of the poor;
- they will defend those parts of the welfare state from which they see themselves as benefiting or likely to benefit, while supporting reductions in those parts from which they do not.

The relevant points recur time and again. Historically, the post-war spurt of growth in welfare state expenditures can be traced to wartime uncertainties, which both poor and non-poor shared (Chapter 3). In the United States, through 'spillovers' of benefits from programmes designed solely to aid the poor, the non-poor as a group seem to recoup fully half of the increased taxes they pay to finance these programmes (Chapter 4). In their day-to-day operations, most of the British 'universalist' social services – education, health, the complex of housing policies, public transport – favour the better off (Chapter 5). In Australia the non-poor make welfare programmes serve their own ends, regardless of means tests or barriers of distance (Chapter 6 and 7). Finally, when under threat, welfare programmes benefiting the non-poor are the least likely to feel the pinch. In Britain, the Conservative Government of Mrs Thatcher has been significantly more generous in its treatment of social programmes characterized by predominantly middle-class beneficiaries than in its treatment of programmes used predominantly by the poor (Chapter 8). In the United States, social insurance programmes – non-means-tested and thus enjoying a broad base of both poor and non-poor beneficiaries – have continued to flourish under the Reagan administration's cutbacks, while the means test for social assistance programmes targeted tightly on the poor has grown progressively meaner (Chapter 9).

Such a consistent pattern of findings constitutes powerful support for our initial hypothesis about the 'beneficial involvement' of the non-poor in the operations of the welfare state. True, we have not conducted a systematic survey of all social programmes in the countries we have examined, much less all the countries of the world. And, true, each of the preceding chapters approaches the problem from a slightly different angle, each employing its own slightly different methodology and emphases. In some obvious respects, that weakens the findings. In other equally obvious respects, it strengthens them. Convergence on similar conclusions from so many different angles, with respect to so many aspects of policy, lends more credibility to the conclusions than could be derived from a more tightly integrated inquiry into some small subset of the policy universe.

That the non-poor are beneficially involved in universalist social welfare programmes is no great surprise. Even the fact that they may benefit *more* than the poor from such programmes is a point that has been made by several writers, including supporters of the welfare state such as Abel-Smith (1958), Titmuss (1968) and Le Grand (1982b), as well as critics such as Stigler (1970) and Friedman and Friedman (1980). What these writers did not discuss in any detail were explanations for the phenomenon. Here, the foregoing chapters provide some of the missing causal links.

Being better educated, the non-poor are better at manipulating complex bureaucratic rules to their advantage. Having more private resources (such as cars and telephones) and more flexible working hours allows them to take better advantage of services that are officially universally available to all alike (Chapters 5 and 7). Even when programmes are notionally targeted on the poor, the non-poor may still be the incidental beneficiaries of tendencies for bureaucracies to grow and for boundaries of 'need' to be ever-expanding. In addition, the middle classes are collectively politically powerful and individually adept at arranging their affairs so as to make themselves appear 'poor' within the terms of any particular programme's means test, both of which might lead to heavy non-poor participation in programmes designed to benefit 'only the poor'. On evidence from Australia, anyway, it is the last of these – individual behavioural responses – that seem most important in accounting for non-poor participation in means-tested programmes (Chapter 6).

These findings, too, are tentative. Much more work might profitably be done on each of these issues, in different locales, using different methodologies, to study different programmes and in different periods. Such work would surely lead to important elaborations and modifications of these results. Still, the basic pattern of the present findings seems to be fairly conclusive. Let us, for now, just take that basic pattern as given.

The questions that then arise are those – deferred from Chapter 1 – of evaluation and reform. Is the beneficial involvement of the non-poor in the operations of the welfare state inevitable? We conclude, in the argument that follows, that it probably is. Is it, then, necessarily undesirable? That, we show in the subsequent section, all depends on your goals. If they are egalitarian, the beneficial involvement of the non-poor will, on at least one defensible counterfactual, necessarily frustrate them; but if they are merely the reduction of poverty and the securing of some minimal standards for all, then beneficial involvement is not (necessarily) a bad thing. Finally, if the beneficial involvement of the non-poor in the welfare state is thought undesirable (i.e. if the goals are egalitarian ones), but is nonetheless considered inevitable, is there anything that can be done to achieve the aim of greater equality? We suggest, in the penultimate section, the focus of the policy should be on measures that would lead to a more acceptable primary income distribution, rather than counting upon institutions like the welfare state to produce a more acceptable secondary distribution. Let us take these three broad questions in turn.

Is it Inevitable?

Perhaps it is best to turn this question inside out. The only way to say conclusively that the beneficial involvement of the non-poor in the welfare state is *not* inevitable would be to try to demonstrate some mechanism by which it could be overcome. Trying to find some such mechanism and failing does not, in itself, prove that one does not exist. Neither, in Popper's terms, does trying to falsify a hypothesis and failing to do so prove, in itself, that the hypothesis is verified. But the more often and the harder you try, and still fail, the more reason you have to believe the hypothesis to be true. Hence the failure of all the obvious mechanisms for guaranteeing the exclusion of the non-poor – if such failure can be established – will rather tend to suggest the inevitablity of their beneficial involvement in the welfare state.

BAD SERVICE

One sure way – perhaps the only sure way – to guarantee that the non-poor will not partake of a service is to make it a bad service. If quality is low, or the conditions of use are disagreeable, or there is some stigma attaching to usage, then the middle classes might be put off using the service. This was the logic of the old principle of 'less eligibility', whereby the non-needy were discouraged from relying on poor relief; say of it whatever else one will, there can be no denying that it worked, for that purpose at least. A similar principle may presently be at work to discourage the middle classes from using British council housing.

There are, of course, a great many things to be said against such a strategy. One is that it is stigmatizing and socially divisive. Of course, in part, this may be precisely what is intended; and, for those who harbour precisely such intentions this will not constitute an objection – or, anyway, not a decisive one.

Instead, let us consider an objection that will have to be accepted as a telling one, even by those who do not mind stigmatizing people. The crux of the objection here in view is that, with the 'bad service' strategy, you are giving with one hand and taking back with the other. That is to say, you are making sure of a larger proportion of the goods being allocated going to the poor by, in effect, allocating fewer goods. Worse goods are, obviously, less good – i.e. the equivalent of fewer goods of greater quality. Even just in terms of the value of redistribution, then, it is an open question whether more will be gained by distributing fewer goods in a way that targets more tightly on the poor, or by distributing more goods in a way that targets less tightly on the poor.[1]

TIGHTER MEANS–TESTING

It may well be that Australians are just plain perverse. Judging, however, from the evidence of Chapter 6, it would seem to be the case that even fairly rigorously means-tested programmes tend to attract an increasingly middle-class clientele over time, as people find a way around the means test. Of course, it may be that we have just not hit on precisely the right formula for the means test yet. But, as with the quest for the Holy Grail, the more we seek and fail to find the Perfect Formula, the less likely it is that there is one ever to be found. At the very least, it is by now clear that the Perfect Formula if it exists will be a finely-balanced affair, and hence would be likely to get out of adjustment fairly easily.

The only moderately promising strategy for means testing grows out of (but is not necessarily confined to) proposals for integrating welfare means tests with the most elaborate assessment of them all: the income tax. Instead of filling out a separate form, people could claim welfare benefits merely upon presentation of their tax returns. One variation on that basic theme is the negative income tax. Another is the proposal to impose 'user fees' based on ability-to-pay as judged through tax returns. In such a scheme, people might be allowed to use a service free of charge at point of provision, but later be charged for it on their tax return if they can afford to pay. This idea grows out of Crosland's (1956, p. 145) distinction, discussed in Chapter 1, between the 'universal availability' of a service and its 'universal *free* availability'; and it emerges in its most worked-out form in proposals for a 'graduate tax' (discussed in Chapter 5); clawing back some of the increased earnings an individual receives thanks to higher education from a surcharge on his subsequent taxes.[2]

Of course it is true that people might fiddle their taxes, just as they might misreport income and assets on specifically social-security means tests. But we have a fair bit of practice in detecting tax cheats, and an experienced bureaucracy is already in place for handling such problems. Partly in consequence, there is a well-established pattern of voluntary compliance with tax laws requiring full reporting of income and wealth. Incentives to misrepresent in either direction (especially when the same return would do double-duty in the social security office) tend to be so complex that most people are likely to throw up their hands, cease trying to calculate an advantageous fiddle, and report honestly. Furthermore, no stigma attaches to filing a tax return, as it does to filing a means or assets test at the social security office.

The obvious advantage of this approach is that, assuming the tax rate is reasonably progressive, the rich will be charged much more for the same service than the non-rich, and the poor will pay less or nothing at all. Any perverse redistributive effect (poor to non-poor) growing out of the tendency of the non-poor to be beneficially involved in the welfare state is thereby cancelled.

There are, however, likely to be political difficulties. Once we start imposing 'user fees', and in that way putting the operations of the welfare state on a 'proper economic basis', it will be difficult to block a move toward assessing everyone the same fee: anything else amounts to 'price discrimination', and runs contradictory to the market ethos. It is one thing to ask 'what is the economic cost of providing this service?' It is quite another to ask, 'how progressive should our rate structure be in assessing charges for it?' The politically adept middle classes will endeavour to ensure that the former is taken to provide the answer to the latter, so that any user fee that is assessed will be uniform across all income classes, thus seriously compromising the redistributive aims of the reform.

GEOGRAPHICAL TARGETING

One further strategy, discussed in Chapters 5 and 7 above, is to decentralize publicly-provided services. There is some evidence that such a strategy could work – British nursery schools, for example, seem to be utilized about equally by all social classes perhaps in part because they were initially sited in predominantly working-class neighbourhoods (Chapter 5).

But while such a strategy can work, it will work only under very special circumstances. Since, as was argued in Chapter 7, distance disadvantages (indeed, differentially disadvantages) poor users, a service that is *perfectly evenly* dispersed throughout the community will still attract rather more middle-class than poor users. Only if the poor cluster tightly together in their neighbourhoods, while the non-poor are dispersed widely and live on average very far from poor neighbourhoods, would this strategy of geographical targeting begin to pay substantial redistributional dividends.

RESISTANCE TO TARGETING

A considerable difficulty with both increased means-testing and geographical dispersion concerns the middle classes' attitudes towards such targeting. The problems encountered by successive British governments in redistributing health care resources from the relatively well-endowed South to the poorly-served North, mentioned in Chapter 5, illustrate how much opposition can be generated by attempts to redistribute within an already existing programme. The fact that, as illustrated in Chapters 8 and 9, the middle classes will fight vigorously any cuts in programmes that already benefit them bodes ill for attempts seriously to improve targeting in existing programmes – particularly in times of slow or negative economic growth when improving the services available to the poor will inevitably involve reducing those available to the better off.

Nor is the situation much better in the case of new programmes. The Australian evidence indicates programmes that initially are heavily targeted on the poor, but that have the potential of benefiting the non-poor, inevitably will end up doing so. On the other hand, programmes from which the middle classes do not perceive themselves as benefiting or likely to benefit are systematically contracted (Chapters 8 and 9), thus reducing the involvement of the poor in the welfare state and (relatively) increasing the beneficial involvement of the non-poor.

We conclude, therefore, that some measure of non-poor beneficial involvement in the welfare state is probably inevitable. But this is only of consequence if it is also undesirable; it is this question we must now consider.

Is it Undesirable?

In assessing whether this apparently inevitable beneficial involvement of the non-poor in the welfare state is actually undesirable, we need to distinguish between two sorts of considerations: pragmatic and principled. Those terms are intended to be descriptive, not judgemental. Low politics is contrasted with high principle. But in marking that distinction, we are not meaning to imply that the latter has any necessary moral priority over the former. On the contrary, 'ought implies can'. Judgements about what it is desirable for us to do must necessarily be powerfully constrained by judgements about what we can and cannot do. Pragmatic considerations can, where they are relevant, be as decisively determinative of moral judgements as can moral principles themselves. Our argument for largely ignoring them here is not that they are in any way inferior considerations in general, but merely that there is no good reason for thinking them particularly relevant in these particular circumstances.

PRAGMATIC POLITICAL CONSIDERATIONS

As a matter of purely pragmatic politics, there seems to be one argument for welcoming the beneficial involvement of the non-poor in the welfare state and one argument for opposing it. The argument for opposing it is just that, in a world of competing political claims and crowded legislative agendas, there are only so many programmes in any given category that we can realistically hope to enact; and 'genuinely redistributive' measures might, in this way, have been crowded out by the enactment of policies that, although ostensibly redistributive, turn out to be largely of benefit to the middle classes.

That argument begs a lot of questions, of course. One is that there is some fixed number of programmes that can get enacted in any given policy area in any given period; another is that there really are some 'genuinely redistributive' measures available to be enacted; yet another is that the same coalitions that enacted the schemes of sham-redistribution would have opted for those genuinely redistributive ones. All of those propositions are contentious, to be sure. But all of them at least have a certain surface plausibility about them.

The political argument for, conversely, welcoming 'beneficial involvement' turns basically on the so-called 'sharp elbows' of the middle classes. The idea here is that if the middle classes benefit from programmes, then they will use their not inconsiderable political skills to obtain more resources for those programmes or to defend them in periods of decline. As a result, the welfare programmes will be better funded – and the poor better off, in consequence – than they would have been had the middle classes not been beneficially involved.

In its simplest form, the argument is not very persuasive. There is no guarantee that the sharp elbows of the middle class will be used, on a programme-by-programme basis, to further the interests of those parts of the welfare state that help the poor exclusively. Indeed, the evidence of Chapters 8 and 9 suggests rather the reverse: that middle-class pressure results in the maintenance or expansion of the middle-class services, while the services for the poor are contracted. Only insofar as the poor benefit from middle-class service will they benefit from the middle classes' beneficial involvement in the welfare state through the political pressure that this generates.

A more sophisticated, whole-system, version of the argument turns on questions of counterfactuals introduced in Chapter 2 above. When asking, 'Is the beneficial involvement of the non-poor in the welfare state desirable?', we must always, implicitly, ask further, 'Compared to what?' Certainly a welfare state without beneficial involvement of the non-poor is better, on redistributive grounds, than one with it. But what if that is not the alternative that is truly available? What if the only real choice is between a welfare state with beneficial involvement of the non-poor and no welfare state at all? Then, on those selfsame redistributive grounds, a welfare state with beneficial involvement of the non-poor may be preferred – especially if it is financed by progressive taxation. Comparisons between the distribution of 'original' income (income from private sources) and the distribution of 'final' income (income after taxes and public expenditure benefits have been taken into account) show that, for most countries with developed welfare states, the latter is more equal than the former (see, e.g., O'Higgins, 1985, for the UK and Pechman, 1985, for the US). Hence, if the current welfare state (even with its beneficial involvement of non-poor) did not exist or was abolished tomorrow, the distribution of income might revert to something close to its 'original', less equal form. Chapter 2 discusses some technical objections to this line of argument – notably, that the distribution of original income is not independent of the distribution of final income. However, it is unlikely that taking this dependence into account would blunt the point significantly.

This is certainly an argument to be taken seriously. But essentially it resolves itself into an argument about what the options really are. Those who defend the beneficial involvement of the non-poor on these grounds are claiming that the welfare state would collapse altogether if the non-poor were denied its benefits.

By their very nature, claims about counterfactuals (i.e., contrary-to-fact conditionals) can never be tested directly, because the conditions they specify have not actually occurred. We can, however, try to make a reasoned choice among the available counterfactual hypotheses on the basis of more general theories of human behaviour derived from other realms.

Those who defend the beneficial involvement of the middle classes in the welfare state say that if denied its benefits, they will deny it their support – support that is politically crucial. That presupposes, first, that the political support of the middle classes is crucial for the continuation of the programmes and, second, that the middle classes will support social institutions only if they derive direct, immediate benefits from them.

As regards that first presupposition, we are inclined to agree (on the basis of the evidence from Chapter 3) that middle-class support probably is crucial for the initial establishment of a programme. But once established, bureaucratic inertia may well take over and sustain a programme even after the initial conditions of its creation have passed. Students of public administration say that programmes – and still more, agencies – tend to be virtually immortal (Kaufman, 1976). And students of welfare state expenditures say, similarly, that one of the best predictors of expenditures is the age of the programmes (Cutright, 1965; Jackman, 1975). There is also evidence in Chapter 3 of just this phenomenon: having been greatly expanded in response to the pervasive uncertainties surrounding the war, the welfare state survived in expanded form even after those uncertainties resolved themselves. More recently, there is also evidence from Scandinavia that welfare states built up in times of economic boom are substantially defended from cutbacks in times of economic stagnation by entrenched bureaucratic interests (Johansen and Kolberg, 1985). Of course, bureaucrats will be *more* effective in defending their programmes if those programmes also serve middle-class interests and have middle-class lobbies behind them: that is the finding of Chapters 8 and 9 above. But even those programmes serving clienteles composed of poor people exclusively have far from disappeared – even under the extraordinary assaults from the Reagan and Thatcher governments. Hence it seems that middle-class support may not be nearly so politically essential for sustaining a programme as for its initial enactment.

As regards the second presupposition, there is much evidence (in this book and elsewhere) to suggest that the great majority of people will indeed support social institutions only if they derive direct, immediate benefits from them. But there is much evidence that people will also lend their support to social institutions whose benefits to them are more indirect, long-term or uncertain. The family is, perhaps, the most obvious example. But even the police can qualify: how often do you call a constable for direct, immediate assistance, after all? The upshot of this argument is that the middle classes may support the welfare state even if they were precluded from realising any direct, immediate benefits from it.

Furthermore, there is another perfectly tenable theory of human behaviour that would tell even more powerfully in that direction. There is evidence – ranging from Titmuss's (1971) study of blood donation to Merton's (1946) study of war bond drives (see generally Goodin, 1982a, ch. 6) – that people will support a moral cause if but only if it is unambigously and indisputably moralistic. If the welfare state were *purely* a matter of helping those less well-off than themselves, then, paradoxically, the non-poor might support it even more strongly than if it were partly of benefit to themselves as well.

None of this is conclusive of course. It is in the nature of counterfactuals that it cannot be. But on balance there seems to be as much – or as little – evidence for supposing that the real alternative to a welfare state with the beneficial involvement of the non-poor is a welfare state without it as there is for supposing that the real alternative is no welfare state at all.

DIFFERENT PRINCIPLES, DIFFERENT CONCLUSIONS

Leaving pragmatic politics to one side and turning to matters of high principle, there seems to be one quite wrongheaded argument saying the beneficial involvement of the non-poor in the welfare state is not at all undesirable, and two persuasive but quite distinct moral principles saying that it is.

Let us first dispose of the fallacious argument in defence of beneficial involvement. This builds on the apparently innocuous principle of equity that 'he who benefits should pay' and, conversely, 'he who pays should benefit'. Since the non-poor pay more in taxes toward welfare-state services, it is perfectly reasonable on those grounds that they should benefit more from the services. Or so the argument goes.

A particular version of this argument concerns the life-cycle redistributive function of the welfare state discussed in Chapter 1. In particular, if the aim of the welfare state is to redistribute income over the life-cycle, and if the average non-poor individual pays more in welfare taxes over his or her life-cycle than the average poor one, then it could be claimed that they should receive more by way of benefit.

It may be of course very difficult in practice to implement this rule. As pointed out in Chapter 2 above, in a world where most public expenditure (welfare and non-welfare) is financed out of general taxation and borrowing, it is impossible to determine who in fact does pay for the welfare state. However, even leaving that to one side, there is another more profound objection to this defence of beneficial involvement.

The argument employs an altogether too narrow understanding of 'equity', and indeed of redistribution. On that account, there would be nothing wrong – nothing inequitable, even – in enormous (even unearned) differentials in income and wealth between the rich and the poor. On that account, equity just amounts to getting what you pay for, and paying for what you get. Any attempt at redistribution between persons is thereby ruled out – and, perversely, it is ruled out on grounds that it is inequitable. That is certainly not how we ordinarily understand the concept of 'equity'. There surely is some place, in ordinary understandings of the notions, for the concept of 'vertical equity'.

Neither does that principle mesh well with our ordinary understandings of what the welfare state is supposed to do. As was discussed in Chapter 1, it is, among other things, officially meant to produce redistribution between persons (either as an end in itself, or as a means to some other goal). Those who defend the beneficial involvement of the non-poor in the welfare state on the grounds that 'he who pays should benefit' present that as a principle for the equitable administration of the welfare state. In truth, it is nothing of the kind. It is an argument against interpersonal redistribution. On that principle, the state should not subsidize and redistribute; instead, it should, wherever possible, charge for public services directly, strictly on the basis of marginal cost.

Having dismissed that fraudulently principled defence of the beneficial involvement of the non-poor in the welfare state, let us next consider the two quite distinct moral principles that might motivate objections to the phenomenon. Both of these are variations on what we have, in Chapter 1, called the 'redistributive goal' of the welfare state. But for present purposes the differences between those two varieties of redistributivist goal turn out really to matter. The strength of our objections to the beneficial involvement of the non-poor in the welfare state – and the reform strategies that we adopt for meeting those objections – will vary, depending on which of these versions of redistributivist principles our objections are based.

The first reason we might have for wanting welfare benefits to go to the poor and only the poor might be that we embrace an ideal of meeting *minimum standards* (as discussed in Chapter 1), but that we want to realize that ideal at minimum cost. The goal in this case is *least-cost* poverty reduction.

That, in effect, is to say we actually have two distinct goals. One is to lift people out of poverty – to put them above the 'minimum standards' threshold, wherever that is set. The other is to do so at least cost – to commit as few resources to the project as possible. It is only the latter goal that is directly foiled by the non-poor's benefiting from welfare state programmes.[3] The more of the programme's benefits that go to the non-poor, the more resources that will have to be pumped into the programme to make sure that enough eventually get to the poor to lift them above the poverty line.

The second reason we might have for wanting welfare-state benefits to go to the poor and only the poor might be that our ideal is an *egalitarian* one. We want to achieve greater equality between poor and non-poor in their command over resources.

This goal, too, could be coupled with a least cost requirement; that is, the aim could be one of achieving a given measure of equality with the minimum resources devoted to the project, or, more generally, at minimum cost in terms of the attainment of other policy objectives. On these grounds, it may once again be argued that the beneficial involvement of the non-poor is simply wasteful, in the sense that it squanders resources that could have been better used on other projects (or, indeed, that could have been given to the poor, and thereby have created greater equality).

In egalitarian terms, however, the beneficial involvement of the non-poor in the welfare state is not merely wasteful – it is actually counterproductive. The more the non-poor benefit, the less the redistributive (or, hence, egalitarian) the impact of the welfare state will be. How counterproductive beneficial involvement is, in egalitarian terms, depends of course upon what the alternatives to beneficial involvement are. As discussed above, it will be very deeply counterproductive indeed if the alternative is thought to be giving all the money directly to the poor rather than sharing it out among poor and non-poor alike. For those who suppose the alternative is not to have a welfare state at all, far from being counterproductive, beneficial involvement has actually done as much as is politically possible in our society to promote equality.

Notice the important difference in the character – and the strength – of each of these objections to the beneficial involvement of the non-poor in the welfare state. On the second, egalitarian argument it may actually be counterproductive; on the first, poverty-reduction argument, it is merely wasteful. On the second argument, the only cure for any counterproductive beneficial involvement of the non-poor in the welfare state is this involvement's elimination; and, while a partial cure is always better than none at all, the egalitarian's end in view must always be its total elimination. On the first argument, there are various alternatives to excluding the non-poor from the pro-grammes. Conspicuous among them would be simply pumping more money into the programmes. Which of these alternatives is to be favoured depends only on which is least wasteful.

To evoke this contrast in a striking way, suppose that the only really effective means test for a particular welfare programme were to install a television camera in every room of beneficiaries' houses, so that all aspects of their life-styles could be monitored perfectly. Suppose this particular form of monitoring were 100 per cent accurate. Suppose further that the next-best means test is considerably cheaper but only 50 per cent accurate, and furthermore that all its errors are 'false positives', i.e. calling people 'poor' when they are really not. Using this means test, then, half the benefits would go to the non-poor.

So long as the costs in terms of loss of privacy and expenditure of resources were not too great, egalitarians would prefer the first scheme to the second. This is true no matter whether the egalitarians are concerned with absolute or proportional differences between people (see Chapter 1). The absolute difference between poor and non-poor beneficiaries of the programme is unchanged, assuming they both receive the same benefits. So even if, *ex hypothesi*, all the poor but only some of the non-poor receive the benefits, the reduction in the absolute difference between the poor as a whole and the non-poor as a whole will be less under the second scheme than under the first, which awards benefits only to the poor. Much the same is true on the proportional-difference test: giving some of the non-poor the same benefits as the poor (as under scheme two) makes less of a contribution towards reducing the proportional difference between poor and non-poor than would a programme of giving benefits only to the poor (scheme one).

Those concerned principally with the reduction of poverty, wanting only to achieve minimal standards of living for all at least cost to society overall, would judge matters differently. They would take firm note of the exorbitant costs of all those television cameras. Even if all questions of privacy were set aside, they would oppose the television surveillance programme on the grounds that it would be simply cheaper to eliminate poverty by allocating all that money that would be spent on cameras to people who, on the less accurate means test, appear to be poor. The fact that the results would be less egalitarian is not their concern. The point, as they see it, is to eliminate poverty cheaply. Hence they would rank the second scheme above the first.

If that example seems fanciful, consider another that is all too real. There is a fair bit of evidence that the distribution of income and wealth *within* families might be almost as inegalitarian as the distribution *between* households. At the very least, there is no good reason just to assume that non-working wives share their husbands' incomes and wealth on anything like equal terms with their spouses (Edwards, 1984; Pahl, 1983; 1985; Piachaud, 1982). Unfortunately, however, we cannot identify poor members of non-poor families at all accurately at present. The means test is, in that respect, highly imperfect.

One response to that situation – the response that would be favoured by egalitarians – would be to mount a major effort to perfect the means test, so that transfers could be made to those who are poor and only to those who are poor. Another response would be to abandon any efforts at means testing at all, and just pay universalist Family or Child Benefits through some administrative mechanism (e.g. distribution through the local sub-post-office during ordinary business hours) that in effect ensures that they end up in the pockets of the poorer, non-working members of households. Those benefits are universalistic, going to both poor and non-poor; and they do less to reduce interpersonal inequality than tightly-targeted benefits would do, in consequence. But if our concern is primarily with reducing poverty and making sure everyone achieves certain minimum standards, then targeting might simply not be worth the cost. From that perspective, there would be nothing fundamentally wrong with 'erring on the side of kindness' (Goodin, 1985a), and paying benefits to some people who do not strictly need them, if that is the least-cost way of guaranteeing that they reach everyone who does need them.

The upshot of these arguments, then, is that whether or not you think the beneficial involvement of the non-poor in the welfare state is undesirable depends on what you suppose the goals of the welfare state to be. If the goal in view is an egalitarian one, then the beneficial involvement is likely to be undesirable. Assuming that the same monies spent on programmes benefiting the non-poor would alternatively have been available to be spent on programmes benefiting the poor exclusively, the more the non-poor benefit, the less redistributive or egalitarian the impact of those programmes will necessarily be. If the goal in view is reducing poverty or guaranteeing everyone minimum standards, however, then the objection to beneficial involvement is not nearly so strong. The most that can be said against the non-poor's benefiting from welfare programmes is, in these terms, that it is wasteful. But if weeding out non-poor beneficiaries is even more costly, then we should in these terms be prepared to accept that level of wastage in pursuit of our poverty-reduction goals.

Alternatives to the Welfare State

Insofar as the aim is ensuring minimum standards and the reduction of poverty, the welfare state might not be such a bad mechanism even though there is, apparently inevitably, heavy beneficial involvement of the non-poor within it. Insofar as the aim is an egalitarian one, however, that beneficial involvement is probably a damning critique. If that is the goal in view, then some other mechanism will have to be sought for accomplishing it.

POLITICAL STRATEGIES

One standard strategy here would be to look for mechanisms to increase the *political* leverage of the poor relative to that of the non-poor (Stephens, 1979; Korpi, 1980; Furniss and Mitchell, 1984; Esping-Andersen, 1985). There is no denying that the middle classes possess enormous political skills and resources, that the poor lack them, or that this differential political power makes an important difference in determining the distributional impact of the welfare state.

Still, attempts to change that distributional impact of the welfare state by changing that balance of political power are likely to prove futile. In part, the poor are weak politically *because* they are weak economically: money is power, both in politics and in markets. And in part, the poor are weak politically *for the same reasons* that they are weak economically: the same social skills and educational and other resources that differentially advantage the non-poor in the one arena differentially advantage them in the other as well. All that makes it highly unlikely that the poor will make any great political strides until they first have made some considerable economic advances. And insofar as that is true, it is idle to recommend that they attempt to make those economic advances through political action designed to make the welfare state more redistributive.

A wide variety of cross-national political research bears out these skeptical conclusions. It is, of course, a familiar hypothesis that the welfare state grows, politically, out of mass democracy. Expansion of the franchise expanded the political power of the lower classes, which in turn led to increased programmes of transfers from rich to poor. Thus, J. S. Mill predicted that the 1832 Reform Bill in Britain would bring in its wake a revolution that would 'exterminate every person in Great Britain and Ireland who has £500 a year' or more (quoted in Hewitt, 1977, p. 451). There is much in the historical record that apparently substantiates this 'simple democratic' hypothesis, linking economic redistribution to political democratization. Most recently, for example, Flora and Alber (1981) have found that growth in social insurance programmes in Western Europe over the past century correlates remarkably well with extensions of the political franchise. But those linkages are more apparent than real, judging from a variety of other cross-national research: once we take into account other variables relating to the level of economic development as well, the link between democratization and redistribution disappears. Studying a variety of different countries, in a variety of different periods, using a variety of different operationalizations, Cutright (1965), Jackman (1975, ch. 4), Wilensky (1975, ch. 2) and Hewitt (1977) all come to this same conclusion.

An important variation on the 'simple democratic' hypothesis would be the 'social democratic' hypothesis. The central idea here is that redistributive policies follow not merely from the fact of the poor's having been given the vote, but from the way in which they then go on to use their votes. Redistributive policies will emerge if, and to a large extent only if, the poor cast their votes for parties of the left that then go on to win government and that then stay in government long enough to make real changes. There is more evidence in support of this hypothesis than the other. The amount of time that labour parties have spent in government in the postwar era does seem to correlate both with social security expenditures and with reductions in inequality (Hewitt, 1977; Dryzek, 1978; Esping-Andersen, 1985, Table 2).

Against the 'social democratic' hypothesis, it must be said that, although the bottom line is as it predicts, there is precious little evidence of the sorts of linkages that it claims to be at work producing those results. Neither the share of the vote going to parties of the left in the postwar era nor the proportion of the workforce unionized in the postwar era has any significant effect on social security spending, taken as a percentage of GDP (Esping-Andersen, 1985, Table 2). The levels of both those variables in the *interwar* period do seem to influence postwar spending levels, suggesting that perhaps predicted links are at work but with a very long lead time. But if the lead time is all that long, then the 'social democratic' hypothesis does not seem to be pointing to anything that can constitute a very effective reform strategy in the here and now.

Furthermore, and perhaps most damaging to the 'social democratic' hypothesis, there is the often unexamined question of whether it is the political wing or the economic wing of the organized labour movement that is doing the work in the model. Jackman's (1975, p. 133) findings suggest that when both factors are entered into a formal model of the process, the labour-party variable seems to fade away as an independent influence on social security expenditures. Labour union strength leads both to socialist-party strength and to redistribution. Any apparent relationship between socialist-party strength and redistribution proves to be almost wholly spurious, in Jackman's (1975) data set, at least.

Finally, studies showing correlations between labour movement mobilization and increases in overall social security expenditures mask important distinctions as to *which* programmes the extra expenditures go on. So far as the beneficial involvement of the non-poor in the welfare state is concerned, the differences clearly matter: social insurance programmes tend to favour the non-poor much more than programmes of social assistance; public subsidies of transport or higher education tend to favour the non-poor much more than expenditures on public housing.

There seem to be good reasons for supposing that, *prima facie*, the political power of organized labour is unlikely to be used to benefit the latter. The political brief of organized labour is, after all, to defend workers and their dependents; given that brief, they might reasonably be expected to use their political power principally in defence of people (or dependents of people) who are, at least intermittently, in the labour force. The problem of poverty is most acute, however, for those who, for one reason or another, stand outside the labour market altogether.

Such evidence as there is offers only weak support, if any at all, for the supposition that organised labour might use its political power to promote programmes of benefit principally to people who are not attached, either directly or indirectly, to the labour market. One way to address this question is to look at the extent to which a state works through 'occupationally exclusive' programmes of pensions or insurance – programmes which, by their very nature, are limited to participants in the labour market. To capture this, Esping-Andersen (1985, p. 239) constructs a 'corporatism' variable that constitutes an 'average of the number of occupationally separate social-insurance schemes across three programmes: pensions, unemployment, and sickness'. A truly redistributive state should try to break these down; and if organized labour is truly redistributive, we should see a negative correlation between measures of labour movement mobilisation and this measure of corporatism. Yet Esping-Andersen (1985, Table 7) finds no correlation at all between the breakdown of these occupationally-specific insurance schemes and either (1) percentage of the workforce unionised or (2) percentage of the vote going for parties of the left, and there is only a very weak correlation with (3) the strength of left-wing parties in governing coalitions.[4]

Of even more importance to the concerns of this book with beneficial involvement of the non-poor, it seems that when in power parties of the left generally promote universalistic programmes. These, by their nature, tend towards more beneficial involvement of the non-poor. Esping-Andersen's (1985, Tables 2 and 3) eighteen-nation study, once again, shows that, while left-wing participation in governing coalitions tends strongly towards increasing social security expenditures as a percentage of GDP, the bulk of that extra expenditure goes on universalistic programmes rather than on programmes targeted on the poor. The correlation between means-tested public assistance as a percentage of social security expenditure in 1974 and left-wing participation in governing coalitions 1950–76 is a whopping $r = -0.674$ ($f = -3.54$).

This finding runs slightly counter to the suggestion, emerging out of Chapter 8 above, that the British Labour Government in the 1970s tended to be more responsive to increasing needs for programmes benefiting the poor than in ones benefiting the non-poor. Perhaps that government was simply unusual in that respect; or perhaps the subsequent statistical warning signals were right to suggest that the equations yielding those conclusions (unlike those concerning the Thatcher Government) were unsound from the start.

The general run of findings, cross-nationally, seems reasonably clear. The political power of organized labour is unlikely to be used in such a way as to reduce substantially the beneficial involvement of the non-poor in the welfare state. Increasing its political power is not, in general, a very promising strategy for fully satisfying the redistributivist goals of egalitarians.

ECONOMIC STRATEGIES

Perhaps a more promising strategy would be economic rather than political. The basic idea here would be to move away from fiscal transfers, and toward measures that would produce desirable effects directly upon the 'primary' income distribution.

> We may look upon social security as a system of secondary income distribution, a system which is different in its distributive principles and primary objectives from the economy's functional income distribution. Functional income payments go to employed factors of production. They perform their productive function when they attract and allocate these factors in accordance with economic efficiency. Income from social security, on the other hand, is oriented, at least in the first instance, to the needs of its beneficiaries rather than the requirements of the production process. Social security payments go chiefly to totally or partially unemployed and unemployable persons, in other words, persons who are in the main separated from productive activity. (Rimlinger, 1961, pp. 105–6)

Thus, the welfare state works on an undesirable primary income distribution that the market throws up, and tries to remedy it in certain respects through fiscal transfers of one sort or another.[5] But it is surely more straightforward (and indeed easier, economically if not necessarily politically) to adopt the less back-handed strategy of intervening directly in the market to try to make sure that it produces the right income distribution in the first place (Atkinson, 1983).

There are a variety of practical policy measures that that might entail. One would be a full employment policy. Another would be a capital-transfer scheme, ensuring that everyone had the capital required to make the sort of functional contribution that the primary income distribution rewards; this might come most dramatically in the form of a poll grant – an allocation of a capital sum to each member of the population, perhaps on reaching maturity – or less dramatically in the form of public investments in 'human capital' through health and education services. Another policy for fixing the primary income distribution would be to remove barriers to otherwise employable people's working by, for example, legislating against discrimination on the basis of sex, race, religion or handicap, or by requiring employers to provide on-site child-minding services. Still another such policy would be to legislate minimum wages.

All such policies would make a relatively more direct contribution to the redistributivist-cum-egalitarian goal than the welfare state's *post hoc* patching up of the secondary income distribution. There are, of course, other values (in many cases, efficiency) that they may offend against. And, of course, those inefficiencies may ultimately end up harming the poor, thereby undermining our egalitarian intentions: less-than-minimum pay is better, and more egalitarian, than no pay, if these two really are the only viable options. Still, for those more concerned with equality than with minimum standards, those surely are the right sort of strategies to investigate.

It is beyond the scope of this book to attempt anything like a complete assessment of the advantages and disadvantages of such strategies. Indeed, such a task would require a book all its own. There is, however, one question that arises directly from this book's basic concerns that must be addressed here: that is, what political obstacles might the middle classes throw in the way of their implementation? Specifically, what grounds might there be for supposing that attempts at intervening in the *primary* income distribution should attract any less resistance from the non-poor than attempts to alter the *secondary* distribution have been shown to suffer?

One answer concerns the way that the existence of a secondary distributional mechanism might undermine political support for policies altering the primary distribution itself. As has been argued elsewhere (Le Grand, 1982b, chapter 8), the fact that there is a welfare state that is allegedly engaging in substantial redistribution reduces the pressure for intervention at the primary level. There is less pressure for full employment policies, for example, in the 1980s than in the 1930s because unemployment benefit is thought to ensure that the unemployed will not suffer too greatly from their joblessness.

How, exactly, we might garner middle-class political support for primary distribution policies is unclear. Various partial answers are readily available. One has to do with something akin to the 'tax illusion': people's objections to primary distribution policies like minimum wages might be less strenuous because it is less clear that they are transfer policies; there is no 'tax' formally assessed against the non-poor to pay for those policies in quite the same way there is in the case of 'the dole', although of course the effect ultimately is much the same. Another partial answer has to do with the distinction (discussed in Chapter 1) that people seem to find intuitively clear and ethically compelling between policies aiming at 'equalization of outcomes' and 'equalization of opportunities or access': by appealing to the latter, more popular principle, policies designed to alter the primary income distribution might win more support.

Ultimately, however, the greatest source of political strength of primary distribution policies might derive from the fact that the middle classes suppose that they might ultimately benefit from them. What is at stake in primary distributions is the basic structure of society; and basic structures, like political constitutions, are enduring features that are hard to manipulate in response to ephemeral circumstances. When asked what basic structure they want their society to have for the indefinite future, people must reflect upon what that future might hold for them. And the evidence suggests that that may be very uncertain indeed: Duncan's (1984) findings in *Years of Poverty, Years of Plenty*, for example, find that one in four Americans lived in households receiving welfare payments in at least one year in the decade straddling the 1970s and 1980s. Thus, the same sort of uncertainty that led people to choose social welfare programmes during the war (as seen in Chapter 3 above) would, perhaps, lead people to favour a more egalitarian primary distribution.

Significantly, once policies correcting the primary distribution get established, they will be more easily sustainable than policies aimed at producing a more acceptable secondary distribution. This is for two reasons. First, the non-poor do not have the same sorts of incentives to 'infiltrate' programmes aimed at the primary distribution than ones aimed at the secondary one. The way such infiltration worked in Chapter 6 above was through the non-poor changing their behaviour so as to appear poor, and hence entitled to benefits under the secondary distribution, according to primary-distribution criteria. There is no analogous way for them to manipulate their affairs to benefit illicitly from many of the primary distribution policies. The only way to benefit from a minimum wage law is not one that would tempt those who would not otherwise be among the poor.

Second, interventions in the primary distribution are likely to be more self-sustaining because they 'empower' the poor politically. As argued above, political power is part derives from economic power; the richer people are, the more and the more effectively they participate politically (Goodin and Dryzek, 1980). Primary distribution policies, by giving more economic resources to those who would otherwise be poor, give them more political resources, too. Secondary distribution policies, on the other hand, often as we have seen benefit the non-poor and thus aid them in maintaining their economic and political hegemony.

Conclusion

Thus we conclude that the beneficial involvement of the non-poor in the welfare state is probably inevitable. Whether or not it is also undesirable – from a redistributivist point of view – depends in part upon what you regard the real alternative to it to be, and in part on which version of the redistributivist ideal you embrace.

For those who suppose that there would be no welfare state at all, or only a very much diminished one, if the non-poor were denied its benefits, beneficial involvement of the non-poor is no bad thing. It would, by them, be regarded as the necessary price to be paid for having the welfare state at all, even in its present flawed form. And from the redistributivist point of view, it would be a price that would indeed be worth paying just so long as the tax-transfer system on balance shifts resources from the non-poor to the poor. That the welfare state is less redistributive than it might be were the non-poor excluded from its benefits is, from this perspective, irrelevant: that is just not an option.

The question, of course, is merely whether that is true. Is the only alternative to a welfare state whose redistributive objectives are compromised by beneficial involvement of the non-poor really no (or virtually no) welfare state at all? Counterfactuals, by their nature, can never be proven. But we find this conjecture implausible. We prefer to assume that much (though not necessarily all) the same resources would be available from much the same sources to fund programmes benefiting the poor exclusively as are presently available for programmes benefiting poor and non-poor alike.

Just how undesirable beneficial involvement of the non-poor in the welfare state is then depends upon which version of the redistributivist ideal you embrace. For those principally concerned to alleviate poverty and ensure minimal standards for all, beneficial involvement is merely wasteful. Naturally, less waste is better than more waste – especially where some of the forms that the 'waste' might take might ultimately turn out to harm the very poor we are trying to help. But the objection to 'mere waste' is only a fairly feeble protest. 'Mere waste' is something that, in many circumstances, poverty-alleviaters might find that they could live with fairly happily.

For those favouring more deeply egalitarian versions of the redistributivist ideal, beneficial involvement of the non-poor is a more serious matter. Given a fixed set of resources to be devoted to the task of reducing inequality, the best way to do that is to give all the resources to the poor and only to the poor. Sharing them with the non-poor as well will only reduce the egalitarian impact of the policy – assuming, of course, that it really is the same set of resources that would be available for distribution, either way.

Given the apparent inevitability of the beneficial involvement of the non-poor in the welfare state, there is little scope for egalitarian-redistributivists who are thus offended by it to eliminate it through any simple reforms to the welfare state. Instead of looking for any such reformed way to patch up the secondary income distribution in ways they would find more congenial, egalitarians should instead be looking at methods of correcting the primary income distribution. There are many independently attractive proposals along those lines. It is those that we ought now be investigating.

Notes

We gratefully acknowledge the comments of John Dryzek, Bob Haveman, John Hills and Des King on earlier drafts of this chapter.

1   The answer depends in part on whether the redistributivist's concern is with 'equality' or just 'minimum standards' (see Chapter 1). In terms of 'equality', the bad-service strategy might have something to be said for it; in 'minimum-standards' terms, it has very little.

2   Just as in the case of National Insurance, this programme would have to be made compulsory if adverse selection is to be avoided: otherwise, those students with above-average expected future incomes would opt for taking out a bank loan instead. We are indebted to John Hills for this point.

3   Indirectly, of course, the former may ultimately be foiled as well, if higher marginal tax rates lead to greater work disincentives that ultimately rebound to the disadvantage of the poor. But that is a trebly 'iffy' proposition, and any one of those 'ifs' may in the end fail to materialize.

4   Moreover, that relationship is more significant ($r = -0.476$, $t = -2.16$) for the influence of 1918–49 coalition participation on 1955 corporatism, but much less so ($r = -0.329$, $t = -1.39$) for 1950–76 coalition participation on 1979 programmes (Esping-Andersen, 1985, Table 7).

5   In a mixed economy, of course, the primary income distribution is determined not just by the market but also by bargaining power and political interventions of various sorts. But for reasons given above, it seems unlikely that we will be able to change any of *that* in ways that would produce any very much more redistributive outcomes.

About the Authors

Robert E. Goodin is a Reader in Government at the University of Essex specializing in problems of political theory, both normative and empirical. He serves as an Associate Editor of the journal *Ethics* and as Co-Editor of the *British Journal of Political Science*. He has authored, most recently, books on *Political Theory and Public Policy*, on *Protecting the Vulnerable,* and on *Reasons for Welfare*.

Julian Le Grand is a Senior Research Fellow at the Suntory–Toyota International Centre for Economics and Related Disciplines, London School of Economics, where he is co-director (with A. B. Atkinson) of the Welfare State Programme. His most recent publications include *The Strategy of Equality* and (ed. with Ray Robinson) *Privatisation and the Welfare State*. He will shortly be taking up a new post as Professor of Public Policy at the University of Bristol.

John Dryzek is an Assistant Professor of Political Science at the University of Oregon. His teaching and research interests include policy analysis, human ecology, political economy and critical theory. He is the author of, most recently, *Rational Ecology* and (with Davis Bobrow) *Policy Analysis by Design*.

D. M. Gibson is a Lecturer in Sociology at the University of Queensland, specializing in medical sociology, problems of ageing and social policy more generally.

Russell L. Hanson is an Associate Professor of Political Science at Indiana University, Bloomington. He is the author of *The Democratic Imagination in America: Conversations with Our Past*, a historical study of democratic ideologies in the United States. Hanson is currently participating in the Ford Foundation's Project on Social Welfare and the American Future, for which he is investigating the impact of interstate economic competition of public assistance policies.

Robert H. Haveman is John Bascom Professor of Economics at the University of Wisconsin, Madison and Research Associate at the Institute for Research on Poverty. His research is in the areas of economics of poverty and income distribution, cost-benefit analysis and the incentive effects of government taxes and transfers. He has published several journal articles on these topics, and most recently has authored *Poverty Policy and Poverty Research: 1965–1980.*

David Winter currently holds a joint appointment in the Department of Economics at Bristol University and at the Suntory–Toyota International Centre for Economics and Related Disciplines at the London School of Economics, where he is a Senior Research Fellow on the Welfare State Programme. He has published several journal articles in applied econometrics, concentrating on the analysis of non-clearing markets and of the behaviour of governments and bureaucracies.

References

Aaron, H. (1977), 'Demographic effects on the equity of social security benefits', in M. Feldstein and R. Inman (eds), *The Economics of the Public Services* (London: Macmillan).

Aaron, H. and McGuire, M. (1970), 'Public goods and income distribution', *Econometrica*, vol. 38, pp. 907–20.

Abel-Smith, B. (1958), 'Whose welfare state?', in N. McKenzie (ed.), *Conviction* (London: McGibbon), pp. 55–73.

Ackerman, B. A. and Hassler, P. (1981), *Clean Air/Dirty Coal* (New Haven, Conn.: Yale University Press).

Acton, J. P. (1975), 'Nonmonetary factors in the demand for medical services: some empirical evidence', *Journal of Political Economy*, vol. 83, pp. 595–614.

Aday, L. A. (1975), 'Economic and noneconomic barriers to the use of needed medical services', *Medical Care*, vol. 8, pp. 447–56.

Addison, P. (1975), *The Road to 1945* (London: Cape).

Aharoni, Y. (1981), *The No-Risk Society* (Chatham NJ: Chatham House).

Albritton, R. B. (1979a), 'Social amelioration through mass insurgency? A reexamination of the Piven and Cloward thesis', *American Political Science Review*, vol. 73, pp. 1003–11.

Albritton, R. B. (1979b), 'Reply to Piven and Cloward', *American Political Science Review*, vol. 73, pp. 1020–23.

Alchian, A. A. and Demsetz, H. (1972), 'Production, information costs and economic organization', *American Economic Review*, vol. 62, pp. 777–95.

Anderson, F. R., Kneese, A. V., Reed, P. D., Stevenson, R. B. and Taylor, S. (1978), *Environmental Improvement Through Economic Incentives* (Baltimore: Johns Hopkins Press).

Anderson, M. (1978), *Welfare: The Political Economy of Welfare Reform in the United States* (Stanford, Calif.: Hoover Institution Press).

Arrow, K, J. (1964), 'Control in large organizations', *Management Science* vol. 10, pp. 397–408.

Arrow, K. J. (1974), *The Limits of Organization* (New York: Norton).

Atiyah, P. S. (1980), *Accidents, Compensation and the Law*, 3rd edn (London : Weidenfeld & Nicholson).

Atkinson, A. B. (1983), 'The commitment to equality', in J. Griffith (ed.), *Socialism in a Cold Climate* (London: Allen & Unwin), pp. 22–36.

Atkinson, A. B. (1987), 'Economics of the welfare state: introductory comments', *European Economic Review* (Papers and Proceedings of the 1986 Annual Congress of the European Economic Association) vol. 31, pp. 171–81.

Atkinson, A. B., Hills, J. and Le Grand, J. (1986), 'The welfare state in Britain

1970–1985: extent and effectiveness', Welfare State Programme Discussion Paper no. 9 (London: London School of Economics).

Bacon, R. W. and Eltis, W. A. (1976), *Britain's Economic Problem: Too Few Producers* (London: Macmillan).

Baker, J. (1979), 'Social conscience and social policy', *Journal of Social Policy*, vol. 8, pp. 177–206.

Barry, B. (1977), 'Justice between generations', in P. M. S. Hacker and J. Raz (eds), *Law, Morality and Society* (Oxford: Clarendon Press), pp. 268–84.

Batson, C. D. and Coke, J. S. (1981), 'Empathy: a source of altruistic motivation for helping?', in J. P. Rushton and R. M. Sorrentino (eds), *Altruism and Helping Behavior* (Hillsdale, NJ: Lawrence Erlbaum Associates), pp. 167–87.

Baum, S. and Sjogren, J. (1983), 'Alternative social security indexing schemes and poverty among the elderly', *Policy Studies Journal*, vol. 12. pp. 79–90.

Baumol, W. (1982), 'Applied fairness theory and rationing policy', *American Economic Review*, vol. 72, pp. 639–51.

Bawden, D. L. and Palmer, J. (1984), 'Social policy: challenging the welfare state', in J. L. Palmer and I. V. Sawhill (eds), *The Reagan Record* (Cambridge, Mass.: Ballinger), pp. 177–215.

Beales, H. L. (1946), *The Making of Social Policy*, L. T. Hobhouse Memorial Trust Lecture no. 15 (London: Oxford University Press).

Becker, G. S. (1965), 'A theory of the allocation of time', *Economic Journal*, vol. 75, pp. 493–517.

Becker, G. S. (1982), *A Treatise on the Family* (Cambridge, Mass.: Harvard University Press).

Becker, G. S. (1983), 'A theory of competition among pressure groups for political influence', *Quarterly Journal of Economics* vol. 98, pp. 371–400.

Bell, W. (1965), *Aid to Dependent Children* (New York: Columbia University Press).

Benn, S. I. (1978), 'The rationality of political man', *American Journal of Sociology*, vol. 83, pp. 1271–6.

Benn, S. I. (1979), 'The problematic rationality of political participation', in P. Laslett and J. S. Fishkin (eds), *Philosophy, Politics and Society*, 5th series (Oxford: Blackwell), pp. 291–312.

Bergmann, B. (1971), 'The effect on white incomes of discrimination in employment', *Journal of Political Economy*, vol. 79, pp. 294–313.

Berkman, M. B. and Hanson, R. L. (1986), 'Containing the "welfare explosion": strategic action in a federal system', paper given at the annual meeting of the Western Political Science Association, Eugene Oreg., March.

Beveridge, W. H. (1907), 'Labour exchanges and the unemployed', *Economic Journal*, vol. 17, pp. 66–81.

Beveridge, W. H. (1942), *Social Insurance and Allied Services*, Cmd 6404 (London: HMSO).

Bixby, A. K. (1983), 'Social welfare expenditures, fiscal year 1980', *Social Security Bulletin*, vol. 46, no. 8, pp. 9–17.

Bixby, A. K. (1986), 'Social welfare expenditures, 1963–1983', *Social Security Bulletin*, vol. 49, no. 2, pp. 12–19.

Black, D. (1980), *Inequalities in Health*, report of a research working party, chaired by Sir Douglas Black (London: Department of Health and Social Security).

Blau, P. (1963), *The Dynamics of Bureaucracy*, 2nd edn (Chicago: University of Chicago Press).

Blaug, M., Dougherty, C. and Psacharopoulos, G. (1982), 'The distribution of schooling and the distribution of earnings: raising the school leaving age in 1972', *Manchester School*, vol. 50, pp. 24–40.

Bluestone, B. and Harrison, B. (1982), *The Deindustrialization of America* (New York: Basic Books).

Booth, C. (1892), *Pauperism and the Endowment of Old Age* (London: Macmillan).

Boreham, A. and Semple, M. (1976), 'Future development of work in the government statistical service on the distribution and redistribution of household income', in A. B. Atkinson (ed.), *The Personal Distribution of Incomes* (London: Allen & Unwin), pp. 269–312.

Breton, A. and Wintrobe, R. (1982), *The Logic of Bureaucratic Conduct* (Cambridge: Cambridge University Press).

Briggs, A. (1961), 'The welfare state in historical perspective', *Archives Européennes de Sociologie*, vol. 2, pp. 221–58.

Brodkin, E., and Lipsky, M. (1983) 'Quality control in AFDC as an administrative strategy', *Social Service Review*, vol. 57, pp. 1–34.

Buchanan, J. M. and Tullock, G. (1962), *The Calculus of Consent* (Ann Arbor, Mich.: University of Michigan Press).

Burns, E. M. (1944), 'Social insurance in evolution', *American Economic Review (Papers and Proceedings)*, vol. 34, pp. 199–211.

Burns, E. M. (1965), 'Social security in evolution: toward what?, *Social Service Review*, vol. 39, pp. 129–40.

Butler, J. (1726), *Fifteen Sermons at the Rolls Chapel* (London: Knapton).

Butlin, S. J. and Schedvin, C. B. (1977), *War Economy 1942–45*, Australia in the War of 1939–45, series 4 (Civil), vol. 4 (Canberra: Australian War Memorial).

Chambers, D. E. (1985), 'Policy weakness and political opportunities', *Social Service Review*, vol. 59, pp. 1–17.

Chartered Institute of Public Finance and Accountancy (CIPFA) (1985), *Education Statistics 1983/84 – Actual* (London: CIPFA).

Coase, R. H. (1937), 'The nature of the firm', *Economica*, vol. 4, pp. 386–405.

Commonwealth of Australia, Australian Bureau of Statistics (ABS) (1982) *Handicapped Persons in Australia, 1981* (Canberra: ABS).

Commonwealth of Australia, Department of Social Security (DSS) (1983) *Developments in Social Security: A Compendium of Legislative Changes since 1908*, Research Paper no. 20, Research and Statistics Branch, Development Division (Canberra: DSS).

Commonwealth of Australia, Social Welfare Policy Secretariat (SWPS) (1980), *Commonwealth Spending on Income Support Between 1968–69 and 1978–79 and Why It Increased* (Canberra: SWPS).

Crosland, C. A. R. (1956), *The Future of Socialism* (London: Jonathan Cape).

Cullis, J. G. and West, P. A. (1979), *The Economics of Health: An Introduction* (Oxford: Martin Robertson).

Cutright, P. (1965), 'Political structure, economic development and national social security programs', *American Journal of Sociology*, vol. 70, pp. 537–50.

Cutright, P. (1967), 'Income redistribution: a cross-national analysis', *Social Forces*, vol. 46, pp. 180–90.

D'Amato, A. (1983), 'Legal uncertainty', *California Law Review*, vol. 71, pp. 1–55.

Dacy, D. C. and Kunreuther, H. (1969), *The Economics of Natural Disasters* (New York: Free Press).

Danziger, S., Gottshalk, P., Rubin, R. J. and Smeeding, T, M. (1984), 'Recent increases in poverty: testimony before the House Ways and Means Committee', Institute for Research on Poverty Discussion Paper no. 740–83 (Madison, Wis.: University of Wisconsin); reprinted in part as 'Poverty in the United States: where do we stand now?' *Focus*, vol. 7, pp. 1–13.

Danziger, S., Haveman, R. and Plotnick, R. (1981), 'How income transfer programs affect work, savings, and the income distribution: a critical review', *Journal of Economic Literature*, vol. 19, pp. 975–1028.

Danziger, S. and Weinberg, D. (eds), (1986), *Fighting Poverty: What Works and What Doesn't* (Cambridge: Harvard University Press).

De Alessi, L. (1967), 'A utility analysis of post-disaster cooperation', *Papers in Non-Market Decision Making*, vol. 3, pp. 85–90.

De Alessi, L. (1968), 'The utility of disasters', *Kyklos*, vol. 21, pp. 525–32.

De Alessi, L. (1975), 'Towards an analysis of postdisaster cooperation', *American Economic Review*, vol. 65, pp. 127–38.

Dolbeare, C. N. (1981), 'Statement on "supply side economics"', *Hearings before the Task Force on Tax Policy of the Committee on the Budget*, US House of Representatives, 97th Congress, 1st Session, 10 March 1981 (Washington, DC: GPO).

Douty, C. M. (1972), 'Disasters and charity: some aspects of cooperative economic behavior', *American Economic Review*, vol. 62, pp. 580–90.

Downs, A. (1957), *An Economic Theory of Democracy* (New York: Harper).

Downs, A. (1960), 'Why the government budget is too small in a democracy', *World Politics*, vol. 12, pp. 541–63.

Downs, A. (1967), *Inside Bureaucracy* (Boston: Little Brown).

Dryzek, J. (1978), 'Politics, economics and inequality', *European Journal of Political Research*, vol. 6. pp. 399–410.

Dryzek, J. and Goodin, R. E. (1986), 'Risk-sharing and social justice: the motivational foundations of the post-war welfare state', *British Journal of Political Science*, vol. 16, pp. 1–34.

Duncan, G. J. (1984), *Years of Poverty, Years of Plenty* (Ann Arbor, Mich.: Institute for Social Research, University of Michigan).

Dunleavy, P. (1985), 'Bureaucrats, budgets and the growth of the state', *British Journal of Political Science*, vol. 15, pp. 299–328.

Dunne, J. P., Pashardes, P. and Smith, R. P. (1984), 'Needs, costs and bureaucracy: the allocation of public consumption in the UK', *Economic Journal*, vol. 94, pp. 1–15.

Durbin, J. (1970), 'Testing for serial correlation in least squares regressions when some of the regressors are lagged dependent variables', *Econometrica*, vol. 38, pp. 410–21.

Edwards, M. (1984), *The Income Unit in the Australian Tax and Social Security Systems* (Melbourne: Institute of Family Studies).

Esping-Andersen, G. (1985), 'Power and distributional regimes', *Politics and Society*, vol. 14, pp. 223–56.

Field, F., Meacher, M. and Pond, C. (1977), *To Him Who Hath* (Harmondsworth: Penguin).

Flora, P. and Alber, J. (1981), 'Modernization, democratization, and the development of welfare states in Western Europe', in Flora and Heidenheimer (1981), pp. 37–80.

Flora, P. and Heidenheimer, A. J. (eds) (1981), *The Development of Welfare States in Europe and America* (New Brunswick, NJ: Transaction Books).

Foster, C. D., Jackman, R. A. and Perlman, M. (1980), *Local Government Finance in a Unitary State* (London: Allen & Unwin).

Fraser, D. (1973), *The Evolution of the British Welfare State* (London: Macmillan).

Freeden, M. (1978), *The New Liberalism* (Oxford: Clarendon Press).

Friedman, M. and Friedman, R. (1980), *Free to Choose* (London: Secker & Warburg).

Friedkin, N. E. (1983), 'Horizons of observability and the limits of informal control in organizations', *Social Forces*, vol. 62, pp. 54–77.

Fuchs, V. (1965), 'Towards a theory of poverty', in *The Concept of Poverty* (Washington, DC: Chamber of Commerce of the United States).

Furniss, N. and Mitchell, N. (1984), 'Social welfare provision in Western Europe', in H. R. Rogers, Jr (ed.), *Public Policy and Social Institutions* (Greenwich, Conn.: JAI Press), pp. 15–54.

Furniss, N. and Tilton, T. (1977), *The Case for the Welfare State* (Bloomington, Ind.: Indiana University Press).

Gibson, D. M. (1983), 'Utilization of medical and paramedical services', in H. L. Kendig, D. M. Gibson, D. T. Rowland and J. Hemer, *Health, Welfare and Family in Later Life* (Sydney: New South Wales Council on the Ageing).

Gibson, D. M. and Aitkenhead, W. (1983), 'The elderly respondent', *Research on Ageing*, vol. 5, pp. 283–96.

Gibson, D. M., Broom, D. H. and Duncan-Jones, P. (1984). 'Access to dental services amongst the aged', *Community Health Studies*, vol. 3, pp. 62–74.

Gibson, D. M., Goodin, R. E. and Le Grand, J. (1985), ' "Come and get it": distributional biases in social service delivery systems', *Policy and Politics*, vol. 13, pp. 109–125.

Gilbert, N. (1977), 'The transformation of social services', *Social Service Review*, vol. 51, pp. 624–41.

Gilbert, N. (1982), 'The plight of universal social services', *Journal of Policy Analysis and Management*, vol. 1, pp. 301–16.

Gilbert, N. (1984), 'Welfare for profit', *Journal of Social Policy*, vol. 13, pp. 63–74.

Gilder, G. (1980), *Wealth and Poverty* (New York: Basic Books).

Glennerster, H. and Le Grand, J. (1986), 'Financing students', *New Society*, 13 December, pp. 421–2.

Glennerster, H., Merrett, S. and Wilson, G. (1968), 'A graduate tax', *Higher Education Review*, vol. 1, pp. 26–38.

Gold, K. A. (1982), 'Managing for success: a comparison of the private and public sectors', *Public Administration Review*, vol. 42, pp. 568–75.

Goldthorpe, J. H. (1964), 'The development of social policy in England, 1800–1914', in *Transactions of the Fifth World Congress of Sociology, Washington DC, September 1962* (Paris: International Sociological Association) vol. 4, pp. 41–56.

Goodin, R. E. (1976), *The Politics of Rational Man* (London: Wiley).

Goodin, R. E. (1982a), *Political Theory and Public Policy* (Chicago: University of Chicago Press).

Goodin, R. E. (1982b), 'Rational politicians and rational bureaucrats in Washington and Whitehall', *Public Administration* (London), vol. 60, pp. 23–41.

Goodin, R. E. (1985a), 'Erring on the side of kindness in social welfare policy', *Policy Sciences*, vol. 18, pp. 141–56.

Goodin, R. E. (1985b), *Protecting the Vulnerable* (Chicago: University of Chicago Press).

Goodin, R. E. (1985c), 'Self-reliance versus the welfare state', *Journal of Social Policy*, vol. 14, pp. 25–47.

Goodin, R. E. (1986), 'Laundering preferences', in J. Elster and A. Hylland (eds), *Foundations of Social Choice Theory* (Cambridge: Cambridge University Press), pp. 75–101.

Goodin, R. E. (forthcoming), *Reasons for Welfare*. (Princeton, NJ: Princeton University Press).

Goodin, R. E. and Dryzek, J. (1980), 'Rational participation: the politics of relative power', *British Journal of Political Science*, vol. 10, pp. 273–92.

Goodin, R. E. and Le Grand, J. (1986), 'Creeping universalism in the Australian welfare state', *Journal of Public Policy*, vol. 6, pp. 255–74.

Goodin, R. E. and Roberts, K. W. S. (1975), 'The ethical voter', *American Political Science Review*, vol. 69, pp. 926–8.

Gowing, M. (1975), 'Obituary notice: R. M. Titmuss', *Proceedings of the British Academy*, vol. 51, pp. 401–28.

Greater London Council (GLC) (1974), *Supplementary Licensing* (London: GLC).

van Gunsteren, H. (1976), *The Quest for Control* (London: Wiley).

Hansen, W. L. (1963), 'Total and private rates of return to investment in schooling', *Journal of Political Economy*, vol. 71, pp. 128–140.

Hansen, W. and Weisbrod, B. (1971), 'Who pays for a public expenditure program?', *National Tax Journal*, vol. 24, pp. 515–17.

Hansmann, H. B. (1980), 'The role of nonprofit enterprise', *Yale Law Journal*, vol. 89, pp. 835–901.

Hanson, R. L. (1983), 'The "content" of welfare policy: the states and Aid to

Families with Dependent Children', *Journal of Politics*, vol. 44, pp. 771–88.

Harman, G. (1975), 'Moral relativism defended', *Philosophical Review*, vol. 84, pp. 3–22.

Harrington, M. (1984), *The New American Poverty* (New York: Penguin).

Harris, J. (1981), 'Some aspects of social policy in Britain during the Second World War', in W. J. Mommsen (ed.), *The Emergence of the Welfare State in Britain and Germany, 1850–1950* (London: Croom Helm).

Harsanyi, J. C. (1953), 'Cardinal utility in welfare economics and in the theory of risk-taking', *Journal of Political Economy*, vol. 61, pp. 434–5.

Harsanyi, J. C. (1955), 'Cardinal welfare, individualistic ethics and interpersonal comparisons of utility', *Journal of Political Economy*, vol. 63, pp. 309–21.

Harsanyi, J. C. (1982), 'Morality and the theory of rational behavior', in A. Sen and B. Williams (eds), *Utilitarianism and Beyond* (Cambridge: Cambridge University Press), pp. 39–62.

Hatry, H. P. (1972), 'Issues in productivity measurement for local governments', *Public Administration Review*, vol. 32, pp. 776–84.

Haveman, R. (ed.) (1977), *A Decade of Federal Anti-Poverty Programs: Achievements, Failures, Lessons* (New York: Academic Press).

Haveman, R. (1984), 'How much have the Reagan Administration's tax and spending policies increased work effort?', in C. R. Hulten and I. V. Sawhill (eds), *The Legacy of Reaganomics: Prospects for Long-Term Growth* (Washington, DC: The Urban Institute).

Haveman, R. and Wolfe, B. (1984), 'Schooling and economic well being: the role of non-market effects', *Journal of Human Resources*, vol. 19, pp. 377–407.

Haveman, R. and Wolfe, B. (1985). 'Uncertainty, transfers, and the economic well-being of the disabled', in M. David and T. Smeeding (eds), *Horizontal Equity, Uncertainty and Economic Well-Being* (Chicago: University of Chicago Press), pp. 293–319.

Hayek, F. A. (1945), 'The use of knowledge in society', *American Economic Review*, vol. 35, pp. 519–30.

Hayek, F. A. (1976), *Law, Legislation and Liberty: The Mirage of Social Justice* (Chicago: University of Chicago Press).

Heclo, H. (1981), 'Towards a new welfare state?', in Flora and Heidenheimer (1981), pp. 383–406.

Heilbrun, J. (1974), *Urban Economics and Public Policy* (New York: St Martins Press).

Helps, A. (1845), *The Claims of Labour: An Essay on the Duties of the Employers to the Employed*, 2nd edn (London: William Pickering).

Hewitt, C. (1977), 'The effect of political democracy and social democracy on equality in industrial societies', *American Sociological Review*, vol. 42, pp. 450–64.

Hirsch, F. (1976), *Social Limits to Growth* (London: Routledge & Kegan Paul).

Hirschleifer, J. (1953), 'War damage insurance', *Review of Economics and Statistics*, vol. 35, pp. 144–53.

Hochman, H. M. and Rogers, J. D. (1969). 'Pareto optimal redistribution', *American Economic Review*, vol. 59, pp. 542–57.

Hood, C. C. (1976), *The Limits of Administration* (London: Wiley).

Hosek, J. R. (1978), *Family Participation in the AFDC–Unemployed Fathers Program*, RAND Report R–2316–HEW (Santa Monica, Calif.: RAND Corporation).

Hotelling, H. (1929), 'Stability in competition', *Economic Journal*, vol. 33, pp. 41–57.

Hume, D. (1739), *A Treatise of Human Nature* (London: J. Noon).

Hume, D. (1777), *An Enquiry Concerning the Principles of Morals* (London: T. Cadell).

International Labour Organisation (ILO) (1952), 'The cost of social security', *International Labour Review*, vol. 54, pp. 726–91.

Jackman, R. W. (1975), *Politics and Social Equality* (New York: Wiley).

Jamrozik, A. (1983), 'The economy, social inequalities and the welfare state: implications for research', paper delivered to ANZAAS Congress, Perth.

Joe, T. and Rogers, C. (1985), *By the Few for the Few: The Reagan Welfare Legacy* (Lexington, Mass.: D. C. Heath).

Johansen, L. N. and Kolberg, J. E. (1985), 'Welfare state regression in Scandinavia? The development of the Scandinavian welfare states from 1970 to 1980', in S. N. Eisenstadt and O. Ahimeir (eds), *The Welfare State and Its Aftermath* (London: Croom Helm), pp. 143–76.

Jones, M. A. (1983), *The Australian Welfare State*, 2nd edn (Sydney: Allen and Unwin).

Kahn, A. J. (1976), 'Service delivery at the neighborhood level: experience, theory and fads', *Social Service Review*, vol. 50, pp. 23–56.

Kahneman, D., Slovic, P. and Tversky, A. (eds) (1982), *Judgment Under Uncertainty: Heuristics and Biases* (Cambridge: Cambridge University Press).

Kaufman, H. (1976), *Are Government Organizations Immortal?* (Washington, DC: Brookings Institution).

Kewley, T. H. (1973), *Social Security in Australia, 1900–72*, 2nd edn (Sydney: Sydney University Press).

King, M. A. and Atkinson, A. B. (1980), 'Housing policy, taxation and reform', *Midland Bank Review* (Spring), pp. 7–15.

Kolm, S.-C. (1976), 'Unequal Inequalities', *Journal of Economic Theory*, vol. 12, pp. 416–442; vol. 13, pp. 82–111.

Korpi, W. (1980), 'Social policy strategies and distributional conflict in capitalist democracies', *West European Studies*, vol. 3, pp. 296–316.

Krefetz, S. P. (1976), *Welfare Policymaking and City Politics* (New York: Praeger).

Lampman, R. (1974), 'What does it do for the poor? – A new test for national policy', *The Public Interest*, no. 34, pp. 66–82.

Lampman, R. (1984), *Social Welfare Spending: Accounting for Changes from 1950 to 1978* (New York: Academic Press).

Le Grand, J. (1982a), 'The distribution of public expenditure on education', *Economica*, vol. 49, pp. 63–8.

Le Grand, J. (1982b), *The Strategy of Equality* (London: Allen & Unwin).

Le Grand, J. (1984), 'The future of the welfare state', *New Society*, vol. 68, pp. 385–6.

Le Grand, J. (1985), 'On measuring the distributional impact of public expenditure', in A. J. Culyer and G. Terny (eds), *Public Finance and Social Policy* (Detroit: Wayne State University Press), pp. 197–208.

Le Grand, J. (1986), 'On researching the distributional consequences of public policies', Welfare State Programme Discussion Paper no. 6 (London: London School of Economics).

Le Grand, J. and Robinson, R. (eds) (1984a), *Privatisation and the Welfare State* (London: Allen & Unwin).

Le Grand, J. and Robinson, R. (1984b), *The Economics of Social Problems*, 2nd edn (London: Macmillan).

Le Grand, J. and Winter, D. (1987), 'The middle classes and the welfare state', Welfare State Programme Discussion Paper no. 14 (London: London School of Economics). Forthcoming in *Journal of Public Policy*.

Lenski, G. (1966), *Power and Privilege* (New York: McGraw-Hill).

Lerner, A. (1944), *The Economics of Control* (New York: Macmillan).

Levin, H. (1977), 'A decade of policy developments in improving education and training for low-income populations', in Haveman (1977).

Liebman, L. (1976), 'The definition of disability in Social Security and Supplementary Security Income', *Harvard Law Review*, vol. 84, pp. 833–67.

Lipsky, M. (1980), *Street-Level Bureaucracy* (New York: Russell Sage Foundation).

Lipsky, M. (1984), 'Bureaucratic disentitlement in social welfare programs', *Social Service Review*, vol. 58, pp. 3–29.

Lloyd, P. and Dicken, P. (1972), *Location in Space* (New York: Harper & Row).

Losch, A. (1954), *The Economics of Location*, trans. W. Woglom and W. Stolper (New Haven, Conn.: Yale University Press).

Margolis, H. (1982), *Selfishness, Altruism and Rationality* (Cambridge: Cambridge University Press).

Margolis, J. (1975), 'Bureaucrats and politicians', *Journal of Law and Economics*, vol. 18, pp. 645–59.

Marris, R. (1964), *The Economic Theory of Managerial Capitalism* (London: Macmillan).

Marris, R. and Mueller, D. C. (1980), 'The corporation, competition and the invisible hand', *Journal of Economic Literature*, vol. 18, pp. 32–63.

Massam, B. (1975), *Location and Space in Social Administration* (London: E. Arnold).

McClure, C. (1972), 'The theories of public expenditure incidence', *Finanzarchiv*, vol. 30, pp. 432–53.

McMillan, A. (1979), 'Social welfare expenditures under public programs, Fiscal Year 1977', *Social Security Bulletin*, vol. 42, no. 6, pp. 3–12.

Meade, J. E. (1971) *The Controlled Economy* (London: Allen & Unwin).

Meade, J. E. (1981), 'The fixing of money rates of pay', in D. Lipsey and D. Leonard (eds), *The Socialist Agenda* (London: Jonathan Cape), pp. 75–106.

Meerman, J. (1979), *Public Expenditure in Malaysia: Who Benefits and Why* (Oxford: Oxford University Press).

Merriam, I. C. and Skolnick, A. M. (1968), *Social Welfare Expenditures under Public Programs in the United States, 1929–1966*, US Department of Health, Education and Welfare, Social Security Administration, Office of Research and Statistics Report no. 25 (Wasington, DC: GPO).

Merton, R. K. (1946), *Mass Persuasion* (New York: Harper).

Mincer, J. (1974), *Schooling, Experience and Earnings* (New York: Columbia University Press).

Monsen, R. J. Jr and Downs, A. (1965), 'A theory of large managerial firms', *Journal of Political Economy*, vol. 73, pp. 221–36.

Mueller, D. C. (1979), *Public Choice* (Cambridge: Cambridge University Press.

Murray, C. (1984), *Losing Ground: American Social Policy 1950–1980* (New York: Basic Books).

Musgrave, R. A (1959), *The Theory of Public Finance* (New York: McGraw Hill).

Musgrave, R. A. and Musgrave, P. B. (1977), *Public Finance in Theory and Practice* (New York: McGraw Hill).

Nelson, B. (1976), 'Residual demand for services: internalized gatekeeping and self-selection out of the public social benefits system in America', PhD. thesis, Ohio State University.

Nichols, A. L. and Zeckhauser, R. (1977), 'Government comes to the workplace: an assessment of OSHA', *Public Interest*, no. 49, pp. 36–69.

Niskanen, W. A. Jr (1971), *Bureaucracy and Representative Government* (Chicago: Aldine-Atherton).

Nozick, R. (1974), *Anarchy, State and Utopia* (Oxford: Blackwell).

Oates, W. E. (1968), 'Theory of public finance in a federal system', *Canadian Journal of Economics*, vol. 1, pp. 37–54.

Oellerich, D. T., and Garfinkel, I. (1983), 'Distributional impacts of existing and alternative child support systems', *Policy Studies Journal*, vol. 12, pp. 119–130.

O'Higgins, M. (1980), 'The distributive effects of public expenditure and taxation: an agnostic view of the CSO analyses', in C. Sandford, C. Pond and R. Walker (eds), *Taxation and Social Policy* (London: Heinemann), pp. 15–46.

O'Higgins, M. (1983), 'Rolling back the welfare state: the rhetoric and reality of public expenditure under the Conservative government', in C. Jones and J. Stevenson (eds), *The Yearbook of Social Policy in Britain, 1982* (London: Routledge & Kegan Paul), pp. 153–78.

O'Higgins, M. (1985), 'Inequality, redistribution and recession: the British experience', *Journal of Social Policy*, vol. 14, pp. 279–308.

Olson, M. Jr (1965), *The Logic of Collective Action* (Cambridge, Mass.: Harvard University Press).

Olson, M. Jr (1982), *The Rise and Decline of Nations* (New Haven, Conn.: Yale University Press).

Olson, M. Jr (1983), 'A less ideological way of deciding how much should be given to the poor', *Daedalus*, vol. 112, no. 4, pp. 217–36.

Organisation for Economic Co-Operation and Development (OECD) (1985), 'Basic statistics: international comparisons', *OECD Economic Surveys: United States* (Paris: OECD).

Ouchi, W. G. (1977), 'The relationship between organizational structure and organizational control', *Administrative Science Quarterly*, vol. 22, pp. 95–113.

Ouchi, W. G. and Dowling, J. B. (1974), 'Defining the span of control', *Administrative Science Quarterly*, vol. 19, pp. 357–65.

Ouchi, W. G. and Maguire, M. A. (1975), 'Organizational control: two functions' *Administrative Science Quarterly*, vol. 20, pp. 559–69.

Overvold, M. C. (1980), 'Self-interest and the concept of self-sacrifice', *Canadian Journal of Philosophy*, vol. 10, pp. 105–18.

Pahl, J. (1983), 'The allocation of money and the structuring of inequality within marriage', *Sociological Review*, vol. 31, pp. 237–62.

Pahl, J. (1985), 'Who benefits from child benefit?' *New Society*, vol. 72, pp. 117–9.

Peacock, A. T. (1960), 'The welfare society', *Unservile State Papers*, no. 2.

Peacock, A. T. (1974), 'The treatment of government expenditure in studies of income redistribution', in W. L. Smith and J. M. Culbertson (eds), *Public Finance and Stabilization Policy* (London: Jonathan Cape), pp. 139–77.

Peacock, A. T. and Shannon, R. (1968), 'The welfare state and the redistribution of income', *Westminster Bank Review* (August), pp. 30–46.

Peacock, A. T. and Wiseman, J. (1961), *The Growth of Public Expenditure in the United Kingdom* (Princeton, NJ: Princeton University Press).

Peacock, A. T. and Wiseman, J. (1979), 'Approaches to the analysis of government expenditure growth', *Public Finance Quarterly*, vol. 7, pp. 3–23.

Pechman, J. (1985), *Who Paid the Taxes 1966–1985?* (Washington DC: Brookings Institution).

Pellechio, A. and Goodfellow, G. (1983), 'Individual gains and losses from Social Security before and after the 1983 Amendments', *Cato Journal*, vol. 3, pp. 417–42.

Peltzman, S. (1980), 'The growth of government', *Journal of Law and Economics*, vol. 23, pp. 209–87.

Peretz, J. (1975), 'Beneficiaries of public expenditure: an analysis for 1971/2', UK Central Statistical Office, mimeo.

Phelps, C. E. and Newhouse, J. P. (1974), 'Coinsurance, the price of time and the demand for medical services', *Review of Economics and Statistics*, vol. 56, pp. 334–42.

Piachaud, D. (1982), 'Patterns of income and expenditure within families', *Journal of Social Policy*, vol. 11, pp. 469–82.

Pissarides, C. (1982), 'From school to university: the demand for post-compulsory education in Britain', *Economic Journal*, vol. 92, pp. 654–667.

Piven, F. F. and Cloward, R. A. (1971), *Regulating the Poor* (New York: Pantheon).

Piven, F. F. and Cloward, R. A. (1977), *Poor People's Movements: Why They Succeed, How They Fail* (New York: Random House).

Piven, F. F. and Cloward, R. A. (1979), 'Comments on Albritton', *American Political Science Review*, vol. 73, pp. 1012–19.

Piven, F. F. and Cloward, R. A. (1981), *The New Class War* (New York: Basic Books).

Plant, R. (1978), 'Community: concept, conception and ideology', *Politics and Society*, vol. 8, pp. 79–107.

Pliatzky, L. (1984), *Getting and Spending*, revised edn (Oxford: Basil Blackwell).

Plotnick, R. (1979), 'Social welfare expenditures: how much help for the poor?', *Policy Analysis*, vol. 5, pp. 261–89.

Plotnick, R. (1984), 'The redistributive impact of cash transfers', *Public Finance Quarterly*, vol. 12, pp. 27–50.

Plotnick, R. and Skidmore, F. (1975), *Progress Against Poverty* (New York: Academic Press).

Powell, E. (1961/1986), *The Welfare State* (London: Conservative Political Centre, 1961); reprinted in part in R. Pope, A. Pratt and B. Holye (eds), *Social Welfare in Britain, 1885–1985* (London: Croom Helm, 1986), pp. 176–9.

Prest, A. R. (1968), 'The budget and interpersonal distribution', *Public Finance*, vol. 23, pp. 80–98.

Projector, D. and Roen, M. P. (1982), *Family Demography and Transfer Payments During the 1970s*, Studies in Income Distribution, no. 12, US Department of Health and Human Services, Social Security Administration, Office of Policy, Office of Research and Statistics, SSA Publication no. 13–11776 (Washington, DC: US DHSS).

Prottas, J. M. (1979), *People Processing: The Street-Level Bureaucrat in Public Service Bureaucracies* (Lexington, Mass.: D. C Heath).

Rabin, R. L. (1970), 'Implementation of the cost-of-living adjustment for AFDC recipients: a case study of welfare administration', *University of Pennsylvania Law Review*, vol. 118, pp. 1143–66.

Raiffa, H. (1968), *Decision Analysis* (Reading, Mass.: Addison-Wesley).

Rawls, J. (1971), *A Theory of Justice* (Cambridge, Mass.: Harvard University Press).

Riessman, C. K. (1974), 'The use of health services by the poor' *Social Policy*, vol. 5, no. 1, pp. 41–9.

Rimlinger, G. V. (1961), 'Social security, incentives, and controls in the US and USSR', *Comparative Studies in Society and History*, vol. 4, pp. 104–24.

Rimlinger, G. V. (1966), 'Welfare policy and economic development: a comparative historical perspective', *Journal of Economic History*, vol. 26, pp. 556–71.

Rimlinger, G. V. (1971), *Welfare Policy and Industrialization in Europe, America and Russia* (New York: Wiley).

Rivlin, A. M. (1971), *Systematic Thinking for Social Action* (Washington, DC: Brookings Institution).

Robinson, R. V. F. (1981), 'Housing tax-expenditures, subsidies and the distribution of income', *Manchester School*, vol. 49, pp. 91–110.

Robinson, R. V. F. (1986), 'Restructuring the welfare state: an analysis of public expenditure, 1979/80–1984/5', *Journal of Social Policy*, vol. 15, pp. 1–21.

Robson, W. (1976), *Welfare State and Welfare Society* (London: Allen & Unwin).

Rose-Ackerman, S. (1983), 'Social services and the market', *Columbia Law Review*, vol. 83, pp. 1405–38.

Rosenberry, S. A. (1982), 'Social insurance, distributive criteria and the welfare backlash: a comparative analysis', *British Journal of Political Science*, vol. 12, pp. 421–47.

Rousseau, J–J. (1762), *Social Contract,* trans. G. D. H. Cole (London: Dent, 1973).

Rowland, D. T., Kendig, H. L. and Jones, R. G. (1984), 'Improving efficiency and coverage in a survey of the aged', *Australian Journal of Ageing*, vol. 3, pp. 34–38.

Samuelson, P. (1958), 'An exact consumption-loan model of interest with or without the social contrivance of money', *Journal of Political Economy*, vol. 66, pp. 467–72.

Schorr, A. (1980), *. . . Thy Father and thy Mother . . .: A Second Look at Filial Responsibility and Family Policy*, Social Security Administration publication no. 13–11953 (Washington, DC: GPO).

Schultze, C. (1977), *The Public Use of Private Interest* (Washington, DC: Brookings Institution).

Sen, A. (1983), 'Poor, relatively speaking', *Oxford Economic Papers*, vol. 35, pp. 153–69.

Shannon, G. W., Bashshur, R. L. and Metzner, C. A. (1969), 'Review article: the concept of distance as a factor in the accessibility and utilization of health care', *Medical Care Review*, vol. 26, pp. 143–61.

Sharkansky, I. (1980), 'Policy making and service delivery on the margins of government: the case of contracts', *Public Administration Review*, vol. 40, pp. 116–23.

Sharp, C. (1981), *The Economics of Time* (Oxford: Martin Robertson).

Skolnick, A. M. and Dales, S. R. (1970), 'Social welfare expenditures, 1969–70', *Social Security Bulletin*, vol. 33, no. 12, pp. 3–17.

Skolnick, A. M. and Dales, S. R. (1977), 'Social welfare expenditures, Fiscal Year 1976' *Social Security Bulletin*, vol. 40, no. 1, pp. 3–19.

Smeeding, T. (1982), *Alternative Methods for Valuing In-kind Transfer Benefits and Measuring their Impact on Poverty*, Technical Report no. 50, US Bureau of the Census (Washington, DC: GPO).

Smeeding, T. (1984), 'Approaches to measuring and valuing in-kind subsidies and the distribution of their benefits', in M. Moon (ed.), *Economic Transfers in the United States* (Chicago: University of Chicago Press), pp. 139–76.

Smeeding, T. and Moon, M. (1980), 'Valuing government expenditures: the case of medical transfers and poverty', *Review of Income and Wealth*, vol. 26, pp. 305–24.

Smiles, S. (1859), *Self-Help* (London: John Murray).

Smith, A. (1970), *The Theory of the Moral Sentiments*, 6th edn (London: A. Strahan and T. Cadell).

Smith, G. and Ames, J. (1976), 'Area teams in social work practice', *British Journal of Social Work*, vol. 6, pp. 43–69.

Smith, R. P. (1980), 'The demand for military expenditure', *Economic Journal*, vol. 90, pp. 811–821.

Steiner, G. Y. (1966), *Social Insecurity: the Politics of Welfare* (Chicago: Rand McNally).

Steiner, G. Y. (1971), *The State of Welfare* (Washington, DC: Brookings Institution).

Steiner, G. Y. (1981), *The Futility of Family Policy* (Washington, DC: Brookings Institution).

Stephens, J. D. (1979), *The Transition to Socialism* (London: Macmillan).

Stigler, G. J. (1970), 'Director's law of public income redistribution', *Journal of Law and Economics*, vol. 13, pp. 1-10.

Stiglitz, J. E. (1975), 'Incentives, risk and information: notes towards a theory of hierarchy', *Bell Journal of Economics*, vol. 6, pp. 552–79.

Stone, D. A. (1984), *The Disabled State* (London: Macmillan).

Sugden, R. (1982), 'On the economics of philanthropy', *Economic Journal*, vol. 92, pp. 341–50.

Sumner, W. G. (1883), *What Social Classes Owe Each Other* (New York: Harper).

Tawney, R. H. (1943), 'The abolition of economic controls, 1918–21', *Economic History Review*, vol. 13, pp. 1–30.

Tawney, R. H. (1971), *Equality* (London: Allen & Unwin).

Taylor, C. L., and Hudson, M. C. (1972), *World Handbook of Political and Social Indicators*, 2nd edn (New Haven, Conn.: Yale University Press).

Thompson, W. (1825), *Appeal of One Half of the Human Race, Women, Against the Pretensions of the Other Half, Men* (London: Longman).

Titmuss, R. M. (1950), *Problems of Social Policy* (London: HMSO and Longman, Green).

Titmuss, R. M. (1958), *Essays on 'The Welfare State'* (London: Allen & Unwin).

Titmuss, R. M. (1968), *Commitment to Welfare* (London: Allen & Unwin).

Titmuss, R. M. (1971), *The Gift Relationship* (London: Allen & Unwin).

Titmuss, R. M. (1974), *Social Policy* (London: Allen & Unwin).

Tullock, G. (1983), *The Economics of Income Redistribution* (Boston: Kluwer-Nijhoff).

UK Central Statistical Office (UK CSO) (1985), 'The effects of taxes and benefits on household income, 1984', *Economic Trends*, no. 386, December, pp. 99–115.

UK Department of Health and Social Security (UK DHSS) (1976), *Sharing Resources for Health in England*, Report of the Resources Allocation Working Party (RAWP) (London: HMSO).

UK Office of Population Censuses and Surveys (1981), *The General Household Survey, 1979* (London: HMSO).

UK Treasury (1984), *The Government's Expenditure Plans 1984–85 to 1986–87*, Cmnd 9143–I,II (London: HMSO).

UK Treasury (1986), *The Government's Expenditure Plans 1986–87 to 1988–89*, Cmnd 9702–I,II (London: HMSO).

US Congress, House of Representatives, Committee on Ways and Means

(1983), *Background Material on Poverty*, Report for Subcommittee on Oversight and Subcommittee on Public Assistance and Unemployment Compensation, 98th Congress, 1st session (Washington, DC: Government Printing Office).

US Congress, House of Representatives, Committee on Ways and Means, Staff (1986), *Background Material and Data on Programs within the Jurisdiction of the Committee on Ways and Means*, 99th Congress, 2nd Session (Washington, DC: Government Printing Office).

US Council of Economic Advisors (1985), *Economic Report of the President, Together with the Annual Report of the Council of Economic Advisors* (Washington, DC: Government Printing Office).

US Department of Commerce, Bureau of the Census (1985), *Economic Characteristics of Households in the United States: First Quarter, 1984*, Current Population Reports, Household Economic Studies, series P–70 (Washington, DC: Government Printing Office).

US Department of Health, Education and Welfare (DHEW) (1969), *Towards a Social Report* (Washington DC: Government Printing Office).

US Department of Health, Education and Welfare (DHEW) (1975), *The Cyclical Behavior of Income Transfer Programs*, Office of Income Security Policy, Technical Analysis Paper no. 7 (Washington DC: DHEW).

US Department of Health, Education and Welfare (DHEW), Social and Rehabilitation Service (1970a), *Findings of the 1967 AFDC Study: Data by State and Census Division. Part II: Financial Circumstances*, National Center for Social Statistics Report AFDC–4 (67) (Washington, DC: DHEW).

US, Department of Health, Education and Welfare (DHEW), Social and Rehabilitation Service (1970b), *Findings of the 1969 AFDC Study: Data by State and Census Division. Part II: Financial Circumstances*, National Center for Social Statistics Report AFDC–4 (69) (Washington, DC: DHEW).

US Department of Health, Education and Welfare (DHEW), Social and Rehabilitation Service (1972), *Findings of the 1971 AFDC Study. Part II: Financial Circumstances*, DHEW Publication no. (SRS) 72–03757, National Center for Social Statistics Report AFDC–2 (71) (Washington, DC: DHEW).

US Department of Health, Education and Welfare (DHEW), Social and Rehabilitation Service (1975), *Findings of the 1973 AFDC Study. Part II: Financial Circumstances*, DHEW Publication no. (SRS) 76–03765, National Center for Social Statistics Report AFDC–5 (73) (Washington, DC: DHEW).

US Department of Health, Education and Welfare (DHEW), Social Security Administration (1978), *AFDC 1975 Recipient Characteristics Study. Part 3: Financial Circumstances.* DHEW Publication no. SSA 78–11777 (Washington, DC: DHEW).

US Department of Health and Human Services (DHHS), Social Security Administration (1980), *AFDC 1977 Recipient Characteristics Study, Part 2: Financial Circumstances of AFDC Families* (Washington, DC: DHHS).

US Department of Health and Human Services (DHHS), Social Security Administration (1982), *AFDC 1979 Recipient Characteristics Study. Part 2: Financial Circumstances of AFDC Families* (Washington, DC: DHHS).

US Department of Health and Human Services (DHHS) (1984–5), 'Annual Statistical Supplement', *Social Security Bulletin* (Washington, DC: GPO).

Varian, H. (1984), *Micro-economic Analysis*, 2nd edn (New York: W. W. Norton).

Vaughan, R. J. (1979), *State Taxation and Economic Development* (Washington, DC: Council of State Planning Agencies).

Victor, C. R. and Evandrou, M. (1986), 'Social class and the elderly: analysis of the 1980 GHS', paper presented at the British Sociological Association Annual Conference, Loughborough, March.

Watts, R. (1980), 'The origins of the Australian welfare state', *Historical Studies*, vol. 19, pp. 175–98.

Webb, A. and Sieve, J. E. B. (1971), *Income Redistribution and the Welfare State*, Occasional Papers in Social Administration, no. 41 (London: Bell).

Wildavsky, A. (1979), *Speaking the Truth to Power* (Boston: Little, Brown).

Wildavsky, A. (1985), 'A cultural theory of government growth and (un)balanced budgets', *Journal of Public Economics*, vol. 28, pp. 349–57.

Wilensky, H. L. (1975), *The Welfare State and Equality* (Berkeley, Calif.: University of California Press).

Williams, G. (1967), *The Coming of the Welfare State* (London: Allen & Unwin).

Williamson, O. E. (1975), *Markets and Hierarchies* (New York: Free Press).

Williamson, O. E. (1981), 'The modern corporation: origins, evolution, attributes', *Journal of Economic Literature*, vol. 19, pp. 1537–68.

Willis, J. R. M. and Hardwick, P. J. W. (1978), *Tax Expenditures in the United Kingdom* (London: Heinemann, for Institute for Fiscal Studies).

Wilson, T. and Wilson, D. (1982), *The Political Economy of the Welfare State* (London: Allen & Unwin).

Witte, J. F. (1983), 'The distribution of federal tax expenditures', *Policy Studies Journal*, vol. 12, pp. 131–53.

Wright, G. C. Jr (1975), 'Interparty competition and state social welfare policy: when a difference makes a difference', *Journal of Politics*, vol. 37, pp. 796–803.

Zeckhauser, R. (1974), 'Risk spreading and distribution', in H. M. Hochman and G. E. Peterson (eds), *Redistribution Through Public Choice* (New York: Columbia University Press), pp. 206–28

Index